THE LONDON DIPLOMATIC LIST

January 2014

GW00703025

CONTENTS

Because of the time necessarily taken in preparation, this List is based on the information notified to the Foreign and Commonwealth Office by Diplomatic Missions and International Organisations approximately two months before publication.

LONDON : TSO

Published by TSO (The Stationery Office) and available from:

Online
www.tsoshop.co.uk

Mail, Telephone, Fax & E-mail
TSO
PO Box 29, Norwich, NR3 1GN
Telephone orders/General enquiries: 0870 600 5522
Fax orders: 0870 600 5533
E-mail: customer.services@tso.co.uk
Textphone 0870 240 3701

TSO@Blackwell and other Accredited Agents

ISBN 978 0 11 591799 8
ISSN 0950 6918

PO002582625   C13   01/14

THE LONDON DIPLOMATIC LIST

Alphabetical list of the representatives of Foreign States & Commonwealth Countries in London with the names & designations of the persons returned as composing their Diplomatic Staff. Representatives of Foreign States & Commonwealth Countries & their Diplomatic Staff enjoy privileges & immunities under the Diplomatic Privileges Act, 1964. Except where shown, private addresses are not available.

m   Married
*   Married but not accompanied by wife or husband

AFGHANISTAN

Embassy of the Islamic Republic of Afghanistan
31 Princes Gate SW7 1QQ
020 7589 8891
Fax 020 7584 4801
contacts@afghanistanembassy.org.uk
www.afghanistanembassy.org.uk
Monday-Friday 09.00-16.00

Consular Section
020 7589 8892
Fax 020 7581 3452
consulate@afghanistanembassy.org.uk
Monday-Friday 09.00-13.30

HIS EXCELLENCY DR MOHAMMAD DAUD YAAR   **m**   *Ambassador Extraordinary & Plenipotentiary (since 07 August 2012)*
            Mrs Sadia Yaar
Mr Ahmad Zia Siamak   **m**   *Counsellor*
Mr M Hanif Ahmadzai   **m**   *Counsellor*
Mr Najibullah Mohajer   **m**   *1st Secretary*
Mr M. Daud Wedah   **m**   *1st Secretary*
Mrs Nazifa Haqpal   **m**   *2nd Secretary*
Miss Freshta Omer   *2nd Secretary*
Mr Hanif Aman   *3rd Secretary*
Mrs Wahida Raoufi   **m**   *3rd Secretary*
Mr Yasir Qanooni   *3rd Secretary*
Mr Ahmad Jawaid   **m**   *Commercial Attaché*
Mr Nezamuddin Marzee   **m**   *Acting Military Attaché*

ALBANIA

Embassy of the Republic of Albania
33 St George's Drive SW1V 4DG
020 7828 8897
Fax 020 7828 8869
embassy.london@mfa.gov.al
www.albanianembassy.co.uk

HIS EXCELLENCY MR MAL BERISHA   **m**   *Ambassador Extraordinary & Plenipotentiary (since 18 March 2013)*
            Mrs Donika Berisha

1

Dr Teuta Starova   **m**   *Minister-Counsellor*
Ms Entela Gjika   *Counsellor*
Mrs Gentjana Nino   **m**   *1st Secretary*
Dr Xhoana Papakostandini   **m**   *3rd Secretary*
Col. Roland Berzani   **m**   *Defence Attaché*

ALGERIA
People's Democratic Republic of Algeria
1 Riding House Street W1W 7DR
020 7221 7800
Fax 020 7221 0448
info@algerianembassy.org.uk

Consular Section
6 Hyde Park Gate SW7 5EW
020 7589 6885
Fax 020 7589 7725
consular@algerianconsulate.org.uk

HIS EXCELLENCY MR AMAR ABBA   **m**   *Ambassador Extraordinary & Plenipotentiary (since 17 December 2010)*
          Mrs Zehra Abba
Mr Noureddine Meriem   **m**   *Minister-Counsellor*
Ms Dalila Samah   *Consul*
Mr Ali Kessai   **m**   *Minister Plenipotentary*
Colonel Menouer Zidane   **m**   *Defence Attaché*
Colonel Hocine Mekaoui   **m**   *Maritime Attaché*
Mr Mohamed Redha Bouchenafa   **m**   *Counsellor*
Mr Boubekere Sedik Anane   **m**   *Deputy Consul*
Mr Ahmed Adib   *Counsellor*
Mr Ali Bouatrous   **m**   *Deputy Consul*
Mr Mohamed Bendjaafar   **m**   *1st Secretary*
Mr Kader Yahia   **m**   *1st Secretary*
Mrs Soraya Yahia   **m**   *Deputy Consul*
Mr Sofiane Hamrouche   **m**   *1st Secretary*
Mr Said Sadouki   **m**   *Chancery Attaché*
Mr Abdelhafid Hachem   *Attaché*
Mr Mohamed Hamdani   **m**   *Attaché*
Miss Fouzia Salhi   *Vice Consul*
Mr Lies Amici   **m**   *Attaché*
Mrs Soumia Hamrouche   **m**   *Attaché*
Mr Yazid Ayachi   **m**   *Attaché*
Mr Abderkader Si Ahmed   **m**   *Attaché*
Mr Laalmi Hoggas   **m**   *Attaché*

ANDORRA
The Principality of Andorra is not currently represented in London. For further information please contact:
Ministry of Foreign Affairs & Institutional Relations, C/ Prat de la Creu 62-64, AD500 Andorra la Vella
Tel: +376 875 704
Fax: +376 869 559
exteriors.gov.andorra.ad

ANGOLA

Embassy of the Republic of Angola
22 Dorset Street W1U 6QY
020 7299 9850
Fax 020 7486 9397
TELEX 8813258 EMBAUK G
embassy@angola.org.uk
Monday-Friday 09.00-12.00 & 13.30-16.00
Visa Section Monday-Friday 09.30-13.00 (Closed Wednesday)

HIS EXCELLENCY MR MIGUEL GASPAR FERNANDES NETO **m** *Ambassador Extraordinary & Plenipotentiary (since 09 February 2012)*
   Ms Emilia Neto
Mr Diogo José Paulo Cristiano * *Counsellor*
Mr Henrique Assis **m** *Counsellor*
Lt Jonatão Augusto Morais **m** *Defence Attaché*
Mrs Rosa Benigna Sobrinho * *Deputy Angolan Representative of the IMO*
Mr Rui Nelson Goncalves **m** *Deputy Defence Attaché*
Mrs Delta Palmira Neves Cadete * *1st Secretary*
Mrs Nsimba Kudimana Nkulo * *1st Secretary*
Mr Ngongo Gomes Maiato * *2nd Secretary*
Mr António dos Santos Nascimento **m** *Press Attaché*
Mr Joao Domingos Pascoal * *Protocol & Ceremonial Attaché*
Mr Adriano Joao Correia de Almeida **m** *Telecommunications Attaché*
Mrs Maria Caetana R. Neto Amado *Financial Attaché*
Mr Samora Moreno Fernandes Neto * *Administrative Attaché*
Ms Eunice Ferreira de Almeida *Attaché & Secretary to Ambassador*

ANTIGUA & BARBUDA

High Commission for Antigua & Barbuda
2nd Floor 45 Crawford Place W1H 4LP
020 7258 0070
Fax 020 7258 7486
enquiries@antigua-barbuda.com
www.antigua-barbuda.com

HIS EXCELLENCY DR CARL B.W. ROBERTS, CMG **m** *High Commissioner (since 03 October 2004)*
   Mrs Pauline Roberts
Mrs Althea Allison Vanderpoole Banahene *Minister-Counsellor (Administration & Consular Affairs)*
Vacant *Counsellor*

ARGENTINA

Embassy of the Argentine Republic
65 Brook Street W1K 4AH
020 7318 1300
Fax 020 7318 1301
www.argentine-embassy-uk.org
info@argentine-embassy-uk.org
trade@ argentine-embassy-uk.org
culture@ argentine-embassy-uk.org
politica@ argentine-embassy-uk.org
pressoffice@ argentine-embassy-uk.org

cooperation@ argentine-embassy-uk.org
protocol@ argentine-embassy-uk.org

Consulate General
27 Three Kings Yard W1K 4DF
020 7318 1340
Fax 020 7318 1349
www.clond.mrecic.gov.ar
clond@mrecic.gov.ar

Defence Attaché's Office (Military, Naval & Air Attachés)
134-136 Buckingham Palace Road Second Floor SW1W 9TR
020 7730 4356
Fax 020 77824 8703
agredefmiluk@hotmail.com

Representation to IMO
2nd Floor 27 Three Kings Yard W1Y 1FL
020 7491 8785
Fax 020 7491 8837
romi@argentine-embassy-uk.org

HER EXCELLENCY MS ALICIA CASTRO   *Ambassador Extraordinary & Plenipotentiary (since 16 March 2012) (Permanent Representative to IMO)*
Mr Oscar Galli   *Minister*
Mr Alejandro Pineiro Aramburu   **m**   *Minister*
Mr Claudio Rojo   **m**   *Minister, Consul General*
Ms Alejandra Pecoraro   *Minister*
Mr Horacio Fernández Palacio   **m**   *Minister*
Mr César Campoy   **m**   *Minister*
Ms Elena Mikusinski   *Counsellor, Deputy Consul General*
Group Captain Alejandro Amorós   **m**   *Defence Attaché*
Mr Mariano Enrico   *Counsellor*
Miss Silvina Murphy   *Counsellor*
Mrs Cristina Hitce   **m**   *1st Secretary*
Mrs Cynthia Mulville   **m**   *2nd Secretary*
Mr Pedro Lopez Godoy   **m**   *3rd Secretary*
Mr Adrian Vernis   **m**   *Adminstrative Attaché*
Captain Germán Cibeira   **m**   *Technical Adviser to the IMO*
Captain Mario Farinon   **m**   *Technical Adviser to the IMO*
Mr Daniel Ruggero   **m**   *Assistant Defence Attaché*

ARMENIA

Embassy of the Republic of Armenia
25A Cheniston Gardens W8 6TG
020 7938 5435
Fax 020 7938 2595
armemb@armenianembassyuk.com
consular@armenianembassyuk.com
www.uk.mfa.am

HIS EXCELLENCY DR ARMEN SARKISSIAN   *Ambassador Extraordinary & Plenipotentiary (since 21 October 2013)*
          Mrs Nouneh Sarkissian
Mr Ara Margarian   *Counsellor*
Mr Hayk Khemchyan   *Attaché (Consular Affairs)*

AUSTRALIA

Australian High Commission
Australia House Strand WC2B 4LA
020 7379 4334
Fax 020 7240 5333
www.uk.embassy.gov.au

HIS EXCELLENCY THE HON MICHAEL DAVID RANN CNZM   *High Commissioner*
(since 02 December 2012)
Mr Andrew Todd   **m**   *Deputy High Commissioner*
Mr Ken Pascoe   **m**   *Minister-Counsellor (Management)*
Mr Peter Calver   **m**   *Minister-Counsellor*
Brigadier William Sowry   **m**   *Head of Australian Defence Staff*
Mr David Richard Crook   **m**   *Minister-Counsellor (Commercial)*
Ms Liesl Maria Jordan   **m**   *Minister-Counsellor (Liaison)*
Ms Elizabeth Beate Hoffmann   *Minister-Counsellor (Immigration)*
Mr James Kelly   **m**   *Minister-Counsellor (Economic)*
Mr David Maclennan   **m**   *Counsellor*
Ms Erika Thompson   *Counsellor*
Ms Corinne McDonald   **m**   *Counsellor*
Colonel Peter Steele   **m**   *Army Adviser*
Group Captain Paul Nicholas   **m**   *Air Force Adviser*
Captain Warren Bairstow   **m**   *Naval Adviser*
Mr Keiran Miller   **m**   *Counsellor (Police Liaison)*
Mr Andrew Ball   **m**   *Counsellor (Defence)*
Mr Anthony Hogan   **m**   *Counsellor (Transport)*
Mr Kevin Pullen   **m**   *Counsellor (Immigration)*
Mr John Baily   **m**   *Counsellor*
Mr Brian Hickey   **m**   *Counsellor (Defence Materiel)*
Mr clint Heinze   **m**   *Counsellor (Defence Science)*
Mr Matthew Black   *1st Secretary*
Ms Helen Taylor   *1st Secretary & Consul*
Mr Stuart Thomson   **m**   *1st Secretary*
Mr Timothy Spiteri   *1st Secretary*
Ms Louise Baker   **m**   *1st Secretary*
Mr Robert Vlazlovski   **m**   *1st Secretary & Consul*
Mr Andrew Conroy   **m**   *1st secretary*
Ms Zoe Thompson   *1st Secretary*
Mr Andrew Brooke   **m**   *1st Secretary*
Commander Richard Donnelly   **m**   *Assistant Defence Adviser*
Ms Morvern Maclean   *1st Secretary (Liaison)*
Mr Bernard Geason   **m**   *1st Secretary (Police Liaison)*
Mr David Haynes   **m**   *1st Secretary (Liaison)*
Ms Sally Reay-Young   **m**   *1st Secretary (Immigration)*
Ms gail McClure   **m**   *1st Secretary (Police Liaison)*
Ms Alison Rosetta   **m**   *2nd Secretary*
Mr Daniel Marina   *2nd Secretary*
Ms Erica Parrington   **m**   *2nd Secretary*
Ms Victoria Margo Benz   **m**   *2nd Secretary (Immigration)*
Ms Angela Feiner   *2nd Secretary*
Ms Katie Hamilton   **m**   *3rd Secretary*
Ms Donna Woodward   *Executive Assistant (Consular)*

AUSTRIA

Embassy of Austria
18 Belgrave Mews West SW1X 8HU
020 7344 3250
Fax 020 7344 0292
london-ob@bmeia.gv.at
www.bmeia.gv.at/london
Monday-Friday 09.00-17.00

Cultural Section
28 Rutland Gate SW7 1PQ
020 7225 7300
Fax 020 7225 0470
culture@austria.org.uk
www.austria.org.uk/culture

Defence Section
18 Belgrave Mews West SW1X 8HU
020 7245 9185
Fax 020 7245 9185
ma.gbr@bmlvs.gv.at

Financial Section
18 Belgrave Mews West SW1X 8HU
020 7344 3255
marlene.krotmayer@bmeia.gv.at

Commercial Section
45 Prince's Gate SW7 2QA
020 7584 4411
Fax 020 7584 2565
london@austriantrade.org
www.advantageaustria.org/gb

HIS EXCELLENCY DR EMIL BRIX m *Ambassador Extraordinary & Plenipotentiary (since 01 April 2010)*
              Mrs Elisabeth Brix
Mr Christoph Weidinger m *Minister Plenipotentiary, Deputy Head of Mission*
Ms Sabine Staffelmayr *Minister Plenipotentiary (Press Affairs)*
Mr Andreas Sumper m *1st Secretary*
Mr Alexander Zenz m *Counsellor (Administration Affairs) & Consul*
Mr Markus Wolfsteiner m *Attaché (Administrative Affairs)*
Mrs Edeltrud Desmond m *Assistant Attaché*
Mrs Barbara Biller-Jisa m *Assistant Attaché*
Mrs Silvia Szücs-Haiden m *Assistant Attaché*
Mrs Bettina Kadoch *Assistant Attaché*
Col Ronald Vartok m *Defence Attaché*
Mrs Elisabeth Koegler m *Director of the Austrian Cultural Forum, Minister Plenipotentiary (Cultural Affairs)*
Mr Ralf Boeckle *Attaché (Finance)*
Mr Georg Karabaczek *Commercial Counsellor & Trade Commissioner*
Mrs Sonja Holocher-Erti *Commercial Attaché*

AZERBAIJAN REPUBLIC

Embassy of the Republic of Azerbaijan
4 Kensington Court W8 5DL
020 7938 3412
Fax 020 7937 1783
london@mission.mfa.gov.az
www.azembassy.org.uk
Consular Section Tel/Fax 020 7938 5482

HIS EXCELLENCY MR FAKHRADDIN ISA OGLU GURBANOV **m** *Ambassador Extraordinary & Plenipotentiary (since 21 September 2007)*
        Mrs Saida Samadova
Lieutenant Colonel Vugar Ahmadov **m** *Defence Attaché*
Mr Vusal Abdullayev **m** *1st Secretary*
Mr Azar Gulabli **m** *1st Secretary*
Mr Farhad Isayev *2nd Secretary*
Mr Alibay Gahramanov *2nd Secretary*
Mr Polad Mammadov **m** *2nd Secretary*
Mr Ayaz Mustafayev *3rd Secretary*
Lieutenant Colonel Muslum Nasirov **m** *Senior Assistant to the Defence Attaché*
Mr Giyasaddin Guliyev **m** *Attaché*
Mr Vagif Musayev **m** *Financial Attaché*

BAHAMAS

High Commission of the Commonwealth of the Bahamas
10 Chesterfield Street W1J 5JL
020 7408 4488
Fax 020 7499 9937
information@bahamashclondon.net
www.bahamashclondon.net
Monday-Friday 09.30-17.30
Visa: Monday-Friday 10.00-13.00
Collection: Monday-Friday 14.00-17.30

HIS EXCELLENCY MR ELDRED EDISON BETHEL **m** *High Commissioner (since 17 December 2012)*
        Mrs Brenda Dawne Libby Bethel
Mr Michael Guy *2nd Secretary & Vice Consul*
Miss Donyelle Shavonne Ward *3rd Secretary & Vice Consul*

BAHRAIN

Embassy of the Kingdom of Bahrain
30 Belgrave Square SW1X 8QB
020 7201 9170
Fax 020 7201 9183
www.bahrainembassy.co.uk
information@bahrainembassy.co.uk
Monday-Friday 09.00 -16.00

Cultural Office
98 Gloucester Road SW7 4AU
020 7341 0770
Fax 020 7373 4210
info@bcao.co.uk

Her Excellency Miss Alice Thomas Yusuf Samaan   *Ambassador Extraordinary & Plenipotentiary (since 19 September 2011)*
Mrs Hayfa Ali Ahmed Matar   **m**   *Minister Plenipotentiary*
Mr Tariq Khalid Mohamed   **m**   *Counsellor*
Mr Hussain Makhlooq   *Counsellor*
Mr Hussain Mohammed Alam   *1st Secretary*
Shaikh Ali Ahmed Al Khalifa   *3rd Secretary*
Miss Lubna Khalifa Ahmed Selaibeekh   *Cultural Counsellor*

BANGLADESH

High Commission for the People's Republic of Bangladesh
28 Queen's Gate London SW7 5JA
020 7584 0081
Fax 020 7581 7477
info@bhclondon.org.uk
www.bhclondon.org.uk
Monday-Friday 10.00-17.30
Consular Section Monday-Thursday 10.00-13.00 & delivery 15.00-16.30
Friday 10.30-12.45 & delivery 15.00-16.30

His Excellency Mr Mohamed Mijarul Quayes   **m**   *High Commissioner (since 01 September 2008)*
          Mrs Naeema Chaudhury Quayes
Mr Rashed Chowdhury   **m**   *Minister (Press)*
Mr Azim Ahmed   **m**   *Minister (Consular)*
Mrs Sharifa Khan   **m**   *Commercial Counsellor*
Mr Ajit Kumar Ghosh   **m**   *Counsellor*
Mr A.K.M. Shahidul Karim   **m**   *Counsellor*
Mr S.M. Mahbubul Alam   **m**   *Counsellor & Head of Chancery*
Mr Kazi Ziaul Hasan   **m**   *1st Secretary*
Ms Nasima Mosharaf   *1st Secretary*
Ms Shirin Akther   *   *2nd Secretary*
Mr Mansurullah Khan   **m**   *2nd Secretary (Protocol)*
Mr Md Mominul Islam   **m**   *Attaché (Consular)*
Brigadier-General Sheikh Pasha Hahib Uddin   **m**   *Defence Adviser*

BARBADOS

Barbados High Commission
1 Great Russell Street WC1B 3ND
020 299 7150
Fax 020 7323 6872
london@foreign.gov.bb
Monday-Friday 09.30-17.30

His Excellency Mr Hugh Anthony Arthur   *High Commissioner (since 01 September 2008)*
Mr Donville Johnson   *Deputy High Commissioner*
Mr Euclid Goodman   *Minister-Counsellor*
Mrs Kendra Gibbons   **m**   *1st Secretary*
Mr Jean-Paul Cumberbatch   **m**   *1st Secretary (Commercial)*
Mrs Petra Roach   *Attaché*
Ms Anica Bostic   *Attaché*
Miss Tanya Brathwaite   *Attaché*
Mr Devon Chase   **m**   *Attaché*

Ms Francoise Lana-Mae Hendy   **m**   *Attaché*
Miss Norene Callender   *Attaché*

BELARUS
Embassy of the Republic of Belarus
6 Kensington Court W8 5DL
020 7937 3288
Fax 020 7361 0005
uk.london@mfa.gov.by
www.uk.mfa.gov.by
Monday-Friday 09.00-13.00 & 14.00-18.00
Economic/Commercial Section
020 7938 1633
Consular Section
020 7938 3677
Monday-Friday except Wednesdays 09.00-12.30

HIS EXCELLENCY MR SERGEI ALEINIK   **m**   *Ambassador Extraordinary & Plenipotentiary (since 18 February 2013)*
        Mrs Ludmila Aleinik
Mr Valery Dougan   **m**   *Chargé d'Affaires a.i.*
Mr Vitali Shumski   **m**   *Counsellor (Economic & Comercial Affairs)*
Mr Vitaly Lysyura   **m**   *Counsellor*
Mr Vitaly Krishtanosov   *1st Secretary (Economic & Commercial Affairs)*
Mr Yury Prudnikovich   **m**   *1st Secretary (Consular Affairs)*
Mr Aleksandr Palchevsky   **m**   *Attaché*

BELGIUM
Embassy of Belgium
17 Grosvenor Crescent SW1X 7EE
020 7470 3700
Fax 020 7470 3795
london@diplobel.fed.be
www.countries.diplomatie.belgium.be/nl/verenigd_koninkrijk
www.countries.diplmatie.belgium.be/fr/royaume_uni
www. countries.diplmatie.belgium.be/en/united_kingdom

Office of the Flemish Community & Region
Flanders House 1A Cavendish Square W1G 0LD

Flemish Community
020 7299 3590
Fax 020 7299 3591

Flanders Trade & Investment
020 7307 7710
Fax 020 7307 7711

HIS EXCELLENCY MR JOHAN VERBEKE   **m**   *Ambassador Extraordinary & Plenipotentiary (since 17 January 2010)*
        Mrs Catherine Dubois
Mrs Véronique Petit   **m**   *Counsellor (Political Affairs)*
Mr Bruno Marien   **m**   *Consul (Head of Consular & Administative Affairs)*
Baroness Carole van Eyll   *1st Secretary (Political Affairs)*
Ms Tine Jacobs   **m**   *2nd Secretary (Political Affairs)*

Mr Pierre-Yves Dumont   **m**   *Consul*
Mr Christiaan Sys   **m**   Vice Consul
Mr Luc Lefere   **m**   *Attaché (Consular Affairs)*
Mr Marc Rogiers   **m**   *Attaché (Consular Affairs)*
Mr Geert De Proost   **m**   *Counsellor for the Flemish Community & the Flemish Region*
Mr Ben De Smit   **m**   *Counsellor for the Flemish Region*
Mr Didier Denayer   **m**   *Counsellor for the Walloon Region*
Mr François de Vrije   **m**   *Counsellor for the Brussels Region*

BELIZE

Belize High Commission
Third Floor 45 Crawford Place W1H 4LP
020 7723 3603
020 7723 9637
info@belizehighcommission.co.uk
www.belizehighcommission.co.uk

HER EXCELLENCY MS PERLA MARIA PERDOMO   *High Commissioner (since 15 July 2012)*
          Ms Carmen Scarleth Ayon Neda
Ms Lou Anne Burns-Martinez   *Minister-Counsellor*
Ms Jolene Kidd   **m**   *1st Secretary*
Mr Andrew Wigmore   **m**   *Trade, Commercial & Press Attaché*

BENIN

Embassy of the Republic of Benin
87 Avenue Victor Hugo 75116 Paris
00 331 45 009882
Fax 00 331 45018202
ambassade.benin@gofornet.com

London Honorary Consulate (see page 125)

Vacant   *Ambassador Extraordinary & Plenipotentiary*
Mr Cosme Arouna   **m**   *Minister-Counsellor*
Mr Jean Clément Deka James   **m**   *Attaché*
Mrs Monique Attolou-Arouna   **m**   *Attaché*
Mr Joël-Marie Lontchedji   **m**   *Attaché*

BOLIVIA

Embassy of Bolivia
106 Eaton Square SW1W 9AD
020 7235 4248/4255/2513
Fax 020 7235 1286
embol@bolivianembassy.co.uk
www.bolivianembassy.co.uk

Consular Section
consulate@bolivianembassy.co.uk

Vacant   *Ambassador Extraordinary & Plenipotentiary*
Ms Veronica Paola Melendres Argote   *2nd Secretary & Chargé d'Affaires a.i.*
Mr David Alejandro Infante Vascones   *Civil Attaché*

BOSNIA & HERZEGOVINA

Embassy of Bosnia & Herzegovina
5-7 Lexham Gardens W8 5JJ
020 7373 0867
020 7373 0915
Fax 020 7373 0871
embassy@bhembassy.co.uk
www.bhembassy.co.uk
Monday-Friday 09.00-17.00
Consular Section: Monday-Friday 10.00-13.00

HIS EXCELLENCY MR MUSTAFA MUJEZINOVIC **m** *Ambassador Extraordinary & Plenipotentiary (since 04 May 2012)*
      Mrs Emina Mujezinovic
Mr Svetozar Maletic **m** *Minister Counsellor*
Ms Ljubica Peric *Counsellor for Consular Affairs*
Mr Nedeljko Gajic **m** *1st Secretary*
Mrs Jasmina Turajlic *2nd Secretary*

BOTSWANA

Botswana High Commission
6 Stratford Place W1C 1AY
020 7499 0031/020 7647 1000
Fax 020 7495 8595/020 7409 7382
bohico@govbw.com
Monday-Friday 09.00-17.00

HIS EXCELLENCY MR ROY WARREN BLACKBEARD *High Commissioner (since 29 December 1998)*
Mrs Poppy Majingo **m** *Minister Counsellor/Head of Chancery*
Mr Mosie Mfolwe **m** *2nd Secretary Political*
Mrs Irene Gofaone Rowland **m** *2nd Secretary*
Col Gaboratanelwe Tshweneetsile **m** *Defence Attaché*
Mr Modisotsile Magaga **m** *Training Attaché*
Mr Bin Matengu **m** *Assistant Commercial Attaché*
Mrs Adalinah Magagane **m** *1st Secretary*
Mrs Ambrosia Matsetse-Chisonta **m** *Administration Attaché*

BRAZIL

Embassy of Brazil
14/16 Cockspur Street SW1Y 5BL
020 7747 4500
www.brazil.org.uk

Commercial Section
14/16 Cockspur Street SW1Y 5BL
020 7747 4500

Consular Section
3-4 Vere Street W1G ODH
020 7659 1550
Fax 020 7659 1554

Office of the Naval Adviser
170 Upper Richmond Road SW15 2SH
020 8246 4400
Fax 020 8246 4475

Office of the Air Adviser
16 Great James Street WC1N 3DP
020 7440 4320
Fax 020 7831 8129

HIS EXCELLENCY MR ROBERTO JAGUARIBE GOMES DE MATTOS   **m**   *Ambassador Extraordinary & Plenipotentiary (since 11 August 2010)*
             Mrs Cinara Maria Fonseca de Lima
Mr Marcos Vinicius Pinta Gama   **m**   *Permanent Representative of Brazil to International Organisations*
Mrs Maria de Lujan Caputo Winkler   **m**   *Consul General*
Mr Eduardo Monteiro de Barros Roxô   *Minister-Counsellor (Deputy Consul General)*
Mr Flavio Marega   **m**   *Minister-Counsellor (Deputy Head of Mission)*
Mr Alexandre Guido Lopes Parola   **m**   *Minister-Counsellor (Political & Multilateral Affairs)*
Ms Rosimar da Silva Suzano   *Minister-Counsellor*
Mrs Cecília Kiku Ishitani   **m**   *Minister (Head of Ambassador's Office & Press Affairs)*
Captain Denilson Medieros Nôga   **m**   *Defence & Naval Attaché*
Colonel Fernando Telles Ferreira Bandeira   **m**   *Army Attaché*
Colonel Saulo Valadares do Amaral   **m**   *Air Attaché*
Mr Valmir Lemos de Oliveira   **m**   *Police Attaché*
Mr Davino Ribeiro de Sena   **m**   *Counsellor (Science & Technology)*
Mr André Chermont de Lima   **m**   *Counsellor (Political Affairs)*
Mrs Liliam Beatris Chagas de Moura   **m**   *Counsellor (Economic)*
Mr Ancelmo César Lins de Góis   *Counsellor (Multilateral Affairs Section)*
Mr João Marcos Senise Paes Leme   **m**   *Counsellor (Political Affairs)*
Mr Joaquim de Oliveira Penna Coelho da Silva   **m**   *Counsellor (Multilateral Affairs Section)*
Mr Evandro de Barros Araújo   *1st Secretary (Environment Affairs)*
Mr Flavio Werneck Noce dos Santos   *1st Secretary*
Mr Felipe Krause Dornelles   *   *2nd Secretary*
Mr Flavio Luis Pazeto   *2nd Secretary*
Ms Alethea Pennati Migita   *   *2nd Secretary (Political Affairs)*
Mr Daniel Souza Costa Fernandes   **m**   *2nd Secretary (Commercial Section)*
Mr Winston Alexander Silva   **m**   *2nd Secretary (Administration Affairs)*
Mr Krishna Mendes Monteiro   **m**   *3rd Secretary*
Mr Paulo Henrique Barauna Duarte Medeiros   *2nd Secretary*
Ms Sandra Myriam Amorim Dantas   *Vice Consul*
Mrs Lucia Naomi Iwakiri   *Vice Consul*
Mrs Nesira Ana Baker   **m**   *Vice Consul*
Mr Eduardo Monteiro Lopes Jr   **m**   *Vice Consul*
Mrs Brasilina de Sousa Santos Mollard   **m**   *Vice Consul*
Miss Juliana Ciccarini Nunes   *Vice Consul*
Captain Antonio Bernardo Ferreira   **m**   *Naval Adviser*
Commander Marcelo Menezes Cardoso   **m**   *Naval Adviser*
Commander Jose Carlos Cavalcanti Sales   **m**   *Naval Adviser*
Commander Paulo Cesar de Barros   **m**   *Naval Adviser*
Commander Sérgio Nahal de Souza   **m**   *Naval Adviser*
Group Captain José Antonio Moraes de Oliveira   **m**   *Air Adviser*
Wing Commander José Antonio Moraes de Oliveira   **m**   *Air Adviser*
Colonel Luiz Carlos de Oliveira Filho   **m**   *Air Adviser*
First Lieutenant Alessandra de Carvalho Malta   **m**   *Air Adviser*

BRUNEI

Brunei Darussalam High Commission
19/20 Belgrave Square SW1X 8PG
020 7581 0521
Fax 020 7235 9717
info@bdhcl.co.uk

Consular Section
20 Belgrave Square SW1X 8PG
020 7581 0521 (ext. 111)

Student Unit
35-43 Norfolk Square W2 1RX
020 7402 0045, 020 7402 0953
Fax 020 7262 8406, 020 7706 0558
Monday-Friday 09.30-13.00 & 14.00-16.30

HIS EXCELLENCY DATO PADUKA MOHD AZIYAN ABDULLAH   **m**   *High Commissioner (since 01 November 2010)*
          Mrs Nur Fadhlina Abdullah
Pg Hajah Siti Jauyah Pg Othman   **m**   *Minister-Counsellor*
Mr Pg Dato Yusof Sepiuddin   **m**   *Counsellor*
Mr Hj Ahmad Tudin   **m**   *Counsellor*
Mr Hj Junai Hj Ismail   **m**   *1st Secretary*
Mr Mohammad Dino Hj Ayup   *2nd Secretary*
Mrs Rizayarni Hj Masri   **m**   *3rd Secretary (Admin)*
Mrs Norsuriaashikin Hj Ismail   **m**   *3rd Secretary (Finance)*
Mr Pg Abd Rahman Pg Hj Damit   **m**   *3rd Secretary (In-Service Training)*
Mr Anuar Hj Mahmud   **m**   *3rd Secretary (Protocol)*
Mr Ak Hj Shahrin Pg Hj Bakar   *3rd Secretary (Protocol)*
Mr Mohammad Alyassa Rosli   *3rd Secretary (Consular)*
Mr Hj Amdani Hj Ismail   **m**   *Attaché (Communication)*
Lt Col Hj Abdur Rahim Hj Abdul Karim   **m**   *Defence Adviser*
Mr Ali Hamdani Md Diah   **m**   *Attaché (Education)*
Mr Khalid Hj Sulaiman   **m**   *Attaché (Education)*
Mr Hj Sammali Hj Adam   **m**   *Attaché (Education)*
Mrs Kamaliah Hj Abdul Rahman   **m**   *Attaché (Education)*
Mr Pg Md Wahab Pg Hj Abdullah   **m**   *Attaché (Education)*
Mrs Azizah Md Tuah   **m**   *Attaché (Education)*
Mr Al-Aseer Hj Md Yussof   *Attaché (Education)*
Mr Nazrul Ajidi Razali   **m**   *Attaché (Finance)*
Mrs Hjh Sahlailawati Hj Mohd Noor   **m**   *Attaché (Finance)*
Mr Mohd Azmi POKLS DSS Hj Abdul Rahman   **m**   *Attaché (Finance)*
Mr Mohammad Hamita Md Taib   **m**   *Attaché (Finance)*
Mr Nurhayani Mohd Tali   *Attaché (Finance)*
Mrs Masrani Abdul Razak   **m**   *Attaché (Finance)*
Mr Muhammad Adibul Amin Pg Hj Marjuki   *Attaché (Finance)*
Mr Kamsul Azrin Mohd Delli   **m**   *Attaché (Finance)*
Mr Md Fuad Hj Mahmud   *Attaché (Finance)*
Ms Rashidah Hj Berudin   *Attaché (Finance)*
Mr Md Ardhini Osman   **m**   *Attaché (Finance)*
Ms Sazianah Hj Sabli   *Attaché (Finance)*

BULGARIA

Embassy of the Republic of Bulgaria
186-188 Queen's Gate SW7 5HL
020 7584 9400, 020 7584 9433, 020 7581 3144
Ambassador's Office 020 7591 0781
Fax 020 7584 4948
info@bulgarianembassy.org.uk
ambass.office@bulgarianembassy.org.uk
www.bulgarianembassy-london.org

Consular Section
020 7589 3763 (Individual Inquiries on Submitted Applications 13.00-15.00)
Fax 020 7581 9073
Monday-Friday 09.30-13.30

Commercial Section
020 7589 4875
Fax 020 7589 4875
trade@bulgarianembassy.org.uk
Monday 10.00-16.00

HIS EXCELLENCY MR KONSTANTIN STEFANOV DIMITROV   **m**   *Ambassador Extraordinary & Plenipotentiary (since 19 March 2012)*
          Mrs Nadya Ivanova Dimitrova
Dr Stoimen Velev   *Minister Plenipotentiary (Deputy Head of Mission)*
Mr Dimitri Pampoulov   **m**   *Minister Plenipotentiary (Head of Consular Section)*
Rear Admiral Nikolay Ivanov Nikolov   **m**   *Minister Plenipotentiary (Defence Attaché)*
Mrs Rositsa Petrova   **m**   *Counsellor (Justice & Home Affairs)*
Mr Malin Messalski   **m**   *Counsellor (Consular Section)*
Mrs Tanya Valova-Kiryakova   **m**   *Counsellor (Commercial Section)*
Ms Svetla Dionisieva   *Counsellor (Director of the Bulgarian Cultural Institute)*
Mr Ivan Pavlov   **m**   *1st Secretary (Political)*
Mr Todor Krastev   *1st Secretary (Social & Labour Affairs)*
Mr Lachezar Valchev   **m**   *2nd Secretary (Administrative Attaché)*
Mr Tsvetin Spasov   **m**   *3rd Secretary (Press,Cultural & Political Affairs)*

BURKINA FASO

Embassy of the Republic of Burkina Faso
16 Place Guy d'Arezzo Brussels B-1180
0032 2 3459912
Fax 0032 2 3450612
ambassade.burkina@skynet.be
www.ambassadeduburkina.be
Monday-Friday 09.00-13.00 & 14.30-17.00

HIS EXCELLENCY MR FREDERIC ASSOMPTION KORSAGA   **m**   *Ambassador Extraordinary & Plenipotentiary (since 07 February 2013)*
          Mrs Kadiatou Korsaga Keita
Mr Ibrahima Toure   **m**   *Minister-Counsellor*
Mr Robert Compaore   **m**   *2nd Counsellor*
Mr Amadou Sagnon   *Counsellor (Economic Affairs)*
Mr Emmanuel Lalsomde   **m**   *Counsellor (Economic Affairs)*
Ms Zoure neé Zagre Clarisse Marie Hortense   *Counsellor*
Mrs Kabore neé Tiendrebeogo Odile   **m**   *Attaché (Treasurer/Financial Affairs)*
Mr Patrice Traore   **m**   *Attaché*
Ms Ouedragogo Berthe Jeanne S.W   *Attaché*

Mrs Abibata Toure   **m**   *Attaché*
Mr Hamado Tankoano   **m**   *Attaché*

BURMA (MYANMAR)
Embassy of the Republic of the Union of Myanmar
19A Charles Street W1J 5DX
General Office 020 7148 0740 / 020 7499 4340
Ambassador's Office 020 7148 0749
Political, Trade, Press & Cultural Affairs Section 020 7148 0741
Consular Section 020 7148 0740
Fax 020 7409 7043
ambassadoroffice@myanmarembassylondon.com
generalenquiries@myanmarembassylondon.com
visa@myanmarembassylondon.com
www.myanmarembassylondon.com

HIS EXCELLENCY KYAW ZWAR MINN   **m**   *Ambassador Extraordinary & Plenipotentiary (since 28 October 2013)*
　　　　Mrs Aye Minn Myat
Mrs Ei Ei Tin   **m**   *Minister Counsellor*
Mrs Sandar Tin   *   *1st Secretary*
Mrs Moe Thuzar   *   *1st Secretary*
Mr Tin Win Aung Moe   *1st Secretary*
Mr Zaw Htut   **m**   *3rd Secretary*
Ms Chaw Kalyar   *   *Attaché*
Mrs Lwin Mar Maung   *   *Attaché*
Mr Lin Moe   *Attaché*

BURUNDI
Embassy of the Republic of Burundi
Uganda House Second Floor 58-59 Trafalgar Square WC2N 5DX
020 7930 4958
Fax 020 7930 4957
www.burundiembassy.org.uk

Vacant   *Ambassador Extraordinary & Plenipotentiary*
Mr Bernard Ntahiraja   *Chargé d'Affaires a.i.*
Mr Kanene Jean Claude   **m**   *1st Secretary*

CAMBODIA
The Royal Embassy of Cambodia
64 Brondesbury Park Willesden Green NW6 7AT
020 8451 7997
Fax 0208 451 7594
cambodianembassy@btconnect.com
www.cambodianembassy.org.uk
Monday-Friday 09.00-12.30 & 14.00-17.30

HIS EXCELLENCY MR NAMBORA HOR   **m**   *Ambassador Extraordinary & Plenipotentiary (since 11 October 2004)*
　　　　Mrs Hor Khemtana
Mr Paul Sengky   **m**   *1st Counsellor (UK & European Affairs Unit)*
Ms Ban Borom   *2nd Counsellor (African & ASEAN Affairs Unit)*

Ms Kuy Yanna   *1st Secretary (Consular Affairs & Administration)*
Mrs Him Sokha   **m**   *2nd Secretary (Consular)*
Mr Chor Samphal   *3rd Secretary (Press & Communications)*

CAMEROON

High Commission for the Republic of Cameroon
84 Holland Park W11 3SB
020 7727 0771
Fax 020 7792 9353
Monday-Friday 09.00-16.00
info@cameroonhighcommission.co.uk
www.cameroonhighcommission.co.uk

HIS EXCELLENCY MR NKWELLE EKANEY   **m**   *High Commissioner (since 03 October 2008)*
　　　　Mrs Janet Mejane Ekaney
Mr Denis Nyuydzewira   **m**   *Minster-Counsellor*
Mr Joel Herve Nguenkam Keumini   **m**   *2nd Secretary*
Col Joseph Ngwafor   **m**   *Defence Adviser*
Mr Henri Steane Dina Imounga Mpollo   **m**   *1st Secretary*
Mr Peter Ngwaya Ekema   **m**   *2nd Secretary*
Lt-Col Guy-Roger Oyono   **m**   *Assistant Defence Adviser*
Major Marthe Tsogo   *Naval Attaché*
Major Gaskreo Reyang   *   *Attaché*
Major Réné Dieudonné Mezang Oyono   **m**   *Attaché*
Major Serges Mabaya   **m**   *Attaché*
Captain Alain Nagmou Pene   **m**   *Attaché*

CANADA

Canadian High Commission
Macdonald House 1 Grosvenor Square W1K 4AB
020 7258 6600
Fax 020 7258 6333
ldn@international.gc.ca
www.UnitedKingdom.gc.ca

Immigration & Visa Section
Consular & Passport Services
38 Grosvenor Street W1K 4AA

Protocol Venue
Canada House Trafalgar Square SW1Y 5BJ

Regional Service Centre (RSC)
3 Furzeground Way Stockley Park Uxbridge UB11 1EZ

London Quebec Government Office
1 Heddon Street W1B 4BD
020 7766 5900
www.quebec.org.uk

HIS EXCELLENCY MR GORDON CAMPBELL   **m**   *High Commissioner (since 15 September 2011)*
　　　　Mrs Nancy Campbell
Mr Alan Kessel   **m**   *Deputy High Commissioner*
Ms Sharon Chomyn   *Minister (Immigration)*
Mr Mark Fletcher   **m**   *Minister-Counsellor & Consul General*
Mr Brian Parrott   **m**   *Minister-Counsellor (Commercial/Economic)*

Mr Douglas Scott Proudfoot **m** *Minister-Counsellor (Political Affiars/Public Diplomacy)*
Mr Edwin Loughlin **m** *Minister-Counsellor*
Ms Debra Spencer *Counsellor*
Mr Joel Godard *Counsellor*
Mr Jeff Sundquist **m** *Counsellor (Commercial - Alberta)*
Mr Aaron Rosland *Counsellor (Commercial – Ontario)*
Mr Benoit Grenier *Counsellor*
Mrs Vera Alexander **m** *Counsellor (Public Affairs)*
Mr Rob Sinclair **m** *Counsellor*
Mr Rouben Khatchadourian **m** *Counsellor*
Ms Emily McLaughlin **m** *Counsellor (Economic)*
Ms Doreen Dyck **m** *Counsellor (Defence Research & Development)*
Mr Ian Wright **m** *Counsellor (Finance)*
Mr Mark Richardson **m** *Counsellor (Commercial)*
Mr Pascal Laurin *Counsellor (Immigration)*
Mr Marc-Andre Jacques **m** *Counsellor (Management)*
Dr René LaMontagne **m** *Attaché (Medical)*
Ms Jane Bird **m** *Attaché*
Mrs Sandra Rossiter **m** *1st Secretary*
Ms Francine Galarneau *1st Secretary (Immigration)*
Mr Gabriel Fradette *1st Secretary*
Mr Michael Ryan **m** *1st Secretary*
Ms Allison Corbett *1st Secretary (Immigration)*
Ms Gaynor Rent *1st Secretary (Immigration)*
Mr Craig Goldsby *1st Secretary (Immigration)*
Ms Mia Williamson *1st Secretary (Immgration)*
Ms Meghan Pendleton **m** *1st Secretary (Immgration)*
Ms Carina Parnham **m** *1st Secretary (Immigration)*
Mr Thom-Kostas Triantafillou **m** *1st Secretary (Immigration)*
Ms Nancy Fummerton **m** *1st Secretary (Immigration)*
Ms Kimberley O'Reilly **m** *1st Secretary (Management)*
Mr Todd Stewart *1st Secretary (Management & Consul)*
Mr Patrick Cyr **m** *Attaché*
Mrs Michelle Wilson **m** *Attaché*
Mr Jonathan Beaudoin **m** *Attaché*
Mr Anthony Hodgson **m** *Attaché*
Mr Frederic Cantin *Attaché*
Mr Craig Kowalik *Attaché*
Mr John White **m** *Attaché*
Ms Gillian Owens *Attaché*
Mr David Matheson **m** *Attaché*
Ms Anna Bretzlaff **m** *2nd Secretary*
Mr William Dunlop *2nd Secretary (Immigration)*
Ms Halleh Koleyni **m** *2nd Secretary (Commercial)*
Mr Kyriakos Nicolaou **m** *2nd Secretary (Immigration)*
WO David Ridley **m** *Attaché*
Mr Mohammed Derkaoui **m** *Attaché*
Ms Tracey Sibbald **m** *Attaché*
BGen Matthew Overton **m** *Commander & Defence Adviser*
Colonel Marv Makulowich **m** *Army Adviser*
Captain *(N)* Thomas Tulloch **m** *Naval Adviser*
Colonel Joseph Bigaouette **m** *Air Force Adviser*
Lieutenant-Colonel Arthur Agnew **m** *Assistant Air Force Adviser*
Commander Alan James **m** *Assistant Naval Adviser*

Lieutenant-Colonel Jean Trudel **m** *Assistant Army Adviser*
Lieutenant-Colonel John Dowell **m** *Attaché*
LCdr Steven St-Amant **m** *Attaché*
Lt (N) Audrey Rivera *Attaché*
PO1 Troy Ricketts **m** *Attaché*

CABO VERDE

Embassy of the Republic of Cabo Verde
Avenue Jeane 29 1050 Brussels
0032 2643 6270
Fax 0032 2646 3385

For visa enquiries, please contact the London Honorary Consulate (see page 125)

Vacant *Ambassador Extraordinary & Plenipotentiary*
Ms Maria de Jesus Mascarenhas *Chargé d'Affaires a.i.*

CENTRAL AFRICAN REPUBLIC

Embassy of the Central African Republic
30 Rue des Perchamps 75016 Paris

HIS EXCELLENCY MR JEAN WILLYBIRO SAKO *Ambassador Extraordinary & Plenipotentiary (since 14 July 2009)*

CHAD

Embassy of the Republic of Chad
Boulevard Lambermont 52 1030 Brussels
0032 2215 1975
Fax 0032 2216 3526
ambassade.tchad@chello.be

Vacant *Ambassador Extraordinary & Plenipotentiary*
Mr Beadrone Nagarbaye Tombalaye *Chargé d'Affaires*
Mr Ahmat Issaka Diar *Minister-Counsellor*
Mr Detomal Nahogoum *Counsellor (Economic)*
Mr Bakhit Mahamat Saleh Brahim *1st Secretary*
Mr Hissein Abdoulaye Hartaka *Attaché*
Mr Mahamat Djourab Mallaye *Attaché (Press)*

CHILE

Embassy of Chile
37-41 Old Queen Street SW1H 9JA
020 7222 2361
Fax 020 7222 0861
embachile@embachile.co.uk
http://chileabroad.gov.cl/reino-unido

Consulate General
37-41 Old Queen Street SW1H 9JA
020 7222 3434

Commercial Office
37-41 Old Queen Street SW1H 9JA
020 7233 2500
Fax 020 7233 2501
info@prochile.co.uk
www.prochile.co.uk

Defence & Naval Attaché's Office
37-41 Old Queen Street SW1H 9JA
020 7292 1500/02
Fax 020 7434 0793

Military Attaché's Office
37-41 Old Queen Street SW1H 9JA
020 7233 3851

Air Attaché's Office
37-41 Old Queen Street SW1H 9JA
020 7930 0028
Fax 020 7930 0499

HIS EXCELLENCY MR TOMÁS E. MÜLLER SPROAT   *Ambassador Extraordinary & Plenipotentiary (since 20 September 2010)*
            Ms Claudia Bobadilla
Mr Rodrigo Espinosa   *Minister-Counsellor, Deputy Head of Mission*
Captain Daniel Aguirre Bueno   **m**   *Defence & Naval Attachè*
Colonel Patricio Torres Aguirre   **m**   *Military Attaché*
Group Captain Sergio Figueroa   **m**   *Air Attaché*
Captain Jaime Leon Del Pedregal   **m**   *Assistant Naval Attaché*
Mr Patricio Diaz   **m**   *Consul*
Captain Carlos Cerda Espejo   **m**   *Alternate Maritime Adviser*
Mr Maximiliano Valdes   *3rd Secretary*

CHINA

Embassy of the People's Republic of China
49-51 Portland Place W1B 1JL
020 7299 4049
Monday-Friday 09.00-12.30, 14.00-17.00
www.chinese-embassy.org.uk

Political Section
49-51 Portland Place W1B 1JL
020 7299 4072

Press and Public Affairs Section
49-51 Portland Place W1B 1JL
020 7299 4097

Administration Section
49-51 Portland Place W1B 1JL
020 7299 4021

Consular Section
31 Portland Place W1B 1QD
020 7631 1430

Defence Section
25 Lyndhurst Road NW3 5PA
020 7794 7595

Commercial Section
16 Lancastar Gate W2 3LH
020 7087 4949

Cultural Section
11 West Heath Road NW3 7UX
020 7431 8830

Education Section
50 Portland Place W1B 1NQ
020 7612 0260

Science & Technology Section
10 Greville Place NW6 5JN
020 7625 0079

Martime Section
31 Portland Place W1B 1QD
020 7299 8439

HIS EXCELLENCY MR LIU XIAOMING   **m**   *Ambassador Extraordinary & Plenipotentiary (since 28 February 2010)*
          Mme Hu Pinghua
Mr Cong Peiwu   **m**   *Minister*
Mr Zhou Xiaoming   **m**   *Minister-Counsellor (Commercial Section)*
Mr Shen Yang   **m**   *Minister-Counsellor (Education Section)*
Mr Chen Futao   **m**   *Minister-Counsellor (Science &Technology Section)*
Mr Xiang Xiaowei   **m**   *Minister-Counsellor (Culture Section)*
Mr Lu Zhi   *   *Counsellor*
Mr Tang Li   **m**   *Counsellor & Consul General*
Major General Cai Yong   **m**   *Defence Attaché (Defence Section)*
Mr Li Feng   **m**   *Counsellor (Commercial Section)*
Mr Li Guangling   **m**   *Counsellor (Maritime Section)*
Mr Zhou Zheng   **m**   *Counsellor*
Mrs Zhu Xiaohong   *   *Counsellor*
Mrs Yang Hua   **m**   *Counsellor*
Mr Li Hui   **m**   *Counsellor*
Mr Zhao Yongren   **m**   *Counsellor*
Mr Meng Mian   *   *Counsellor*
Mr Miao Deyu   **m**   *Counsellor*
Ms Li Shan   **m**   *Counsellor*
Mr Hu Zhangliang   *   *Counsellor*
Mrs Su Liya   *   *Counsellor*
Senior Colonel Liu Fangjian   **m**   *Military Attaché (Defence Section)*
Colonel He Furong   *   *Navy Attaché (Defence Section)*
Colonel Sun Hongjun   *   *Air Attaché (Defence Section*
Colonel Sheng Dashuai   **m**   *Deputy Defence Attaché (Defence Section)*
Lieutenant Colonel Yin Lu   **m**   *Deputy Defence Attaché (Defence Section)*
Lieutenant Colonel Wang Hui   *   *Deputy Defence Attaché (Defence Section)*
Major Yan Lei   **m**   *Assistant to Defence Attaché (Defence Section)*
Senior Colonel Han Yantong   **m**   *Secretary to Defence Attaché (Defence Section)*
Major Zhu Xian   *Assistant to Military Attaché (Defence Section)*
Mr Zhang Liuan   **m**   *1st Secretary*
Mr Cheng Haoquan   **m**   *1st Secretary*
Ms Li Guizhi   *   *1st Secretary*
Mr Fan Zhonghua   **m**   *1st Secretary*
Mr Zhang Guolong   **m**   *1st Secretary*
Ms Huang Song   **m**   *1st Secretary*

Mr Wu Xiaoqing   **m**   *1st Secretary*
Ms Zhang Tong   **m**   *1st Secretary*
Ms Li Fanghui   *   *1st Secretary*
Mr Lin Fumin   **m**   *1st Secretary*
Ms Li Yan   **m**   *1st Secretary*
Ms Wu Ying   *   *1st Secretary*
Ms Zhu Jing   *   *1st Secretary*
Mr He Shiqing   **m**   *1st Secretary*
Ms Liu Fang   **m**   *1st Secretary*
Ms Li Jie   *   *1st Secretary*
Ms Li Yi   *   *1st Secretary*
Ms Wang Luxin   **m**   *1st Secretary*
Ms Li Chunzhao   *   *1st Secretary*
Mr Chen Jianping   *   *1st Secretary*
Mr Zhang Peng   *   *1st Secretary (Commercial Section)*
Mr Pan Jiansheng   *   *1st Secretary (Commercial Section)*
Ms Xu Rongrong   **m**   *1st Secretary (Commercial Section)*
Mr Peng Yuan   **m**   *1st Secretary (Commercial Section)*
Ms Gui Yun   *   *1st Secretary (Commercial Section)*
Ms Yan Li   **m**   *1st Secretary (Education Section)*
Mr Jiang Zhengwang   *   *1st Secretary (Education Section)*
Mr Qiao Fenghe   **m**   *1st Secretary (Education Section)*
Mr Chen Wei   **m**   *1st Secretary (Education Section)*
Ms Sun Yan   *1st Secretary (Cultural Section)*
Mr Zhang Renbi   **m**   *1st Secretary (Cultural Section)*
Mr Dai Tieshan   **m**   *2nd Secretary*
Ms Zhu Lin   *2nd Secretary*
Mr Qian Meng   **m**   *2nd Secretary*
Ms Zhang Yu   *2nd Secretary*
Ms Liu Qian   *2nd Secretary*
Mr Ma Yongchao   **m**   *2nd Secretary*
Mrs Wang Dan   **m**   *2nd Secretary*
Mr Yang Yaoyun   **m**   *2nd Secretary (Science & Technology Section)*
Mr Li Zhenxin   **m**   *2nd Secretary (Science & Technology Section)*
Mr Sun Jun   **m**   *2nd Secretary (Maritime Section)*
Mr Song Wei   **m**   *2nd Secretary (Maritime Section)*
Ms Dai Lili   **m**   *2nd Secretary (Commercial Section)*
Mr Yu Xiang   **m**   *2nd Secretary (Commercial Section)*
Ms Hu Guolei   *   *2nd Secretary (Commercial Section)*
Mr Kuang Jianiang   **m**   *2nd Secretary (Cultural Section)*
Ms Feng Xinzeng   *   *2nd Secretary (Cultural Section)*
Mrs Du Fang   *   *2nd Secretary*
Mr Chen Lekang   **m**   *2nd Secretary (Cultural Section)*
Mr Li Wei   **m**   *3rd Secretary*
Mr Zhang Fuqiang   **m**   *3rd Secretary*
Mr Liu Licheng   **m**   *3rd Secretary*
Mr Wang Mang   *   *3rd Secretary*
Mr Liu Huaibiao   **m**   *3rd Secretary*
Mr Gao Fengyi   *   *3rd Secretary*
Mr Zhuang Lekun   **m**   *3rd Secretary*
Mr Deng Ming   **m**   *3rd Secretary*
Ms Zuo Jian   *   *3rd Secretary*
Mrs Li Tao   **m**   *3rd Secretary*
Ms Zhang Li   **m**   *3rd Secretary (Commercial Section)*

Mr Pan Hao   **m**   *3rd Secretary (Commercial Section)*
Mr Li Qiang   **m**   *3rd Secretary (Commercial Section)*
Ms Zheng Rui   *3rd Secretary (Commercial Section)*
Mr Xu Hongri   *3rd Secretary (Commercial Section)*
Ms Cai Hong   *   *3rd Secretary (Education Section)*
Mr Feng Zhi   *3rd Secretary (Education Section)*
Ms Gong Chunhong   *   *3rd Secretary (Education Section)*
Mr Sun Min   *3rd Secretary (Education Section)*
Mr Hu Zhiyu   **m**   *3rd Secretary (Science & Technology Section)*
Mr Guo Dongbo   **m**   *3rd Secretary (Science & Technology Section)*
Ms Wang Xi   *Attaché*
Mr Yan Zhuang   *   *Attaché*
Mr Xing Dong   **m**   *Attaché*
Mr Guan Jinwei   **m**   *Attaché*
Mr Shuai Guipeng   **m**   *Attaché*

COLOMBIA

Embassy of Colombia
3 Hans Crescent SW1X 0LN
020 7589 9177/5037
Fax 020 7581 1829
elondres@cancilleria.gov.co
www.colombianembassy.co.uk

Consulate General
3rd Floor 35 Portland Place W1B 1AE
020 7637 9893 or 020 7927 7121
Fax 020 7637 5604
clondres@cancilleria.gov.co
www.consuladocolombia.net

Commercial Office
6th Floor 2 Conduit Street W1S 2XB
020 7491 3535
Fax 020 7491 4295
london@proexport.com.co

Military, Naval & Police Attaché's Office
3rd Floor 83 Victoria Street SW1H 0HW
020 3170 6012/6013

Vacant   *Ambassador Extraordinary & Plenipotentiary*
Mr Juan Manuel Uribe-Robledo   *Deputy Head of Mission & Chargé d'Affaires*
Ms Ximena Garrido-Restrepo   *Consul General*
Miss Beatriz-Asserias   *Minister Counsellor*
Mrs Andrea Jiménez-Herrera   **m**   *Counsellor for Foreign Affairs*
Mrs Nelsy Munar-Jaramillo   **m**   *Deputy Consul*
Mrs Anyurivet Daza-Cuervo   **m**   *Deputy Consul*
Mrs Ines Elvira Herrera-Ramirez   **m**   *1st Consul*
Captain Esteban Uribe-Alzate   **m**   *Naval Attaché*
Colonel Juan carlos Lozano   **m**   *Military & Air Attaché*
Mr Juan Guillermo Pérez   *Commercial Attaché*
Mrs Mercedes Osma-Peralta   **m**   *Press Attaché-1st Secretary*
Miss Laura Querubin-Borrero   *Cultural Attaché-2nd Secretary*
Mrs Nelsy Munar-Jaramillo   **m**   *Deputy Consul*
Mrs Anyurivet Daza-Cuervo   **m**   *Deputy Consul*

Miss Laura Querubin-Borrero   *2nd Secretary*
Miss Mercedes Osma-Peralta   *Press Attaché*

CONGO

Embassy of the Republic of Congo
37 bis Rue Paul Valéry 75116 Paris, France
0033 1 4500 6057
Fax 0033 1 4067 1733

London Honorary Consulate (see page 139)

HIS EXCELLENCY MR HENRI MARIE JOSEPH LOPES   **m**   *Ambassador Extraordinary & Plenipotentiary (since 27 July 1999)*
        Mrs Nirva Lopes
Mr Jean-Marie Mowelle   **m**   *Minister-Counsellor*
Mr Paul Adam Dibouilou   **m**   *Counsellor (Economic & Commercial Affairs)*
Mr Daniel Ibarra   **m**   *Counsellor (Cultural)*
Mr René Oyandza   *1st Secretary*
Mr Alfred Roland Taty   *1st Secretary*
General Jean-Jacques Morlende Ayaogningat   **m**   *Defence Attaché*
Mr Alain Benoit Itoua   **m**   *Finance Counsellor*

CONGO (DEMOCRATIC REPUBLIC)

Embassy of the Democratic Republic of the Congo
45-49 Great Portland Street W1W 7LD
020 7580 3931
Fax 020 7580 8713
missionrdclondres@gmail.com
www.ambardc-londres.gouv.cd

HIS EXCELLENCY MR BARNABE KIKAYA BIN KARUBI   **m**   *Ambassador Extraordinary & Plenipotentiary (since 24 August 2009)*
        Mrs Josette I.M Kikaya
Mrs Ndjeka Opombo Marie Marguerite   *1st Counsellor*
Mrs Marie-Louise Kafenge Nanga   *2nd Counsellor*
Mr Djo Manianga   *1st Secretary*
Mrs Brigitte Bisumbula Tshishimbi   **m**   *2nd Secretary*

COSTA RICA

Embassy of Costa Rica
14 Lancaster Gate W2 3LH
020 7706 8844
Fax 020 7706 8655
info@costaricanembassy.co.uk
Monday-Friday 10.00-15.00

Consular Section
14 Lancaster Gate W2 3LH
020 7706 8844
Fax 020 7706 8655
consul@costaricanembassy.co.uk

Her Excellency Mrs Pilar Saborio De Rocafort   *Ambassador Extraordinary & Plenipotentiary*
(since 09 January 2007)
Mr Rafael Sáenz Rodriguez   *Minister-Counsellor & Consul General*
Mr Carlos Federico Garbonzo Blanco   **m**   *Counsellor/Consul*

CÔTE D'IVOIRE

Embassy of the Republic of Côte d'Ivoire
2 Upper Belgrave Street SW1X 8BJ
020 7235 6991
Fax 0207 259 5320
TELEX 23906 Ivory Coast
Monday-Friday 09.30-13.00 & 14.00-17.00

Consular Section
2 Upper Belgrave Street SW1X 8BJ

Commercial & Economic Section (Commodities)
Morley House 3rd Floor 314-322 Regent Street W1B 3BE
020 7462 0086
Fax 020 7462 0087

His Excellency Mr Claude Stanislaus Bouah-Kamon   **m**   *Ambassador Extraordinary &*
Plenipotentiary (since 05 August 2011)
            Mrs Marie-Claire Bouah-Kamon
Mr Yapi Dodo   **m**   *1st Counsellor*
Colonel Major Martin Gnonsekan   **m**   *Defence Attaché*
Mr Ali Toure   **m**   *Counsellor (International Organisations Section Commodities)*
Mr Diomande Gondo Serge Siaba   **m**   *Counsellor (Economic)*
Mr Daouda Sako   **m**   *Counsellor (Cultural Affairs)*
Mr Euloge Innocent Atse   **m**   *Counsellor (International Organisations)*
Mrs Maman Toure Kone   **m**   *Counsellor (Political)*
Mr David Jacques Mimran   **m**   *Counsellor (Economic)*
Mr Diagne Mamadou N'Diaye   **m**   *Counsellor (Commercial)*
Mr Gadji Rabe   **m**   *Counsellor (Consular Affairs)*
Mrs Roselyne Salomé Vanié Nee Bede   **m**   *Counsellor*
Mr Dramane Kone   **m**   *Financial Counsellor*
Mr Mory Diarrassounba   **m**   *Counsellor (Commercial)*

CROATIA

Embassy of the Republic of Croatia
21 Conway Street W1T 6BN
020 7387 2022
Fax 020 7387 0310
vrhlon@mvep.hr
http://uk.mvp.hr
Monday-Friday 09.00-17.00

Consular Section
21 Conway Street W1T 6BN
Fax 020 7387 0936
conlon@mvep.hr

His Excellency Dr Ivan Grdešić   **m**   *Ambassador Extraordinary & Plenipotentiary (since*
10 October 2012)
            Mrs Elena Grdešić

Colonel Neven Cugelj **m** *Defence Attaché*
Mr Ivan Tojčić * *Minister-Counsellor*
Ms Ivana Porges *1st Secretary (Political)*
Ms Iva Gudelj *2nd Secretary (Consular)*
Ms Ana-Marija Žuvan **m** *2nd Secretary (Political & Press)*
Ms Helena Majetić *3rd Secretary (Political and Economics)*

CUBA
Embassy of the Republic of Cuba
167 High Holborn WC1 6PA
020 7240 2488
Fax 020 7836 2602
embacuba@cubaldn.com
www.cubaldon.com

Consular Section
15 Grape Street WC1 6PA
020 7240 2488
Fax 020 7379 4557

HER EXCELLENCY MRS ESTHER GLORIA ARMENTEROS CARDENAS **m** *Ambassador Extraordinary & Plenipotentiary (since 12 October 2010)*
        Mr Angel Ramón Ramirez Fonseca
Mr Jorge Luis Garcia Garcia **m** *Counsellor (Deputy Head of Mission)*
Mr Ivan Docampo Felipe **m** *Counsellor*
Mr Miguel Chang German **m** *Counsellor (Tourism)*
Mrs Olena Estela Navas Pērez **m** *Counsellor (Economic Affairs)*
Mrs Irelia López Díaz **m** *First Secretary (Head of Consular Affairs)*
Mr Ricardo Lamas Camejo **m** *Attaché (Consular Affairs)*
Mr Robert Ricardo de la Peña Pino **m** *Attaché*
Mr Alexis Blanco Rodríguez **m** *Attaché*

CYPRUS
High Commission for the Republic of Cyprus
13 St James's Square SW1Y 4LB
020 7321 4100
Fax 020 7321 4164/5
cyphclondon@btconnect.com
Monday-Friday 09.00-16.30

High Commissioner's Private Secretary
020 7321 4112
highcommissioner@chclondon.org.uk

Consular Section
020 7321 4101/3/6
Fax 020 7321 4165
Monday-Friday 09.30-13.00

Maritime Section
020 7321 4129
dmslo@tiscali.co.uk

Cultural Section
020 7321 4111
cultural_chc@btconnect.com

Press Section
020 7321 4141
Fax 020 7321 4167
pressoffice@chclondon.org.uk

Health Section
020 7321 4152
Fax 020 7930 7536
mnikolaou@mfa.gov.cy

Commercial Section
020 7321 4148/4145
Fax: 020 7321 4169
info@cyprustrade.co.uk

Cyprus Tourism Organisation
020 7321 4181+
Fax 020 7321 4165
informationcto@btconnect.com

HIS EXCELLENCY MR EURIPIDES L. EVRIVIADES **m** *High Commissioner (since 31 October 2013)*
        Mrs Anastasia Iacovidou-Evriviades
Mr Yiorgos Christofides **m** *Deputy High Commissioner*
Mrs Kypriani Stavrinaki **m** *1st Secretary*
Mr Georgios Georgiou **m** *Consul General*
Mr Filippos Christofi * *Counsellor (Commerce)*
Dr Christos Atalianis **m** *Counsellor (Maritime Affairs)*
Mr Nicolaos A. Charalambous *Counsellor (Maritime Affairs)*
Mr Kypros Charalambous **m** *Counsellor (Cultural Affairs)*
Mrs Panayiota Ioannou **m** *Attaché (Communications, Security & Labour Affairs)*
Mr Emilios Melis *Attaché (Accounts)*
Mr Orestis Rossides *Attaché (Information & Tourism)*
Mrs Maria Papalouca **m** *Attaché (Educational Affairs)*

CZECH REPUBLIC

Embassy of the Czech Republic
26-30 Kensington Palace Gardens W8 4QY
020 7243 1115
Fax 020 7727 9654
london@embassy.mzv.cz
www.czechembassy.org.uk

HIS EXCELLENCY MR MICHAEL ŽANTOVSKY **m** *Ambassador Extraordinary & Plenipotentiary*
(since 02 October 2009)
        Mrs Jana Žantovská
Mr Antonín Hradilek * *Minister-Counsellor, Deputy Head of Mission*
Colonel Roman Siwek **m** *Defence Attaché*
Mrs Jana Brazdova * *1st Secretary (Political Affairs)*
Mr Jan Tomášek **m** *1st Secretary (Political Affairs)*
Mr Pavel Bobek **m** *2nd Secretary (Head of Economic & Commercial Affairs)*
Mr David Steinke *2nd Secretary (Political Affairs)*
Mr Pavel Hajfler * *2nd Secretary (Consular Affairs)*
Miss Tereza Porybna *2nd Secretary (Director of the Czech Centre)*
Mrs Jana Brázdová * *2nd Secretary (Political Affairs)*
Mrs Jana Přikrylová * *3rd Secretary (Political Affairs)*
Mr Jiri Fejgl **m** *3rd Secretary (Head of Administration)*

Lieutenant Colonel René Klapáč m *Military Attaché*
Mr Ales Adam *Attaché (Administration)*

DENMARK
Royal Danish Embassy
55 Sloane Street SW1X 9SR
020 7333 0200
Fax 020 7333 0270
lonamb@um.dk
www.storbritannien.um.dk
Monday-Thursday 09.00-16.30 & Friday 09.00-16.00

Consular Section
Monday-Friday: By appointment only
Passports 020 7333 0200
Visas 020 7333 0200
Fax 020 7333 0266

Defence Attaché's Office
020 7333 0228/0229
Fax 020 7333 0231

HIS EXCELLENCY MR CLAUS GRUBE m *Ambassador Extraordinary & Plenipotentiary (since 25 September 2013)*
  Mrs Susanne Fournais Grube
Mr Christian Grønbech-Jensen m *Minister Counsellor, Deputy Head of Mission*
Mr Christian Stenberg Jensen m *Counsellor (European Policy & Financial Affairs)*
Mrs Helle Margrethe Sejersen Myrthue m *Counsellor (Commercial Affairs)*
Mr Jannich Sloth m *Consul/Attaché (Administrative & Consular Affairs)*
Captain (RDN) Martin La Cour-Andersen m *Defence Attaché*
Mr Ole Blöndal *Minister-Counsellor (European Financial Institutions)*
Pastor Else Hviid m *Attaché (Social Affairs)*

Representation of the Faroes
Tel. 020 7333 0227/0207
Fax 020 7333 6707
info@tinganes.fo
www.faroes.org.uk

Mr Jóannes Vitalis Hansen m *Minister-Counsellor (Representative of the Government of the Faroes)*

DJIBOUTI
Embassy of the Republic of Djibouti
26 Rue Emile Ménier 75116 Paris
0033 1 4727 4922
Fax 0033 1 4553 5053
webmaster@amb-djibouti.org
www.ambdjibouti.org

HIS EXCELLENCY MR RACHAD FARAH m *Ambassador Extraordinary & Plenipotentiary (since 21 March 2005)*
  Mrs Tazuko Hala Farah
Mr Mourad Houssein Mouti m *Chargé d'Affaires a.i. & 1st Counsellor*
Mr Aden Ali Mahamade m *2nd Counsellor (Economic & Commercial Affairs)*
Mr Hassan Moussa Omar m *Counsellor*

Mrs Amina Djama Set **m** *Counsellor (Protocol)*
Mr Amir Adaweh Robleh **m** *Counsellor (Cultural)*

DOMINICA, COMMONWEALTH OF

Office of the High Commissioner for the Commonwealth of Dominica
1 Collingham Gardens SW5 0HW
020 7370 5194
Fax 020 7373 8743
info@dominicahighcommission.co.uk
www.dominicahighcommission.co.uk
Monday-Friday 09.30-17.30

HER EXCELLENCY MRS FRANCINE BARON *High Commisisoner (since 31 August 2012)*
Mrs Janet Charles **m** *2nd Secretary*
Ms Nakinda Daniel *3rd Secretary*
Mr Omar Murtuzalieu **m** *Trade Attaché*

DOMINICAN REPUBLIC

Embassy of the Dominican Republic
139 Inverness Terrace W2 6JF
020 7727 7091
Fax 020 7727 3693
info@dominicanembassy.org.uk
www.dominicanembassy.org.uk
Monday-Friday 10.00-17.00

Consular Section
020 7727 6285
Monday-Friday 10.00-14.00

HIS EXCELLENCY DR FEDERICO ALBERTO CUELLO CAMILO **m** *Ambassador Extraordinary & Plenipotentiary (since 14 July 2011)*
         Mrs Natalia Maria Federighi de Cuello
Mrs Katia McKenzie **m** *Minister-Counsellor (Commercial Affairs)*
Mrs Alejandra Hernández **m** *Minister-Counsellor (Political Affairs)*
Ms Carolina Castro *Counsellor (Maritime Affairs)*
Mrs Aralis Rodríguez **m** *Counsellor (Consular Affairs)*
Ms Marlen Vásquez *Counsellor (Cultural Affairs)*
Mrs Johanna Sánchez Mawkin **m** *Counsellor (Political Affairs*

ECUADOR

Embassy of Ecuador
Flat 3B 3 Hans Crescent SW1X 0LS
020 7584 136 7 / 020 7590 2501 / 020 7590 2507
Fax 020 7590 2509
eecugranbretania@mmrree.gov.ec

Office of the Naval Assistant & Permanent Rep. to the IMO
6 Aspen Lodge 61 Wimbledon Hill Road SW19 7QP
020 8715 3595
Fax 020 8715 3594
ecuadorian.imo@armada.mil.ec

Consular Section
1st Floor Uganda House
58/59 Trafalgar Square WC2N 5DX
020 7451 0040
Fax 020 7451 0049
ceculondres@mmrree.gov.ec
www.consuladoecuador.org.uk

Commercial Section
Flat 3b 3 Hans Crescent SW1X 0LS
Tel: 020 7590 2506
e-mail:ocelondres@mmrree.gob.ec

HIS EXCELLENCY MR JUAN EDUARDO FALCONI PUIG   *Ambassador Extraordinary & Plenipotentiary*
(since 30 August 2013)
Mrs Maria Cleotilde Garcia Merino   **m**   *Minister & Deputy Head of Mission*
Mr Fidel Narváez Narváez   **m**   *Minister (Consul General)*
Mr Juan Diego Stacey   **m**   *Counsellor (Trade Commissioner)*
Mrs Maria Eugenia Avilés Zevallos   **m**   *1st Secretary (Consul)*
Mrs Jessica Eliana Bermudez Ronquillo   **m**   *2nd Secretary (Trade Executive)*
Mr Juan Carlos Yepez Franco   **m**   *2nd Secretary (Trade Executive)*
Mrs Diana Estefania Tello Reinoso   **m**   *3rd Secretary (Multilateral, Bilateral, Educational Affairs)*
Miss Maria Cristina Muños Vallejo   *3rd Secretary*
Mr Mauricio Fabian Dalgo Bernis   **m**   *3rd Secretary Vice Consul*

EGYPT

Embassy of the Arab Republic of Egypt
26 South Street W1K 1DW
020 7499 3304
Fax 020 7491 1542
egyemblondon@mfa.gov.eg
egtamboff@gmail.com
Monday-Friday 09.00-17.00

Consulate General
2 Lowndes Street SW1X 9ET
020 7235 9719
Fax 020 7235 5684
info@egyptianconsulate.co.uk

Defence Office
24 South Street W1K 1DN
020 7493 2649
Fax 020 7495 3573
mgm339@hotmail.com

Commercial Office
23 South Street W1K 2XD
020 7499 3002
Fax 020 7493 8110
london@ecs.gov.eg

Press & Information Office
299 Oxford Street W1C 2DZ
020 7409 2236
Fax 020 7493 7456
info@egpressoffice.com

Cultural Office
4 Chesterfield Gardens W1J 5BG
020 7491 7720
Fax 020 7408 1335
egypt.culture@btconnect.com

Medical Office
47 Longridge Road SW5 9SD
020 7370 6944
Fax 020 7370 3641
samiehamer@egmedoffice.org

HIS EXCELLENCY MR ASHRAF ELKHOLY   m   *Ambassador Extraordinary & Plenipotentiary (since 04 December 2012)*
          Mrs Alya Zein
Ms Nahla M E Elzawahry   *Minister Plenipotentiary, Deputy Chief of Mission*
Mr Khaled M A M Azmi   m   *Counsellor*
Mr Hassan Ahmed Shawky   *Counsellor*
Mr Ahmed M.A. Elsawy   m   *Counsellor*
Mr Hisham H.A.M. Abdelghani   m   *Counsellor*
Mr Khaled M.S. Saoud   m   *Counsellor*
Mr Amr H.R. Mohamed   m   *1st Secretary*
Mr Khaled M.S. Shaalan   m   *2nd Secretary*
Mr Mahmoud M.A. Hamdy   m   *2nd Secretary*
Miss Yasmeen A-F. Khattab   *3rd Secretary*
Mr Amr M.M. Nouh   *3rd Secretary*
Mrs Eman M.D. Mohamed   *   *Administrative & Financial Attaché*
Mr Mohamed M.M. Elgendy   m   *Administrative & Financial Attaché*
Mr Yasser S D Soliman   m   *Administrative & Financial Attaché*
Mr Ashraf A.K. Elrasasi   m   *Administrative & Financial Attaché*
Mr Mahmoud I.M. Rashwan   m   *Administrative & Financial Attaché*
Mr Mohamed A.R. Torky   m   *Administrative & Financial Attaché*
Mr Zakaria B.S. Shafe   *   *Administrative & Financial Attaché*
Mr Sherif A.M Naeem   m   *Administrative & Financial Attaché*
Mr Ahmed S.A. Abdelmageed   *   *Administrative & Financial Attaché*
Mr Ashraf L.A. Hussein   *   *Administrative & Financial Attaché*
Mr Mohamed A.A. Sayed   *   *Administrative & Financial Attaché*
Dr Hesham M.A.I. Khalil   m   *Consul General*
Mr Maher R.R. Aboukada   m   *Consul*
Mrs Dahlia M.N.M Tawakol   m   *Consul*
Mr Alaaeldin A.M. Eldwiny   m   *Consul*
Mr Ahmed F.A. Shahin   m   *Vice Consul*
Mr Mohamed A.O. Abdalla   *Administrative & Financial Attaché*
Mr Mohamed M.M.E. Ghanim   m   *Administrative & Financial Attaché*
Mr Fathi I.M. Hamouda   *Administrative & Financial Attaché*
Mrs Hanan A.A. Easa   *   *Administrative & Financial Attaché*
Mr Abdellatif N A Elshenawy   m   *Administrative & Financial Attaché*
Mr Mohamed N. A. Elkabbany   m   *Administrative & Financial Attaché*
Mr Mostafa I I Hammad   m   *Administrative & Financial Attaché*
General Gamal A. M.A. Abu Ismail   m   *Defence Attaché*
Col Dr Tarek E.A. Abdelhady   m   *Assistant Defence Attaché (Medical Affairs)*
Col. Mohamed H.I. Hamad   m   *Assistant Defence Attaché*
Lt Col Hany S.M. Geith   m   *Assistant Defence Attaché*
Lt Col. Tamer A.I. Moustafa   m   *Assistant Defence Attaché*
Lt Col. Walid N.E. Abdelfattah   m   *Assistant Defence Attaché*
Major Mohamed E.A. Elhadad   m   *Assistant Defence Attaché*

Major Mohammed A.M. Gebreil   **m**   *Assistant Defence Attaché*
Major Hisham M.I. Zaher   **m**   *Assistant Defence Attaché*
Dr Samieh A. Amer   **m**   *Medical Counsellor*
Mr Waleed W S El-Zomor   **m**   *Counsellor (Commercial)*
Mr Mohamed A.M.A. Ibrahim   **m**   *2nd Secretary (Commercial)*
Mr Sherif A.E. Abdelmaksoud   **m**   *2nd Secretary (Commercial)*
Mr Osama Sharafeldin   *   *Administrative & Financial Attaché (Commercial)*
Mrs Sohair H.H. Younis   *   *Press & Information Counsellor*
Mr Meky A.M. Meky   **m**   *Press & Information Attaché*
Dr Nadia Elkholy   **m**   *Cultural Counsellor*
Dr Rasha Sharaf   **m**   *Cultural Attaché*
Mrs Suad M A Abdo   *   *Administrative & Financial Attaché*
Mrs Marwa H.M. Abdelrahman   *   *Administrative & Financial Attaché*
Mrs Omayma M.A.H. Elhusseini   *   *Tourism & Information Counsellor*
Mr Mohamed A.S. Elnaggar   **m**   *Tourism Attaché*

EL SALVADOR

Embassy of El Salvador
8 Dorset Square 1st & 2nd Floors NW1 6PU
020 7224 9800
Fax 020 7224 9878
embajadalondres@rree.gob.sv
elsalvador.embassy@gmail.com
Monday-Friday 10.00-17.00

HIS EXCELLENCY MR WERNER MATÍAS ROMERO   *Ambassador Extraordinary & Plenipotentiary*
(since 21 December 2009)
          Mr Roger Atwood
Miss Gilda Velásquez   *Minister-Counsellor (Political and Cooperation Affairs). Deputy Head of Mission*
Mrs Lucía Rosella Badía de Funes   **m**   *Minister-Counsellor (Economic Affairs and International Organisations)*
Ms Beatriz Alfaro   *Counsellor (Consular and Cultural Affairs)*
Colonel Héctor Manuel Alas-Lūquez   *Defence Attaché (non-resident)*

EQUATORIAL GUINEA

Embassy of the Republic of Equatorial Guinea
13 Park Place St James' SW1A 1LP
020 7499 6867
Fax 020 7499 6782
embarege-londres@embarege-londres.org
www.embarege-londres.org
Monday-Friday 09.00-16.00

HER EXCELLENCY MRS MARI-CRUZ EVUNA ANDEME   *Ambassador Extraordinary & Plenipotentiary*
(since 01 July 2012)
          Mr Amadou Bah
Mr Simeon Edjang Mangue   **m**   *Counsellor*
Mr Ben Djibril Ballingha Balinga Alene   **m**   *1st Secretary*
Mr Francisco Nve Osa Afang   **m**   *2nd Secretary*
Ms Mc Dolores Judith Ondo Matogo   *3rd Secretary*
Mr Juda Ngam Obama Ayingono   *   *Financial Attaché*

ERITREA

Embassy of the State of Eritrea
96 White Lion Street N1 9PF
020 7713 0096
Fax 020 7713 0161
www.eritrean-embassy.org.uk
eriemba@eriembauk.com

HIS EXCELLENCY MR TESFAMICAEL GERAHTU OGBAGHIORGHIS **m** *Ambassador Extraordinary & Plenipotentiary (since 21 November 2007)*
        Dr Alem Teclu Hagos

ESTONIA

Embassy of the Republic of Estonia
16 Hyde Park Gate SW7 5DG
020 7589 3428
Fax 020 7589 3430
london@mfa.ee
www.estonia.gov.uk

Consular Section
Monday-Friday 10.00-13.00 Tuesday & Thursday 13.00-16.00
020 7838 5388

HER EXCELLENCY MRS AINO LEPIK VON WIRÉN **m** *Ambassador Extraordinary & Plenipotentiary (since 30 August 2010)*
        Mr Jorma Von Wirén
Ms Karmen Laus *Deputy Head of Mission, Public Affairs*
Mr Sven Tolp **m** *Consul*
Ms Helen Rits *Press & Public Affairs Officer*
Ms Eva-Liisa Jaanus *Economic Affairs*
Ms Kristel Oitmaa *Cultural Counsellor*
Colonel Vahur Väljamäe **m** *Defence Attaché*

ETHIOPIA

Embassy of the Federal Democratic Republic of Ethiopia
17 Princes Gate SW7 1PZ
020 7589 7212
info@ethioembassy.org.uk
www.ethioembassy.org.uk
Monday-Friday 09.00-17.00

Consular Section
020 7838 3895
Monday-Friday 09.00-16.00

Commercial Section
020 7838 3878

Press Section
020 7838 3884

HIS EXCELLENCY MR BERHANU KEBEDE * *Ambassador Extraordinary & Plenipotentiary (since 13 March 2006)*
Mr Demeke Antnafu Ambulo **m** *Minister-Counsellor*
Mr Tewolde Mulugeta Ambaye *Minister-Counsellor*

Mr Hirut Zemene Kassa　*　*Minister-Counsellor*
Mr Berhane Fesseha Woldeselassie　m　*Minister-Counsellor*
Mr Feseha Zeryhun Woldu　*Counsellor*
Mr Shegaw Abate Yimer　*Counsellor*
Mr Alemseged Tekelhaimanot Tesfay　m　*1st Secretary*
Mrs Netsanet Tseganeh Mekonnen　m　*2nd Secretary*

FIJI

High Commission of the Republic of Fiji
34 Hyde Park Gate SW7 5DN
020 7584 3661
Fax 020 7584 2838
mail@fijihighcommission.org.uk
www.fijihighcommission.org.uk
Monday-Friday 09.30-13.00 & 14.00-17.00

Consular Section
020 75843661 ext 5340/5347

HIS EXCELLENCY MR RATU NAIVAKARURUBALAVU SOLO MARA　m　*High Commissioner (since 25 September 2011)*
　　　　　Mrs Kerry Megan Mara
Mr Seniteli Wainiu　m　*2nd Secretary*
Mr Hansel Whippy　m　*2nd Secretary*

FINLAND

The Embassy of Finland
38 Chesham Place SW1X 8HW
020 7838 6200
Fax 020 7235 3680
Consulate Fax 020 7838 9703
sanomat.lon@formin.fi
www.finemb.org.uk
Monday-Friday 08.30-16.30

Finland Trade Centre
Lyric House 149 Hammersmith Road W14 0QL
020 7371 6005
Fax 020 7471 3581

HIS EXCELLENCY MR PEKKA HUHTANIEMI　m　*Ambassador Extraordinary & Plenipotentiary (since 31 May 2010)*
　　　　　Mrs Liisa Huhtaniemi
Mrs Leena Gardemeister　m　*Minister*
Ms Paivi Nevala　*Counsellor*
Mr Pekka Isosomppi　m　*Counsellor (Press Affairs)*
Mr Juho Simpura　m　*1st Secretary*
Mr Lasse Sinikallas　m　*1st Secretary*
Ms Tiina Nelin　*2nd Secretary (Consular & Administrative Affairs)*
Colonel Simo Hautala　m　*Defence Attaché*
Mr Mika Eriksson　m　*Head of Trade Centre*

FRANCE

Embassy of France
58 Knightsbridge SW1X 7JT
020 7073 1000
Fax 020-7073 1004
www.ambafrance-uk.org

Consular Section
21 Cromwell Road SW7 2EN
020 7073 1200
Fax 020 7073 1201

Visa Section
6A Cromwell Place SW7 2EW
020 7073 1250
Fax 020-7073 1246

Cultural Section
23 Cromwell Road SW7 2EL
020 7073 1300
Fax 020 7073 1326

Science & Technology Section
6 Cromwell Place SW7 2JN
020 7073 1380
Fax 020 7073 1390

Trade Commission – UBIFRANCE
28-29 Haymarket SW1 YSP
020 7024 3610
Fax 020 7024 3669

Paymaster & Financial Comptroller Section
30 Queen's Gate Terrace SW7 5PH
020 7589 4909
Fax 020 7581 1360

Taxation Section
58 Knightsbridge SW1X 7JT
020 7073 1000
Fax 020 7073 1196

Customs Section
58 Knightsbridge SW1X 7JT
Tel 020 7073 1000
Fax 020 7073 1159

Economic Section
58 Knightsbridge SW1X 7JT
Tel 020 7073 1000
Fax 020 7073 1189

HIS EXCELLENCY MR BERNARD EMIÉ   *Ambassador Extraordinary & Plenipotentiary (since 04 April 2011)*
          Mrs Isabelle Emié
Mr Antoine Anfré   *Minister-Counsellor*
Mr Patrick Pascal   *   *1st Secretary*
Mr Xavier Chatel   **m**   *Press Counsellor*
Mr Cyril Blondel   **m**   *1st Secretary*
Mr Emmanuel Loriot   **m**   *1st Secretary*
Mrs Madeleine Courant   **m**   *2nd Secretary*

Mr Francois Courant   **m**   *2nd Secretary, Deputy Press Counsellor*
Mr Quentin Teisseire   *2nd Secretary*
Mr Bruno Aguesse   **m**   *1st Secretary (Administrative Affairs)*
Mr Marc Efchin   **m**   *1st Secretary*
Mr Henri Jourdon   **m**   *1st Secretary*
Mrs Cécile Driesbach   *2nd Secretary*
Mrs Anne Nguyen-Robion   **m**   *3rd Secretary (Administrative Affairs)*
Mr Franck Schaal   **m**   *3rd Secretary*
Mr Olivier Robby   **m**   *3rd Secretary*
Mr Dominique Yeddou   *3rd Secretary*
Mrs Valérie Leignel   *Attaché (Protocol)*
Admiral Henri Schricke   *Defence Attaché*
Colonel Alain Bayle   **m**   *Army Attaché*
Captain Yves Le Corre   **m**   *Naval Attaché*
Senior Engineer for Armaments Mr Nicolas Fournier   **m**   *Defence Equipment Attaché*
Colonel Nicolas Chambaz   **m**   *Air Attaché*
Ms Laurence Dubois Destrizais   *Minister-Counsellor (Economic & Financial Affairs)*
Mr Emmanuel Betry   *Counsellor (Financial Affairs)*
Ms Laure Meyssonnier   *Counsellor (Economic Affairs)*
Miss Soraya Oquab   *Attaché (Economic Affairs)*
Miss Marion Chich   **m**   *Attaché (Financial Affairs)*
Mr Hervé Ochsenbein   **m**   *Counsellor (Commercial Affairs)*
Mr Olivier Prothon   **m**   *Attaché (Commercial Affairs)*
Mr Christophe Desplanches   **m**   *Attaché (Commercial Affairs)*
Mrs Caroline Laporte   *Commercial Counsellor (Investment)*
Mr Ludovic Halbwax   *Attaché (Taxation)*
Mr Marc Cesari   **m**   *Deputy Attaché (Taxation)*
Mr Laurent Burin des Roziers   **m**   *Cultural Counsellor*
Mr Laurent Batut   *Cultural Attaché*
Mr Michel-Louis Richard   *Cultural Attaché*
Ms Marie-Doha Besancenot   *Cultural Attaché (Art Department)*
Mr Yves Letournel   **m**   *Cultural Attaché*
Mr Daniel Pirat   **m**   *Cultural Attaché (Administrative Affairs)*
Mr Odran Trumel   *Cultural Attaché (Administrative Affairs)*
Ms Hélène Fiamma   **m**   *Cultural Attaché (Book Department)*
Mr Cyrille van Effenterre   *Counsellor (Science & Technology)*
Mrs France Henry   *Counsellor (Social Affairs)*
Mr Jean-Marc Capdevila   **m**   *Counsellor (Nuclear)*
Mr Jean-Jacques Richard   **m**   *Customs Attaché*
Mr Olivier Chambard   **m**   *Minister-Counsellor & Consul General*
Mr Eric Bayer   *   *Counsellor (Deputy Consul General)*
Mr Jean-Baptiste Girard   *Vice Consul*
Ms Annabelle Averty   *Vice Consul*
Mr Olivier Tulliez   **m**   *Vice Consul*
Mr Francis Lagoutte   *Counsellor (Paymaster & Financial Comptroller)*
Mr Jean-Marc Fumat   **m**   *Attaché (Paymaster & Assistant Financial Comptroller)*
Mr Olivier Deparis   **m**   *Counsellor (Judicial Affairs)*
Ms Nadine Joly   *Counsellor (Police)*
Mr Franck Chaix   *Attaché (Police)*

GABON

Embassy of the Gabonese Republic
27 Elvaston Place SW7 5NL
020 7823 9986
Fax 020-7584 0047
www.gaboneseembassy.org

Vacant   *Ambassador Extraordinary & Plenipotentiary*
Mr Nzé-Ekome   **m**   *1st Counsellor Chargé d' Affaires*
Mr Jean Ngye   **m**   *Counsellor to the IMO*
Mrs Adeline Ngye   **m**   *2nd Counsellor*
Miss Emma Charlotte Akiremy   *Cultural Counsellor*
Mr Pierre Francis Moubikou   **m**   *Economic Counsellor*
Mr Lie Patrick Mouvogny   **m**   *Economic Counsellor*
Mrs Ruth Mouvogny   **m**   *2nd Secretary*
Miss Antoinette Pitty   *Counsellor in Charge of Chancery*

THE GAMBIA

Embassy of The Gambia
92 Ledbury Road W11 2AH
020 7229 8066
Fax 020 7229 9225
gambiahighcomuk@btconnect.com
Monday-Thursday 09.30-17.00, Friday 09.30-13.00

HER EXCELLENCY MRS ELIZABETH YA ELI HARDING   *Ambassador Extraordinary & Plenipotentiary*
(since 04 October 2013, High Commissioner between 20 August 2007 and 03 October 2013)
Mr Yusupha Bojang   **m**   *Deputy Head of Mission*
Ms Ndeye Binta Jobe   *Counsellor*
Mr Gaston Sambou   *1st Secretary*
Mr Ebrima John   **m**   *Finance Attaché*
Mrs Georgina Gomez   **m**   *Protocol/Welfare Officer*

GEORGIA

Embassy of Georgia
4 Russell Gardens W14 8EZ
020 7348 1941
Fax 020 7603 6682
embassy@geoemb.plus.com
www.uk.mfa.gov.ge

Consular Section
020 7348 1942
consular@geoemb.plus.com

Vacant   *Ambassador Extraordinary & Plenipotentiary*
Ms Tamara Kapanadze   *Minister, Deputy Head of Mission*
Mr David Javakhishvili   **m**   *Consul*
Mr Alexander Khvtisiashvili   **m**   *Senior Counsellor*
Ms Nino Kharadze   *Counsellor*
Mrs Ia Makharadze   **m**   *Counsellor*

GERMANY

Embassy of the Federal Republic of Germany
23 Belgrave Square/Chesham Place SW1X 8PZ
020 7824 1300
Fax 020 7824 1449
Monday-Thursday 08.30-17.00 & Friday 08.30-15.30
info@london.diplo.de
www.london.diplo.de

Passport & Visa Section by appointment only
Visa Appointments online or 0871 3762101
Passport Appointments online only
Fax 020 7824 1449
Visa Information Service 020 7824 1465
Passport Information Service 020 7824 1463

Vacant   *Ambassador Extraordinary & Plenipotentiary*
Dr Rudolf Adam   **m**   *Chargé d'Affaires a.i.*
Rear Admiral Karl-Wilhelm Ohlms   **m**   *Defence Attaché*
Dr Gerhard Conrad   **m**   *Minister-(Political Affairs)*
Dr Norman Walter   **m**   *Minister*
Dr Andreas Prothmann   **m**   *Minister*
Mr Stefano Weinberger   **m**   *Minister (Cultural Affairs)*
Mr Thomas F Schneider   **m**   *Minister Counsellor (Legal Consular Affairs)*
Mrs Sibylle Sorg   **m**   *Minister Counsellor (Political Affairs)*
Colonel Michael J Haller   **m**   *Military Attaché*
Col. Andreas Pfeiffer   **m**   *Air Attaché*
Mr Robert Arthur Speicher   **m**   *First Counsellor (Defence Technology)*
Mr Stefan Kordasch   **m**   *Counsellor (Economic Affairs)*
Mr Andreas Schlüter   *Counsellor (Social Affairs)*
Mr Marc Eichhorn   **m**   *Counsellor (Scientific Affairs)*
Mrs Silvana Reimann   **m**   *Counsellor (Political Affairs)*
Mr Martin Vetter   **m**   *Counsellor (Administration)*
Commander Jan Hackstein   **m**   Assistant Naval Attaché
Dr Peter Gullo   *1st Secretary*
Mr Michael Schubert   **m**   *1st Secretary*
Ms Christina Kornblum   *2nd Secretary*
Mrs Anna Katharina Ziegler   **m**   *2nd Secretary*
Mr Jakob Orthacker   *2nd Secretary*
Mrs Bettina Ferrand   *   *2nd Secretary*
Mr Rudolf Konrad Buck   **m**   *2nd Secretary (Police Liaison Officer)*
Mr Joerg Rainer Rousselli   **m**   *2nd Secretary (Cultural Liaison Officer)*
Mrs Rosemarie Hille   **m**   *3rd Secretary*
Ms Ingrid Malcomess   *3rd Secretary*
Ms Melanie Jankovic   *3rd Secretary (Administration)*
Mrs Karin Schroeder   **m**   *3rd Secretary (Press Section)*
Mr Holger Ferdinand Wibe   **m**   *3rd Secretary (Political Affairs)*
Mr Uwe Koppel   **m**   *3rd Secretary (Administration)*
Mr Holger Primas   **m**   *Attaché (Police Liaison Officer)*
Mr Hanno Hille   **m**   *Attaché (Consular Affairs)*
Mr Andreas Doehmen   **m**   *Attaché (Consular Affairs)*
Mrs Nina Walter   **m**   *Attaché (Consular Affairs)*
Mr Theodor Vortkamp   *Attaché (Consular Affairs)*
Mr Kennat Hingst   **m**   *Attaché (Consular Affairs)*
Mr Nino Schramm   *Attaché* (Consular Affairs)

Mr Sven Koegel   *Attaché*
Mrs Susanne Eichhorn   **m**   *Attaché*
Ms Uta Buschmann *Assistant Attaché*
Mrs Antje Waegenbaur   *   *Assistant Attaché*
Mrs Manuela Kirchberg-Welby   **m**   *Assistant Attaché*
Mr Maik Eisbrenner   **m**   *Assistant Attaché*
Mrs Susanne Weyrich-Miller   Assistant *Attaché*
Mr Thorsten Harnys   **m**   *Assistant Attaché (Consular Affairs)*
Warrant Officer II Joachim Auth   **m**   *Chief Petty Officer*
Flight Sergeant Jürgen Pauli   **m**   *Flight Sergeant*
Warrant Officer Dirk Weber   **m**   *Warrant Officer 2*
Sergeant Martin Ernst   *Sergeant*
Ms Melanie Meinköhn *Assistant Attaché*
Mrs Kerstin Malin   **m**   *Assistant Attaché*
Ms Daniela Krause   *Assistant Attaché*
Mr Peter Andresen   **m**   *Assistant Attaché*
Ms Annette Hentschel   *Assistant Attaché*
Ms Carola Penz Assistant   *Attaché*

GHANA
Office of the High Commissioner for Ghana
13 Belgrave Square SW1X 8PN
020 7201 5900
Fax 020 7245 9552
gh.donlon@yahoo.com; ghmfa31@ghc-uk.org
www.ghanahighcommissionuk.com
Monday-Friday 09.30-13.00 & 14.00-17.30

Passports, Immigration, Recruitment, Education, Trade & Investment, Police Liaison, & International Maritime Organization
104 Highgate Hill N6 5HE
020 8342 7501
gh.donlon@yahoo.com
www.ghanahighcommissionuk.com
Monday-Friday 09.30-13.00 & 14.00-17.30

HIS EXCELLENCY PROFESSOR KWAKU DANSO-BOAFO   *   *High Commissioner (since 27 September 2009)*
          Mrs Dorothy Danso-Boafo
Mr Edwin Nii Adjei   *   *Minister/Head of Chancery*
Mr George Blankson   **m**   *Minister (Consular & Welfare)*
Commodore seth Vincent Aidoo Coomson   **m**   *Defence Adviser*
Mrs Wilhelmina Asamoah   **m**   *Minister (Education)*
Mr George Kobina Fynn   **m**   *Minister (Trade)*
Mrs Azara Al-hassan Prempeh   **m**   *Minister (IMO Affairs)*
Mrs Beatrice Zakpaa Vib-Sanziri   *   *Minister-Counsellor (Police Liaison)*
Ms Zuweira Ibrahimah Mohammed   *   *Minister-Counsellor (Head of Information)*
Mr Peter Taylor   **m**   *Minister-Counsellor (Political & Economic)*
Mr Thomas Mbun   **m**   *Minister-Counsellor (Treasury)*
Wing Commander (CDR) Eric Agyen-Frempong   *   *Deputy Defence Adviser*
Mr Ale Owiredu Adu   *   *Minister-Counsellor (Passport & Immigration)*
Mr Jojo Bruce-Quansah   *   *Counsellor (Information)*
Ms Neematu Ziblim Adam   *   *Counsellor (Protocol & Administration)*
Mr Daniel Nsiah   **m**   *Counsellor (Finance)*

Mr Bennet Gyau-Yeboah **m** *Counsellor (Consular & Welfare)*
Mrs Anita Osei Poku * *Counsellor (Education)*
Mrs Linda Hogba-Adzanku * *1st Secretary (Finance)*
Mrs Georgina Ankora * *1st Secretary (Finance)*
Mrs Abigail Brown * *1st Secretary (Administration)*
Mrs Matylda Bondzie * *1st Secretary (Consular & Welfare)*
Ms Elizabeth Nkansah * *1st Secretary (Passports & Immigration)*
Ms Elsie Awuku * *1st Secretary (Education)*
Mr Emmanuel Bebaako-Mensah * *1st Secretary (Passport & Immigration)*
Mr Richard Opata Sackitey * *2nd Secretary (Finance)*
Mr Godfred Azure * *2nd Secretary (Protocol)*
Mr Eric Nyarku * *3rd Secretary (Protocol)*
Ms Rose A. Agyapong *3rd Secretary (Administration)*
WOI Lambert Ponedong **m** *Chief Clerk (Defence)*
WOI Tetteh Adico **m** *Finance (Defence)*
Sgt Daniel Appiatu Adom **m** *Movement Clerk*
Mr George Amarh * *Attaché Technical*
Mr Isaac Oteng Adusei * *Attaché Technical*
Mr Joseph Nortey **m** *Attaché Technical*
Mr Henry Osae **m** *Attaché Technical*

GREECE

Embassy of Greece
1A Holland Park W11 3TP
020 7229 3850
Fax 020 7229 7221
political@greekembassy.org.uk
www.greekembassy.org.uk
Monday-Friday 09.00-16.30

Consular Section
1A Holland Park W11 3TP
02073135600 – 5609
Fax 020 7243 3202
consulate@greekembassy.org.uk

Defence Attaché's Office
1A Holland Park W11 3TP
020 7727 3785
Fax 020 7221 2818
hellenicdasecretary@yahoo.gr

Economic & Commercial Office
1A Holland Park W11 3TP
020 7727 8860
Fax 020 7727 9934
commercial@greekembassy.org.uk

Maritime Affairs Office
1A Holland Park W11 3TP
020 7727 0507
Fax 020 7727 0509
maritime@greekembassy.org.uk

Press & Communications Office
1A Holland Park W11 3TP
020 7727 3071
Fax 020 7727 8960
pressoffice@greekembassy.org.uk

Educational Affairs Office
1A Holland Park W11 3TP
020 7221 5977
Fax 020 7243 4212
education@greekembassy.org.uk

Police Liaison Office
1A Holland Park W11 3TP
020 7313 8951
Fax 020 7229 7221
grpoliceliaison@greekembassy.org.uk

National Tourism Organisation Office
4 Conduit Street W1S 2DJ
020 7495 9300
Fax 020 7495 4057
info@gnto.co.uk

HIS EXCELLENCY MR KONSTANTINOS BIKAS   **m**   *Ambassador Extraordinary & Plenipotentiary (since 08 October 2012)*
        Mrs Maria Gogka-Bikas
Mr Nicolaos Argyros   **m**   *Minister Plenipotentiary (Deputy Head of Mission)*
Captain (Hellenic Navy) Apostolos Trivlidis   **m**   *Defence Attaché*
Dr Victoria Solomonidis   **m**   *Minister-Counsellor (Cultural)*
Mr Antonios Katepodis   **m**   *1st Counsellor (Economic & Commercial)*
Mrs Varvara Kampouridi   **m**   *Counsellor (Education)*
Captain Efstathios Kalyvas   **m**   *Maritime Attaché*
Mr Yorgos Dardavilas   **m**   *1st Counsellor (Press & Communications)*
Major Antonios Samouris   *Police Liaison Officer*
Mrs Evdokia Fournatzopoulou   **m**   *Expert Counsellor 1st Class*
Ms Georgia Soultanopoulou   *2nd Counsellor (Political)*
Lt Colonel (Hellenic Air Force) Georgios Tsiotsis   **m**   *Assistant Defence Attaché*
Major Ilias Chatzichamperis   **m**   *Assistant Defence Attaché*
Mr Dimitrios Dohtsis   *1st Secretary*
Mrs Despina Chasirzoglou   **m**   *2nd Secretary (Head of Consular Office)*
Ms Eleni Makrypidi   **m**   *2nd Secretary (Economic & Commercial)*
Mrs Lambrini-Marina Koltsida   **m**   *Secretary for Press*
Mrs Dimitra Panagiotopoulou   **m**   *Secretary for Press*
Ms Irini Kioulafi   *Secretary for Press*
Mrs Maria Helen Andriotou   **m**   *Attaché*
Mrs Dimitra Kouka   **m**   *Attaché*
Mrs Veronia Lo   **m**   *Attaché*
Mrs Calomira Perdikari   *Attaché*
Mrs Maria Monoyoudi   **m**   *Attaché*

GRENADA

High Commission for Grenada
The Chapel Archel Road West Kensington W14 9QH
020 7385 4415
Fax 020 7381 4807
office@grenada-highcommission.co.uk
www.grenadahclon.co.uk
Monday-Friday 09.00-17.00
Consular Hours: Monday-Friday : 10.00-14.00

HIS EXCELLENCY MR JOSLYN RAPHAEL WHITEMAN m *High Commissioner (since 05 August 2013)*
          Mrs Lydia Whiteman
Ms Feona Sandy *1st Secretary (Political & Economic Affairs)*
Mr Richard Leslie Winston Hall * *Attaché (Immigration & Consular Affairs)*
Ms Lornie Bartholomew *Attaché (Administration)*

GUATEMALA

Embassy of Guatemala
13 Fawcett St SW10 9HN
020 7351 3042
inglaterra@minex.gob.gt
info@guatemalanembassy.co.uk

Consular Section
13a Fawcett St SW10 9HN
020 7351 3042
consul@guatemalanembassy.co.uk

HIS EXCELLENCY MR ACISCLO VALLADARES MOLINA m *Ambassador Extraordinary & Plenipotentiary (since 05 January 2010)*
          Mrs Raquel Urruela de Valladares
Mr Lesther Antonio Ortega Lemus *Minister-Counsellor (Deputy Head of Mission)*
Mr Henning Andres Droege *Counsellor (Deputy Head of Mission)*
Miss Lizzi Maffioli *First Secretary and Consul*

GUINEA

Embassy of the Republic of Guinea
258 Belsize Road NW6 4BT
020 7316 1861
Fax 020 7316 1868
ambaguilondres@mae.gov.gn

HIS EXCELLENCY MR PAUL GOA ZOUMANIGUI * *Ambassador Extraordinary & Plenipotentiary (since 08 November 2013)*
Mrs Ramatoulaye Sy Sangare * *Counsellor*
Mr Jean Emile Curtis m *First Secretary*
Mrs Fatoumata Diaraye Balde * *Administrative Attaché*

GUINEA-BISSAU

Embassy of the Republic of Guinea-Bissau
94 Rue St. Lazare 75009 Paris
0033 1 48 74 36 39

Vacant *Ambassador Extraordinary & Plenipotentiary*

Mrs Maria Filomena Embalo Araujo Vieira **m** *Counsellor (Economic)*
Mr José Filipe Fonseca **m** *Counsellor*
Mr Oscar Batica Ferreira **m** *1st Secretary*

GUYANA

High Commission for Guyana
3 Palace Court Bayswater Road W2 4LP
020 7229 7684
Fax 020 7727 9809
guyanahc1@btconnect.com
www.guyanahclondon.co.uk

His Excellency Mr Laleshwar K.N. Singh **m** *High Commissioner (since 16 July 1993)*
　　　　Mrs Latchmin Singh
Ms Marion Elizabeth Herbert *Counsellor*
Miss Keishanna Sullivan *2nd Secretary*
Miss Yolla Sharon Lewis *Attaché (Finance)*

HAITI

The Embassy of the Republic of Haiti
14 Cavendish Place W1G 9DJ
020 7637 8985

Mrs Valerie F. Pompee * *Chargé d'Affaires*
Mr Jean Joseph Léandre **m** *Counsellor*

HOLY SEE

Apostolic Nunciature
54 Parkside SW19 5NE
020 8944 7189
Fax 020 8947 2494
Monday-Friday 09.00-17.00

His Excellency Archbishop Antonio Mennini *Apostolic Nuncio (since 21 February 2011)*
Rt Rev. Monsignor Eloy Alberto Santiago Santiago *First Secretary*

HONDURAS

Embassy of Honduras
4th Floor 136 Baker Street W1U 6UD
020 7486 4880
Fax 020 7486 4550
hondurasuk@lineone.net
Monday-Friday 10.00-1300 & 14.00-17.00

His Excellency Mr Ivan Romero-Martinez **m** *Ambassador Extraordinary & Plenipotentiary (since 22 January 2008)*
　　　　Mrs Mirian Nasser de Romero
Miss Andrea Argueta-Scheib *Minister-Counsellor*
Miss Elisa Bennaton-Jimenez *Minister-Counsellor*

HUNGARY

Embassy of Hungary
35 Eaton Place SW1X 8BY
020 7201 3440
Fax 020 7823 1348
mission.lon@mfa.gov.hu
www.mfa.gov.hu/emb/london
Monday-Thursday 08.30-17.00 & Friday 08.30-14.00

Consular Department
35B Eaton Place SW1X 8BY
020 7235 5218
Fax 020 7235 8630
konz.lon@mfa.gov.hu
Monday-Friday 09.30-12.00

Economic, Investment & Trade Commission
46 Eaton Place SW1X 8AL
020 7235 8767
Fax 020 7235 4319
london@hita.hu

Hungarian Cultural Centre
10 Maiden Lane WC2E 7NA
020 7240 8448
Fax 020 7240 4847
Andrea.kos@hungary.org.uk

Hungarian National Tourist Office
46 Eaton Place SW1X 8AL
020 7823 1032
Fax 020 7823 1459
london@gotohungary.co.uk
www.gotohungary.co.uk

HIS EXCELLENCY MR JÁNOS CSÁK   **m**   *Ambassador Extraordinary & Plenipotentiary (since 31 January 2011)*
      Mrs Júlia Márton
Dr Maria Vass-Salazar   **m**   *Envoy Extraordinary & Minister Plenipotentiary (Deputy Head of Mission)*
Ms Andrea Norman-Walker   **m**   *1st Counsellor*
Colonel József Gulyás   **m**   *Defence Attaché*
Mrs Eszter Mária Pataki   *   *1st Counsellor (Press & Culture)*
Mr László Riskó-Nagy   *Counsellor (Head of Consular Section)*
Mr Zoltan Varga   **m**   *Counsellor (Political)*
Dr Beata Klara Paszthy   *   *Counsellor (Hungarian Cultural Centre)*
Mr Andras Juhasz   *Counsellor (Political)*
Mrs Ildikó Márkus   **m**   *Counsellor (Consular Affairs)*
Mrs Katalin Kapócsné Haás   **m**   *1st Secretary (Economic, Investment and Trade Commission)*
Mr Csaba Gele'nyi   *1st Secretary (Economic, Investment and Trade Commission)*
Ms Eszter Kovacs   *1st Secretary (EU Affairs)*
Ms Aniko Dobi-Rózsa   *1st Secretary (Scientific and Technology Affairs)*
Ms Edina Cserjés   *2nd Secretary (Consular Affairs)*
Mr László Weidlich   **m**   *1st Secretary (Chancellor)*

ICELAND

Embassy of Iceland
2A Hans Street SW1X 0JE
020 7259 3999
Fax 020 7245 9649
Emb.london@mfa.is
www.iceland.is/uk
Monday-Friday 09.00-16.30

HIS EXCELLENCY MR BENEDIKT JÓNSSON **m** *Ambassador Extraordinary & Plenipotentiary (since 05 October 2009)*
         Mrs Adalheidur Oskarsdóttir
Mr Axel Nikulasson **m** *Counsellor*
Ms Petrina Bachmann *Attaché*

INDIA

Office of the High Commissioner for India
India House Aldwych WC2B 4NA
020 7836 8484
Fax 020 7836 4331
administration@hcilondon.in
www.hcilondon.net

(Vacant) *High Commissioner*
Mr Virander Kumar Paul **m** *Acting High Commissioner*
Mrs Sangeeta Bahadur **m** *Minister (Culture)*
Mr Samant Kumar Goel **m** *Minister (Consular)*
Mr Sukhdev Singh Sidhu **m** *Minister (Coordination)*
Mr Rajesh Singh **m** *Minister (Audit)*
Mr Prashant Pise **m** *Counsellor (Political/Head of Chancery) and Special Adviser to High Commissioner*
Ms Jasminder Kasturia **m** *Counsellor (P&I & IO)*
Dr Shailesh K Singh **m** *Counsellor*
Air Commodore Ashok Lal **m** *Air Adviser*
Brigadier Sandeepan Handa **m** *Military Adviser*
Commodore Sandeep Beecha **m** *Naval Adviser*
Ms Padmaja **m** *1st Secretary (P & I)*
Mr Tara Chand **m** *1st Secretary (P&M)*
Mr Balvinder Humpal **m** *1st Secretary (Protocol)*
Mr T V Vasudevan **m** *1st Secretary (Education & Political)*
Mr Pritam Lal **m** *1st Secretary (Coord)*
Mr S.R. Chowdhury **m** *1st Secretary (Consular)*
Mr Ramesh Kumar Raman **m** *1st Secretary (Trade)*
Mr Amitabh Prasad **m** *1st Secretary (Audit)*
Mr Pradeep Kumar Patel ***** *1st Secretary*
Mrs Smita Pant ***** *1st Secretary*
Mr Mohinder Pratap Singh **m** *1st Secretary*
Mr Avtar Singh **m** *2nd Secretary (Visa)*
Mr Brajabashi Sarkar **m** *2nd Secretary (Political)*
Mr Edauazhipurath Krishnan Revi **m** *2nd Secretary (Passport)*
Mr Prithvi Raj Singh **m** *2nd Secretary (Administration)*
Mrs Tara Pathak **m** *2nd Secretary (PPS)*
Mrs Mantravadi Bhanumati **m** *2nd Secretary (PPS)*
Mr Gowri Shankar Sulapu **m** *2nd Secretary (Cultural Centre)*

Mr Ravindran Gopalakrishnan **m** *2nd Secretary*
Mrs Alka Sarkar **m** *2nd Secretary*
Ms Kiran Negi **m** *2nd Secretary*
Mr Puran Mehra **m** *Attaché (Passport)*
Mr Ajay Kumar Ajmani **m** *Attaché (PS)*
Mr Shiv Kumar Sundaramurthy **m** *Attaché (PS)*
Mr Deepak Bellani **m** *Attaché (Protocol)*
Mr Ravi Kumar **m** *Attaché (Pol)*
Mr Sanjay Kumar Bihani **m** *Attaché (P&I)*
Mr Parmanand Sinha **m** *Attaché (Visa)*
Mr Vijay Pal Singh **m** *Attaché (Political)*
Mr Ram Saran Rawat **m** *Attaché (Political)*
Mr Dharmender Kumar **m** *Attaché (Consular)*
Mr Binod Kumar **m** Attaché
Mr G. Srinivasan **m** *Attaché*
Mr Naresh Kumar Sharma **m** *Attaché*
Mr Manoj Sahu **m** *Attaché*
Mr Pradyumna Kumar Sahu **m** *Attaché*
Mr Sankaranarayanan Ramamurthy **m** *Attaché*

INDONESIA
Embassy of the Republic of Indonesia
38 Grosvenor Square W1K 2HW
020 7499 7661
Fax 020 7491 4993
kbri@btconnect.com
www.indonesianembassy.org.uk
Monday-Friday 09.00-17.00

Consular Department & Visa Section
38A Adam's Row W1K 2HW
Fax 020 7491 4993
Monday-Friday 10.00-13.00 (submission of passports/visas), 14.30-16.00 (collection of passports/visas)

His Excellency Mr T M Hamzah Thayeb **m** *Ambassador Extraordinary & Plenipotentiary (since 01 February 2012)*
       Mrs Lastry Thayeb
Mr Harry R J Kandou **m** *Minister*
Mrs Masriati Lita Saadia Pratama **m** *Minister Counsellor (Economic Affairs)*
Mr Eka Aryanto Suripto **m** *Minister Counsellor (Protocol and Consular Affairs)*
Mr Dino Kusnadi **m** *Counsellor (Information, Social & Cultural Affairs)*
Mr Dindin Wahyudin **m** *Minister Counsellor (Political Affairs)*
Col. Jonni Mahroza **m** *Defence Attaché*
Mrs Merry Maryati **m** *Trade Attaché*
Dr Tubagus Ahmad Fauzi Soelaiman **m** *Education Attaché*
Capt Sahattua Simatupang **m** *Transportation Attaché*
Mrs Rossy Verona **m** *Counsellor*
Miss Heni Hamidah *1st Secretary*
Mr Wandi Adriano Syamsu * *1st Secretary*
Mr Hastin Dumadi **m** *1st Secretary*
Mr Fadjar Tjahjanto **m** *2nd Secretary*
Ms Silvia Juliana Malau *2nd Secretary*
Mrs Veronika Vonny Handayani **m** *3rd Secretary*

Mr Yudho Priambudhi Asruchin   *3rd Secretary*
Mr Fajar Narfian   **m**   *Attaché*
Ms Bitaria Citra Dewi   *Attaché*

IRAN

(Temporarily closed)

Embassy of the Islamic Republic of Iran

16 Prince's Gate SW7 1PT
020 7225 4208
Fax 020 7589 4440
consulate@iran-embassy.org.uk
www.iran-embassy.org.uk

Consular Section

50 Kensington Court W8 5DB
020 7937 5225
Fax 020 7938 1615

IRAQ

Embassy of the Republic of Iraq

21 Queens Gate SW7 5JE
020 7590 7650
Fax 020 7590 7679
lonemb@mofaml.gov.iq
www.mofamission.gov.iq
Monday-Friday 09.00-16.00

Consular Section

3 Elvaston Place SW7 5QH
020 7590 9220
Fax 020 7590 9226
Monday-Friday 10.00-13.00

Military Attaché Office

48 Gunnersbury Avenue W5 4HA
020 8752 1314
Fax 020 8896 0356
newiraq2ma@yahoo.com

Cultural Attaché's Office

14-15 Child's Place SW5 9RX
020 7370 2940
Fax 020 7370 2941
office@iraqculturalattache.org.uk

Commercial Attaché Office

7-10 Leadenhall Street EC3V 1JX
020 7725 7007
uk@iraqcomattache.org

HIS EXCELLENCY MR FAIK FERIK ABDILEZIZ NERWEYI   **m**   *Ambassador Extraordinary & Plenipotentiary (since 03 June 2013)*
        Mrs Sinikka Anneli Nerweyi
Dr Muhieddin Al-Taaie   **m**   *Minister Plenipotentiary*
Mr Sherwan Dizayee   **m**   *Minister Plenipotentiary*
Dr Abdulhamid M.H. Hamid   **m**   *Counsellor*

Mrs Tania A. Hussein   *1st Secretary*
Mr Wael Al-Robaaie   **m**   *1st Secretary*
Mr Qusay Alkoubaisi   **m**   *2nd Secretary*
Mr Aiman Abdulmajeed   **m**   *2nd Secretary*
Mrs Kani Abdulkader Abdulkarem Hadad   **m**   *3rd Secretary*
Mr Abduljabbar Abd   **m**   *3rd Secretary*
Mr Bilal Al-Hasirahchi   **m**   *Attaché*
Mr Ammar Farhan   **m**   *Attaché*
Major General Ali Al-Najati   **m**   *Military Attaché*
Dr Mosa Al-Mosawe   **m**   *Cultural Attaché*
Mr Abdul-Hassan Abdul-Amir   **m**   *Commercial Attaché*

IRELAND

Embassy of Ireland
17 Grosvenor Place SW1X 7HR
020 7235 2171
Fax 020 7201 2515
londonembassymail@dfa.ie
www.embassyofireland.co.uk
Monday-Friday 09.30-17.00

Passport & Visa Office
114A Cromwell Road SW7 4ES
Passport enquiries 020 7373 4339
Visa enquiries 090 6661 0197
Diplomatic visa appointments 020 7341 5424
Fax 020 7373 4589
Passport Office Monday-Friday 09.30-16.30
Visa Office Monday-Friday 09.00-12.00 (Lodge applications), 14.30-16.00 (Collections)

His Excellency Mr Daniel Mulhall   **m**   *Ambassador Extraordinary & Plenipotentiary (since 05 September 2013)*
             Mrs Greta Mulhall
Mr John McCullagh   **m**   *Counsellor (EU & External Relations)*
Mrs Barbara Cullinane   **m**   *Counsellor (Anglo Irish & Political Affairs)*
Mr Declan Morrin   **m**   *Counsellor (Economic & Trade Affairs)*
Ms Elizabeth McCullough   **m**   *Acting Counsellor (Press & information)*
Ms Jane Connolly   *1st Secretary (Irish Community& Culture)*
Mr Terry O'Sullivan   **m**   *1st Secretary (Customs & Revenue)*
Ms Noeleen Curran   *   *1st Secretary (Consular & Corporate Services)*
Ms Mary McCarthy   *1st Secretary (Agriculture)*
Ms Clare Brosnan   *Acting 1st Secretary (Press & Political Affairs)*
Ms Cathy Barnicle   *3rd Secretary*
Mr Joe O'Flynn   **m**   *Attaché*
Mr Dermot Keehan   *Attaché (Economic & Trade Affairs)*
Ms Assumpta Griffin   *Attaché (Passport Services)*
Ms Jean McManus   **m**   *Attaché (Consular & Corporate Services)*
Mr David O'Rourke   *   *Attaché (Visa Services)*

ISRAEL

Embassy of Israel
2 Palace Green Kensington W8 4QB
020 7957 9500
Fax 020 7957 9555
www.london.mfa.gov.il
Monday-Thursday 08.30-17.30 & Friday 08.30-13.30

Defence Section
2a Palace Green Kensington W8 4QB
020 7957 9548

Consular Section
15a Old Court Place Kensington W8 4QB
020 7957 9516

HIS EXCELLENCY MR DANIEL TAUB   **m**   *Ambassador Extraordinary & Plenipotentiary (since 05 September 2011)*
       Mrs Zehava Taub
Mr Eitan Na'eh   **m**   *Minister Plenipotentiary*
Mr Marcos Christian Cantor   **m**   *Counsellor*
Mrs Iris Ambor   **m**   *Counsellor (Cultural Affairs)*
Mr Ismail Khaldi   *Counsellor*
Mrs Rony Yedidia   **m**   *Counsellor (Public Affairs)*
Mr Yiftah Curiel   **m**   *Counsellor (Public Affairs)*
Mr Noah Shani   **m**   *Minister (Commercial Affairs)*
Mrs Naama Oryan   **m**   *1st Secretary*
Mrs Judith Raby-Mermer   **m**   *Minister (Administration) & Consul General*
Mr Joseph Alfassy   **m**   *Minister (Administration)*
Mrs Tamar Fillar Frenkel   **m**   *1st Secretary*
Colonel Eytan Arad   **m**   *Defence Attaché & Ministry of Defence Representative*

ITALY

Embassy of Italy
14 Three Kings' Yard Davies Street W1K 4EH
020 7312 2200
Fax 020 7312 2230
ambasciata.londra@esteri.it
www.amblondra.esteri.it

Consular Section
Harp House, 83-86 Farringdon Street, EC4A 4BL
020 7936 5900
Fax 020 7583 9425
consolato.londra@esteri.it
www.conslondra.esteri.it

Cultural Section
39 Belgrave Square SW1X 8NX
020 7235 1461
Fax 020 7235 4618
icilondon@esteri.it
www.icilondon.esteri.it

Defence Section (Military, Naval & Air Attaché's Offices)
7-10 Hobart Place SW1W 0HH
020 7259 4500
Fax 020 7259 4511
segr_dif@difeitalia.co.uk

Financial Section
2 Royal Exchange EC3V 3DG
020 7606 4201
Fax: 020 7606 4065
bilondon@btclick.com

Trade Commission
14 Waterloo Place SW1Y 4AR
020 7389 0300
 Fax: 020 7389 0301
londra@ice.it
www.italtrade.com

HIS EXCELLENCY PASQUALE Q. TERRACCIANO   **m**   *Ambassador Extraordinary & Plenipotentiary (since 01 May 2013)*
        Mrs Karen Terracciano Lawrence
Mr Vincenzo Celeste   **m**   *Minister (Deputy Head of Mission)*
Mr Massimiliano Mazzanti   **m**   *Consul General*
Rear Admiral Dario Giacomin   **m**   *Defence & Naval Attaché*
Mr Nicola Todaro Marescotti   *1st Counsellor (Press Affairs)*
Mrs Silvia Limoncini   *   *1st Counsellor*
Mr Lorenzo Fanara   *Counsellor*
Mr Dante Brandi   *Counsellor*
Mr Edoardo Napoli   **m**   *1st Secretary (Protocol & Secretarial Affairs)*
Mr Franco Giordani   **m**   *Attaché (Administrative Affairs)*
Prof Salvator Roberto Amendolia   *Attaché (Scientific Affairs)*
Col. Mauro Gabetta   **m**   *Air Attaché*
Col. Stefano Mannino   **m**   *Army Attaché*
Lt Col. Emilio Renzo Fiora   **m**   *Attaché (Customs, Excise & Tax Affairs)*
Mr Giampietro Moscatelli   *Attaché (Police Affairs)*
Mrs Caterina Colapietro   **m**   *Attaché (Administrative Affairs)*
Miss Laura Albanese   *Attaché (Economic Affairs)*
Mrs Antonella Airoldi   *   *Attaché (Economic Affairs)*
Mrs Sarah Eti Castellani   **m**   *1st Secretary (Consul)*
Ms Lidia Polmonari   *Attaché (Consular Affairs)*
Ms Marisa Liserre   *Attaché (Consular Affairs)*
Mrs Giuseppina Bove   **m**   *Attaché (Consular Affairs)*
Ms Caterina Cardona   *Attaché (Cultural Affairs - Director)*
Mr Fortunato Celi Zullo   *Attaché (Trade Commissioner)*
Ms Anna Marra   *Attaché (Finance)*
Mrs Carla Babini   **m**   *Attaché (Cultural Affairs)*

JAMAICA

Jamaican High Commission
1-2 Prince Consort Road SW7 2BZ
020 7823 9911
Fax 020 7589 5154
jamhigh@jhcuk.com
www.jhcuk.com
Monday-Thursday 09.00-17.00 & Friday 09.00-16.00

Passport & Visa Section
Monday-Friday 09.30-13.30

HER EXCELLENCY MS ALOUN NDOMBET-ASSAMBA   *High Commissioner (since 24 May 2012)*
Mrs Diedre Nichole Mills   **m**   *Deputy High Commissioner*
Mr Lincoln Downer   **m**   *Minister-Counsellor (Consular Affairs & Diaspora Development)*
Ms Christine Allison Dale   *Counsellor*
Mr Laurence Jones   *Counsellor (Commercial Affairs)*
Mr Trevor Pinnock   *1st Secretary (Finance & Administration)*
Ms Carol Stewart   *1st Secretary (Consular Affairs)*
Mrs Natalie McIntosh-Carroo   **m**   *Attaché*

JAPAN

Embassy of Japan
101-104 Piccadilly W1J 7JT
020 7465 6500
Fax 020 7491 9348
Monday-Friday 09.30-18.00
Visa Section 020 7465 6565 Fax 020 7491 9328
Information Section 020 7465 6500 Fax 020 7491 9347
www.uk.emb-japan.go.jp

HIS EXCELLENCY MR KEIICHI HAYASHI   **m**   *Ambassador Extraordinary & Plenipotentiary (since 21 January 2011)*
　　　　Mrs Hiroko Hayashi
Mr Akio Miyajima   *   *Envoy Extraordinary & Minister Plenipotentiary*
Mr Naoki Ito   **m**   *Minister (Economic)*
Mr Noriyuki Shikata   **m**   *Minister (Political)*
Mr Hideki Asari   *   *Minister (Information)*
Mr Masao Uno   **m**   *Minister (Finance)*
Mr Noriyoshi Yamagami   **m**   *Minister (Transport)*
Mr Hiroshi Kawamura   *   *Minister & Consul General*
Miss Mitsuko Hayashi   *Counsellor (Political)*
Mr Naoto Nakahara   **m**   *Counsellor (Administation)*
Mr Kazuya Mori   *Counsellor (Information)*
Mr Katsushi Iwatani   **m**   *Counsellor (Telecommunications)*
Mr Teruo Iwasaki   **m**   *Counsellor (Accounts)*
Mr Fumiaki Tonoki   **m**   *Counsellor (Commercial)*
Mr Kunihiko Tanabe   **m**   *Counsellor (Consular)*
Mr Junichiro Yamakuchi   **m**   *Counsellor (Economic)*
Mr Eiji Watanabe   **m**   *Counsellor (Information)*
Mr Hiroyuki Hanaoka   **m**   *Counsellor & Medical Attaché*
Mr Kazuyoshi Onishi   **m**   *1st Secretary (Political)*
Captain Keizo Kitagawa   **m**   *Defence Attaché*
Mrs Akiko Shikata   **m**   *1st Secretary (Information)*
Mr Katsumi Funayama   *   *1st Secretary (Administration)*

Mr Katsuhiko Kita   **m**   *1st Secretary (Economic)*
Mr Mitsuru Ikeda   *   *1st Secretary (Economics)*
Mr Koji Maruyama   **m**   *1st Secretary (Economic)*
Mr Makoto Katayama   **m**   *1st Secretary (Political)*
Mr Yasufumi Onishi   **m**   *1st Secretary (Transport)*
Mr Shuntaro Netsu   **m**   *1st Secretary (Political)*
Mr Masahiro Oshima   **m**   *1st Secretary (Political)*
Mr Shunsuke Nakamura   **m**   *1st Secretary (Political)*
Mr Atsushi Oku   *   *1st Secretary (Economic)*
Mr Tatsuya Ito   **m**   *1st Secretary (Economic)*
Mr Kazunari Kotake   **m**   *1st Secretary (Consular)*
Mr Hiroyuki Orita   **m**   *1st Secretary (Political)*
Mr Kanji Totokawa   **m**   *1st Secretary (Political)*
Mr Hiromasa Kurokawa   **m**   *1st Secretary (Consular)*
Mr Yoshitake Naraoka   **m**   *1st Secretary (Political)*
Mr Daisuke Ito   **m**   *1st Secretary (Finance)*
Mrs Mayuri Ide   **m**   *1st Secretary (Economic)*
Mr Misato Tanaka   **m**   *2nd Secretary (Administration)*
Mr Haruhiro Tsunashima   **m**   *2nd Secretary (Telecommunications)*
Miss Chika Imaizumi   *2nd Secretary (Protocol)*
Mr Hidehiko Takase   **m**   *2nd Secretary (Security)*
Mr Hajime Furukawa   **m**   *2nd Secretary (Telecommunications)*
Miss Akiko Tamura   *2nd Secretary (Consular)*
Mr Yasuyuki Matsuda   *2nd Secretary (Finance)*
Mr Shinichi Ishikawa   **m**   *2nd Secretary (Political)*
Mr Makoto Shimamura   **m**   *2nd Secretary (Accounts)*
Mr Go Toriyama   **m**   *2nd Secretary (Consular)*
Mrs Yukina Gonda   **m**   *2nd Secretary (Information)*
Mrs Mami Onishi   **m**   *2nd Secretary (Accounts)*
Mr Shunsuke Nomura   *2nd Secretary*
Mr Tatsuya Ito   **m**   *2nd Secretary (Security)*
Mr Kosuke Furutani   *2nd Secretary*
Mr Hideyuki Suzuki   *3rd Secretary (Information)*
Miss Tomoko Koroki   *Attaché (Accounts)*
Mr Makoto Hirayama   *Attaché (Administration)*
Miss Risa Irikita   **m**   *Attaché (Telecommunications)*
Miss Kaori Kodato *Attaché (Administration)*
Miss Ayako Hitomi *Attaché (Information)*

JORDAN
Embassy of the Hashemite Kingdom of Jordan
6 Upper Phillimore Gardens W8 7HA
020 7937 3685
Fax 020 7937 8795
london@fm.gov.jo
www.jordanembassy.org.uk
Monday-Friday 09.00-16.00

Consular & Visa Section
6 Upper Phillimore Gardens W8 7HA
Monday-Friday 10.00-13.00 & 14.30-16.00

Defence Attaché's Office
16 Upper Phillimore Gardens W8 7HA
020 7937 9611
Fax 020 7937 7505
Monday-Thursday 09.00-15.00, Friday 09.00-12.00

Press Office
6 Upper Phillimore Gardens W8 7HA
020 7937 3685
Fax 020 7937 8795
Monday-Friday 09.00-16.00

HIS EXCELLENCY MR MAZEN KEMAL HOMOUD   m   *Ambassador Extraordinary & Plenipotentiary (since 17 June 2011)*
    Mrs Alia Armouti Homoud
Mr Khalid Al-Kadi   *Counsellor (Deputy Head of Mission)*
Miss Rulan M Samara   *Counsellor*
Mr Mohammad Al Aqeel   *2nd Secretary*
Mr Mohammed Elayan Salman Qatarneh   *2nd Secretary (Consular Affairs)*
Mr Mohammed Ahmad Sataan Alradaidah   *3rd Secretary*
Brig. Gen. Ahmad A. Al Muhaisen   m   *Assistant Military, Naval and Air Attaché*
Colonel Hani Awad Ahmad Al-Wardat   m   *Liaison Officer*
Colonel Ayman Ibrahim Alabbadi   *   *Procurement Officer*
Lt. Colonel Yahya Abdel Karim Alnasr   *   *Finance Officer*
Lt. Colonel Naser Abdallah Alkhalaileh   m   *Finance Officer*
1st Lt. Emad M. Suliman Almomani   m   *Medical Officer*

KAZAKHSTAN

Embassy of the Republic of Kazakhstan
125 Pall Mall SW1Y 5EA
020 7590 3490
Fax 020 7584 8481
london@kazembassy.org.uk
www.kazembassy.org.uk
Monday-Friday 09.00-13.00 & 14.30-18.00

Consular Section
020 7590 3485/84
Fax 020 7584 9905
consulate@kazembassy.org.uk
Monday-Friday 09.00-12.00 (except Wednesday)

HIS EXCELLENCY MR KAIRAT ABUSSEITOV   m   *Ambassador Extraordinary & Plenipotentiary (since 25 March 2008)*
    Mrs Rosa Aidarova
Mr Arkin Akhmetov   m   *Minister-Counsellor*
Mr Daulet Batrashev   m   *Minister-Counsellor*
Mr Talgat Bazarbekov   m   *Counsellor*
Mr Arman Narbayev   m   *Counsellor*
Mr Yesbol Abenov   *   *Counsellor*
Lt. Colonel Abay Sadibekov   m   *Defence Attaché*
Mr Seikzhan Medeuov   m   *1st Secretary Consul*
Mr Vagiz Teberikov   m   *1st Secretary*
Mr Mikhail Aubakirov   *   *2nd Secretary*
Mr Kair Tezekbayev   m   *Assistant to the Defence Attaché*
Mrs Ainur Karbozova   m   *2nd Secretary*

Mr Murat Rustemov   *2nd Secretary*
Ms Moldr Amreyeva   *3rd Secretary*
Mr Bauyrzhan Nurbalin   **m**   *3rd Secretary & PA to Ambassador*
Mr Khaknazar Smailov   *Attaché*
Mrs Kamshat Kumisbay   **m**   *Attaché*

KENYA

Kenya High Commission
45 Portland Place W1B 1AS
020 7636 2371
Fax 020 7323 6717
kcomm45@aol.com
www.kenyahighcom.org.uk
Monday-Friday 09.00-13.00 & 14.00-17.00
Visa Section: Monday-Friday 09.30-12.00 & 14.00-15.30

HIS EXCELLENCY MR EPHRAIM W NGARE   **m**   *High Commissioner (since 05 November 2009)*
           Mrs Jane Muthoni Waweru
Ms Jackline Yonga   *Deputy High Commissioner*
Col. Peter Muteti   **m**   *Defence Adviser*
Mrs Grace Cerere   **m**   *Minister Counsellor II*
Mr Benson Wakhule   **m**   *Immigration Attaché*
Mrs Jayne Toroitich   *1st Counsellor*
Ms Margaret Lesuuda   *Education Attaché*
Mr Michael S. Mandu   **m**   *Commercial Counsellor*
Mr Lazarus Muganda   *1st Secretary*
Mr Hilary Limo   **m**   *Financial Attaché*
Mr Nathaniel Taama   **m**   *2nd Secretary*
Ms Catherine Nyakoe   **m**   *2nd Secretary*
Mr Ibrahim Mwanjumwa   **m**   *Assistant Immigration Attaché*
Ms Ruth Macharia   *Administrative Attaché*
Mrs Esther Mugita   **m**   *Administrative Attaché*
Mr Mutinda Musee   **m**   *Administrative Attaché*

KIRIBATI
High Commissioner c/o Office of the President P.O. Box 68 Bairiki Tarawa Kiribati

Vacant   *High Commissioner*
Mrs Makurita Baaro   *Acting High Commissioner*

KOREA (REPUBLIC OF)

Embassy of the Republic of Korea
60 Buckingham Gate SW1E 6AJ
020 7227 5500/2
Fax 020 7227 5503
Website http://gbr.mofat.go.kr
Monday-Friday 09.30-12.30 & 14.00-17.30

Visa Section
Monday-Friday 10.00-12.00 & 14.00-16.00

Press & information Office
020 7227 5500 (ext. 615)

Korean Cultural Centre
Grand Buildings 1-3 Strand WC2N 5BW
020 7004 2600
Fax 020 7004 2619
www.kccuk.org.uk
Monday-Friday 10.00-18.00 & Saturday 11.00-17.00

HIS EXCELLENCY MR SUNGNAM LIM   **m**   *Ambassador Extraordinary & Plenipotentiary (since 20 September 2012)*
            Mrs Hyun Joo Shim
Mr Kwon Yong Kyu   **m**   *Minister*
Mr Kim Chulsoo   **m**   *Minister-Counsellor*
Mr Lee Beom-Chan   **m**   *Minister*
Mr Bae Byoung-Jun   **m**   *Minister-Counsellor*
Mr Kim Byungkyoo   **m**   *Minister-Counsellor (Financial)*
Mr Kim Kab-Soo   **m**   *Minister-Counsellor (Cultural)*
Mr Cho Seung-Hwan   **m**   *Minister-Counsellor (Maritime)*
Mr Yun Il Kim   *   *Counsellor*
Mr Yang Keum-Suk   **m**   *Minister-Counsellor*
Mr Kim Chang-Sik   **m**   *Counsellor*
Mr Ho Byoung-Kwon   **m**   *Counsellor (Administative)*
Mr Park Jong Won   **m**   *Commercial Attaché*
Mr Shin Jin-Chang   **m**   *Counsellor*
Mr Shin Jae-Shik   **m**   *1st Secretary (Science & Technology)*
Mr Song Yoon-Seog   **m**   *1st Secretary (Press & Information)*
Mr Kang Sung Min   **m**   *1st Secretary (Procurement)*
Mr Kim Hyon Du   **m**   *1st Secretary*
Mr Hong Soon Bok   **m**   *1st Secretary*
Mr Seo Yong Won   *   *1st Secretary*
Mr Shin Seok-Hong   **m**   *1st Secretary*
Mr Im, Byung-Ho   **m**   *1st Secretary (Police)*
Mr Lee Jung-Hyun   **m**   *2nd Secretary*
Mr Kim Chang Soo   **m**   *2nd Secretary*
Mr Kim Hyung-Seok   *3rd Secretary*
Mr Kang Soon-Na   **m**   *Education Director*
Captain Park Ju-Hyeon   **m**   *Defence Attaché*
Lt. Col. Yi Kwang-Jo   **m**   *Air Attaché*

KOREA (DEMOCRATIC PEOPLE'S REPUBLIC OF)

Embassy of the Democratic People's Republic of Korea
73 Gunnersbury Avenue W5 4LP
020 8992 4965
Fax 020 8992 2053
Monday-Friday 09.00-12.30 & 14.00-17.00
prkinfo@yahoo.com

HIS EXCELLENCY MR HAK BONG HYON   **m**   *Ambassador Extraordinary & Plenipotentiary (since 05 January 2012)*
            Mrs Choe Jin Ok
Mr Yong Ho Thae   **m**   *Minister*
Mr Myong Sin Mun   **m**   *1st Secretary*
Mr Kun Song Choe   **m**   *Counsellor (Maritime Affairs)*
Mr Kwang Song Yu   **m**   *1st Secretary (Maritime Affairs)*

KOSOVO (REPUBLIC OF)

Embassy of the Republic of Kosovo
100 Pall Mall St James SW1Y 5NQ
020 7659 6140/020 7664 8607
Fax 020 7659 6137
embassy.uk@ks-gov.net
Monday-Friday 09.00-17.00

Consular Section
020 7659 6138
consulate.london@ks-gov.net

HIS EXCELLENCY MR LIRIM GREIÇEVCI **m** *Ambassador Extraordinary and Plenipotentiary (since 01 December 2012)*
       Mrs Lindita Greiçevci
Mr Bejtullah Destani **m** *Minister-Counsellor*
Mr Arion Krasniqi **m** *1st Secretary*
Mr Mustafè Avdiu **m** *Vice Consul*

KUWAIT

Embassy of the State of Kuwait
2 Albert Gate SW1X 7JU
020 7590 3400/3406/3407
Fax 020 7823 1712
Monday-Friday 09.00-16.00

Cultural Office
Hyde Park House 60A Knightsbridge SW1X 7JX
020 7761 8500
Fax 020 7761 8505
www.kuwaitculturaluk.com

Military Office
Hyde Park House 60A Knightsbridge SW1X 7LF
020 7761 2800/2811
Fax 020 7761 2810/2820

Health Office
40 Devonshire Street W1G 7AX
020 7307 1700
Fax 020 7323 2042

Investment Office
Wren House 15 Carter Lane EC4V 5EY
020 7606 8080
Fax 020 7332 0755

HIS EXCELLENCY MR KHALED AL-DUWAISAN GCVO **m** *Ambassador Extraordinary & Plenipotentiary (since 29 April 1993)*
       Mrs Dalal Al-Duwaisan
Mr Faisal Al Houli **m** *Counsellor*
Mr Meshal Almodaf **m** *1st Secretary*
Mr Nawaf Boshaibah **m** *1st Secretary*
Mr Mohammed Aljran *2nd Secretary*
Mr Khaled Al-Azemi **m** *2nd Secretary*
Mrs Baderalduja Almudhayan **m** *Attaché*
Mr Abdullah Alateeqi *Attaché*
Mrs Nour Alruwaih **m** *Attaché*

Mr Abdullah Al-Hajeri   *Attaché*
Mr Ahmad Alsaqoby   *Attaché*
Mr Mohammad Saleh   *Attaché*
Mr Khaled AlAli   **m**   *Attaché*
Sheikh Faisal Al-Sabah   **m**   *Attaché*
Mr Meshaal Abuajel   **m**   *Attaché*
Dr Mohammad Alhajeri   **m**   *Head of Cultural Office*
Dr Nibal Bouresli   **m**   *Cultural Attaché*
Mr Robah Alrabah   **m**   *Attaché*
Mr Ahmad Majed AlMajed   **m**   *Attaché*
Brigadier Fahad Albaz   *Chief Military Attaché*
Lt Col Adil AlRoujaib   **m**   *Assistant Military Attaché*
Major Salah Alnoumas   **m**   *Assistant Military Attaché for Medical Affairs*
Major Yousef Ahmad Boqambar   *Assistant Military Attaché for Finance & Technical Affairs*
Lt Col Yousef Marafi   *Assistant Military Attaché for Administration*
Dr Fawzia Al-Sayegh   **m**   *Medical Adviser*
Mrs Eqbal Jaber   **m**   *Medical Attaché*
Lt Col Yaqoub AlKandary   *   *Assistant Military Attaché for Training*
Dr Yaqoub Al-Tammar   *   *Health Counsellor*
Mr Ahmad Saeidi   **m**   *Assistant Health Attaché*
Mr Yaseen Al-Yaseen   *   *Health Attaché*
Mr Osama Abdullah Alayoub   **m**   *Financial Attaché*
Mr Abdul Aziz Al-Bader   **m**   *Financial Attaché*
Sheikh Khaled Al-Sabah   *Financial Attaché*
Mr Marwan Al-Saleh   **m**   *Financial Attaché*
Mr Moutez Bishara   *Financial Attaché*
Mr Abdul Razak Al-Buaijan   **m**   *Financial Attaché*
Mr Nawaf Al-Rifai   *   *Financial Attaché*
Mr Abdulrahman Al-Rabaian   *Financial Attaché*
Mr Khaled Al-Mogahwi   *Financial Attaché*
Mr Ahmed Al-Shehab   *Financial Attaché*
Mr Basel Assiri   *Financial Attaché*
Mr Mohammed Al Kharafi   *Financial Attaché*
Mr Omar Al-Sallal   **m**   *Financial Attaché*
Mr Fuad Al-Majed   *   *Financial Attaché*
Mr Abdulrahim Al-Awadi   *   *Financial Attaché*
Mr Saud Al-Qemlas   *   *Financial Attaché*
Mr Kalid Hamadah   *Financial Attaché*
Miss Sarah Al-Sane   *Financial Attaché*
Mr Abdulah Al-Shamlan   *Financial Attaché*
Mr Fahad AlSahli   *Financial Attaché*
Mr Ali Ibraheem AlQadhi   *Financial Attaché*
Mr Mohammad Alderbass   *Financial Attaché*

KYRGYZSTAN

Embassy of the Kyrgyz Republic
Ascot House 119 Crawford Street W1U 6BJ
020 7935 1462
Fax 020 7935 7449
mail@kyrgyz-embassy.org.uk
www.kyrgyz-embassy.org.uk

Vacant *Ambassador Extraordinary & Plenipotentiary*
Mr Aibek Tilebaliev **m** *Chargé d'Affaires a.i*
Ms Saikal Esengeldieva *2nd Secretary (Consul)*

LAOS

Embassy of the Lao People's Democratic Republic
74 Ave Raymond-Poincaré 75 116 Paris
0033 (0) 1 4553 0298
Fax 0033 (0) 1 4727 5789
ambalaoparis@wanadoo.fr

HIS EXCELLENCY MR KHOUANTA PHALIVONG **m** *Ambassador Extraordinary & Plenipotentiary*
(since 18 October 2011)
        Mrs Bouakheua Phalivong
Mr Bounnheuang Songnanvong *Minister-Counsellor & Deputy Head of Mission*
Mr Houmpheng Khamphasith * *Economic & Commercial Counsellor*
Mr Bounnhalith Southichak * *1st Secretary (Cooperation, Francophonie & ASEAN)*
Mr Bounchanh Siphanthong *1st Secretary (Education & Culture)*
Mr Phetsakhone Sysounthone * *1st Secretary (Consular Affairs)*
Ms Sisounthay Keophoxay *2nd Secretary (Consular Affairs)*
Mr Phetsamone Keovongvichith *3rd Secretary (Protocol)*

LATVIA

Embassy of the Republic of Latvia
45 Nottingham Place W1U 5LY
020 7312 0041
Fax 020 7312 0042
embassy.uk@mfa.gov.lv
www.mfa.gov.lv/london

Consular Section
020 7312 0040
Fax 020 7312 0042
consulate.uk@mfa.gov.lv
Monday-Friday 10.00-13.00

HIS EXCELLENCY MR ANDRIS TEIKMANIS **m** *Ambassador Extraordinary & Plenipotentiary (since*
15 May 2013)
        Mrs Inguna Penike
Mr Martins Kreitus **m** *Deputy Head of Mission (EU Issues and Economic Affairs)*
Mrs Sanda Silite-Galina **m** *2nd Secretary (Head of Consular Section)*
Mrs Ieva Jirgensone *1st Secretary (Bilateral Issues & Security Policy)*
Ms Solveiga Latkovska *2nd Secretary (Consular Affairs)*
Mr Andris Livmanis **m** *3rd Secretary (Consular Affairs, Administration & Finance)*

LEBANON

Embassy of Lebanon
21 Kensington Palace Gardens W8 4QN
020 7727 6696/7792 7856
Fax 020 7243 1699
emb.leb@btinternet.com

Consular Section
15 Palace Gardens Mews W8 4RB
020 7229 7265

HER EXCELLENCY MRS INAAM OSSEIRAN   *Ambassador Extraordinary & Plenipotentiary (since 09 June 2008)*
Mr Toni Frangie   *Counsellor*
Mr Mazen Kabbara   **m**   *1st Secretary*
Mr Raed El Khadem   *1st Secretary*

LESOTHO

High Commission of the Kingdom of Lesotho
7 Chesham Place Belgravia SW1X 8HN
020 7235 5686
Fax 020 7235 5023
lhc@lesotholondon.org.uk
www.lesotholondon.org.uk
Monday-Friday 09.00-16.00

HER EXCELLENCY MRS FELLENG MAMAKEKA MAKEKA   *High Commissioner (since 30 September 2013)*
Mrs Maana Mapetja   **m**   *1st Secretary*
Mrs Matiisetso Ramoholi   **m**   *3rd Secretary*

LIBERIA

Embassy of the Republic of Liberia
23 Fitzroy Square W1T 6EW
020 7388 5489
Fax 020 7388 2899
info@embassyofliberia.org.uk
www.embassyofliberia.org.uk
Monday-Friday 10.30-17.00 Spring-Autumn (Chancery closed at 1600 during winter months)

HIS EXCELLENCY MR WESLEY M. JOHNSON   **m**   *Ambassador Extraordinary & Plenipotentiary (since 12 April 2007)*
            Mrs Isabella Cassell Johnson
Ms Genevieve A. Kennedy   *Minister Counsellor & DCM*
Mr Harry Conway   **m**   *Policy Officer and Maritime Attaché*
Mr Anthony Selmah   **m**   *Minister-Counsellor (Press & Public Affairs)*
Mr Chester Barh   **m**   *Minister*
Mr Napoleon Toquie   **m**   *1st Secretary & Consul*
Mr Morris S. Barsee   **m**   *2nd Secretary & Vice Consul*
Ms Winifred y. Nelson-Gaye   **m**   *Attaché*

LIBYA

Embassy of the State of Libya
15 Knightsbridge SW1X 7LY
020 7201 8280
Fax 020 7245 0588
Telex 266767
Monday-Friday 09.30-15.30

Consular Section
61-62 Ennismore Gardens SW7 1NH
020 7589 6120
Fax 020 7589 6087

Cultural Affairs
61-62 Ennismore Gardens SW7 1NH
020 7581 2393

Medical Office
22 Read Lion Street WC1R 4PS
020 7269 6190
Fax 020 7581 2393

Press Office
15 Knightsbridge SW1X 7LY
020 7201 8280
Fax 020 7245 0588

HIS EXCELLENCY MR MAHMUD MOHAMMED NACUA   *Ambassador Extraordinary & Plenipotentiary (since 27 September 2012)*
                    Mrs Fatima Nacua
Dr Saad Elshlmani   **m**   *Minister Plenipotentiary*
Mrs Wedad Serrah   *****   *Counsellor*
Mr Mohamed M.A. Benjama   **m**   *1st Secretary*
Mrs Rowaida.T.A. Ebrish   **m**   *1st Secretary*
Mr Mohamed E.A. Elmahmoudi   **m**   *1st Secretary*
Mr Abdulmunam M.A. Kremed   **m**   *2nd Secretary*
Mr Hamed G.A. Saif Al Nasair   *3rd Secretary*
Mr Tarek Zenbou   **m**   *Liaison Officer*
Mr Faisal A.A Abid   **m**   *2nd Secretary*
Mr Mustafa S.M Elghannai   **m**   *Admin Counsellor*
Miss Samah S.R. Ismail   *****   *Financial Attaché*
Miss Munira M.S. Elosta   *3rd Secretary*
Mr Jamal F.A. Elmalhouf   **m**   *Representative to International Maritime Organisation*
Mrs Samah S.R. Ismail   **m**   *Financial Attaché*
Mr Mohamed M.A. Tomi   **m**   *Financial Attaché*
Mr Mansour A.M. Eldagheili   **m**   *Assistant Financial Observer*
Dr Abdelbasit A. Gadour   **m**   *Cultural Attaché*
Mr Tarek M. Zenbou   **m**   *Liaison Officer*
Mr Osama S.A. Elmijrab   **m**   *Consular Attaché*
Mr Mahmoud M.A. Gsais   **m**   *Commercial Attaché*
Mr Adbulmenam E.M. Tunsi   **m**   *Technical Attaché*
Mr Guima O.M. Bukleb   **m**   *Press Counsellor*
Mr Naser E.I. Elmagtuf   **m**   *Consular Attaché*
Mr Abdullah A.E. Elneihum   **m**   *Medical Attaché*
Mr Ali T.M. Elkarom   *Defence Attaché*
Mr Abderazzaq A.A. Abdalmula   **m**   *Technical Attaché*
Mr Fouzi A.H. Benalhaj   **m**   *Technical Attaché*
Lt Col Abulgasem I Kh. Karir   **m**   *Technical Attaché*
Mr Mosbah S.M. Alzhrani   *Technical Attaché*
Mr Alsadeg M.A. Altrablssi   *Technical Attaché*

LITHUANIA

Embassy of the Republic of Lithuania
Lithuania House 2 Bessborough Gardens SW1V 2JE
020 7592 2840
Fax 020 7592 2864
amb.uk@urm.lt
http://uk.mfa.lt

Commercial Attaché's Office
020 7486 8912
Fax 020 7486 9368

Consular Section
Monday-Friday 09.00-13.00, Monday-Thursday 15.00-16.00

Visa Section
Tuesday, Wednesday & Thursday 14.00-15.00

HER EXCELLENCY MRS ASTA SKAISGIRYTE LIAUSKIENE   *   *Ambassador Extraordinary & Plenipotentiary (since 16 November 2012)*
Mr Sigitas Mitkus   **m**   *Minister-Counsellor (Political & Economic Affairs)*
Mr Tomas Bliznikas   *Minister-Counsellor (Political Affairs)*
Ms Gitana Kilinskaite   **m**   *Counsellor (Diaspora)*
Mr Uginus Labutis   **m**   *Counsellor (Consular Affairs)*
Mr Sigitas Cirtautas   **m**   *1st Secretary (Consular Affairs)*
Mr Martynas Juškus   **m**   *3rd Secretary (Consular Affairs)*
Mr Linas Verbusaitis   **m**   *Chief Officer (Finance & Administration)*
Mr Ričardas Rickus   **m**   *Chief Officer (Finance & Administration)*
Miss Rita Valiukonyte   *Cultural Attaché*
Mr Andrius Nikitinas   *   *Commercial Attaché*

LUXEMBOURG

Embassy of Luxembourg
27 Wilton Crescent SW1X 8SD
020 7235 6961
Fax 020 7235 9734
londres.amb@mae.etat.lu
Monday-Friday 09.00-17.00

Consular Section
Visa Office Monday-Friday 10.00-11.45

HIS EXCELLENCY MR PATRICK JEAN-MARIE ENGELBERG   **m**   *Ambassador Extraordinary & Plenipotentiary (since 13 August 2013)*
          Mrs Christine Engleberg
Ms Béatrice Kirsch   *Counsellor/Deputy Head of Mission*
Mr Miguel Marques   **m**   *Counsellor (Financial Affairs)*

MACEDONIA

Embassy of the Republic of Macedonia
Suites 2.1 & 2.2 Second Floor Buckingham Court 75-83 Buckingham Gate SW1E 6PE
020 7976 0535 / 020 7976 0538
Fax 020 7976 0539
sek.london@mfa.gov.mk
www.macedonianembassy.org.uk

His Excellency Mr Jovan Donev   *   *Ambassador Extraordinary & Plenipotentiary (since 05 March 2013)*
Mrs Biljana Gligorova   *   *Minister Counsellor (Political & Economic)*
Mr Mile Prangoski   *Counsellor*
Mr Oliver Sam   *2nd Secretary*
Goran Siljanovski   *3rd Secretary*

MADAGASCAR
Embassy of the Republic of Madagascar
4 Avenue Raphael Paris XVIII FRANCE
0033145046211
Fax: 0033145035870
info@ambassade-madagascar.fr

Vacant   *Ambassador Extraordinary & Plenipotentiary*

MALAWI
High Commission of the Republic of Malawi
36 John Street WC1N 2AT
020 7421 6010
Fax 020 7831 9273
malawihighcommission@btconnect.com
www.malawihighcommission.co.uk
Monday-Friday 09.30-13.00 & 14.00-17.00

His Excellency Mr Bernard H Sande   m   *High Commissioner (since 21 September 2012)*
       Mrs Gladys Sande
Mr John L Tembo   m   *Deputy High Commissioner*
Mr Vupe Kunkwenzu   m   *Counsellor (Development)*
Mr Mufwa Munthali   m   *Counsellor (Trade)*
Mr Ian Musyani   m   *Counsellor (Tourism)*
Brig Gen McChristie Lazarus Sikwese   m   *Defence Advisor*
Mrs Mirriam Mwapasa   m   *1st Secretary (Finance)*
Mrs Nellia Mkandawire   *1st Secretary (Consular)*
Mrs Jean Machinjili   *3rd Secretary (General Duties)*
Mr Mwayi Dausi   *3rd Secretary (Consular)*

MALAYSIA
Malaysian High Commission
45 Belgrave Square SW1X 8QT
020 7235 8033
Fax 020 7235 5161
mwlon@btconnect.com
Monday-Friday 09.00-17.00
Visa/Consular Monday-Friday 09.00-12.00

Adminstration
020 7919 0254

Protocol
020 7919 0253

Consular
020 7919 0210

Immigration
020 7919 0230

Defence
020 7919 0274

Economic
020 7499 4644 (Trade)
020 7919 0616 (Investment)

Education
020 7985 1252

Maritime
020 7919 0249

HIS EXCELLENCY MR DATUK ZAKARIA SULONG   **m**   *High Commissioner (since 26 May 2010)*
          Mrs Datin Hazizah Zakaria
Mr Nasir Zakaria   **m**   *Deputy High Commissioner*
Brigadier General Othman Hj Jamal   **m**   *Defence Adviser*
Mr Ibrahim Jaafar   **m**   *Minister-Counsellor (Political)*
Dr Mohad Anizu Moh Nor   **m**   *Minister Counsellor (Education)*
Mr Nik Abd Aziz Nik Abd Razak   **m**   *Counsellor (Police Liaison)*
Mrs Najihah Abas   **m**   *Counsellor (Investment)*
Mr Khairul Nizam Moonier   **m**   *Counsellor (Commercial)*
Mr Mr Zaki Zakaria   **m**   *Counsellor (Education)*
Miss Zalikha Moslim   *Counsellor (Immigration)*
Mr Abd Wahab Yusoff   **m**   *Counsellor (Education)*
Mr Mohd Shahfree Mohd Yusof   **m**   *Counsellor (Education)*
Mr Rdzween Abdul Razak   **m**   *1st Secretary*
Mr Khairul Gadafi Kamaludin   *1st Secretary (Political)*
Mrs Engku Puteri Suraya Engku Mohd Afandi   **m**   *1st Secretary*
Mr Wan Liang Lum   *1st Secretary*
Miss Nazlinda Zamani   *Education Attaché*
Mr Nagalingam Murugayah   **m**   *1st Secretary (Police Liaison)*
Mr Shahzul Jayawirawan Mohd Yunus   **m**   *Vice Counsellor (Investment)*
Mr Ahmad Tarmizi Mohd Asarani   **m**   *Education Attaché*
Major Ahmad Rashidi Ithnin   **m**   *Assistant Defence Adviser*
Mr Noorkhairan Nordin   **m**   *Education Attaché*
Mr Mohd Syahidin Mohd Arifin   **m**   *Education Attaché*
Mr Shahrul Nizam Mahfudz   **m**   *Education Attaché*
Miss Zaihasra Zainol Abidan   *Education Attaché*
Mr Dzulkarnain Ismail   **m**   *3rd Secretary (Administration)*
Mrs Emeliana Zainol   **m**   *2nd Secretary (Commercial)*
Mr Wan Mohd Azmi Wan Awang   **m**   *2nd Secretary*
Mr Hussin Shaukat   **m**   *3rd Secretary*

MALDIVES

High Commission of the Republic of Maldives
22 Nottingham Place W1U 5NJ
020 7224 2135
Fax 020 7224 2157
www.maldiveshighcommission.org
Monday-Friday 09.30-17.00

(Vacant)   *High Commissioner*
Mr Ahmed Shiaan   **m**   *Acting High Commissioner*

Mr Mohamed Nazeer   **m**   *Minister (Trade Representative)*
Mrs Aishath Fareena   *   *Attaché (Administrative, Consular & European Affairs)*
Mr Ismail Niyaz   *Attaché (Finance & Protocol)*

MALI
Embassy of the Republic of Mali
Avenue Molière 487 1050 Brussels BELGIUM
00 322 345 74-32
Fax 00 322 344 57 00

Vacant   *Ambassador Extraordinary & Plenipotentiary*
Mr Mamounou Toure   **m**   *Minister Counsellor*
Ms nana Aissa Toure   **m**   *2nd Counsellor*
Mr Cheick Oumar Coulibaly   **m**   *2nd Counsellor*
Mr Baba Cheibani Maiga   **m**   *3rd Counsellor*
Mr Thierno Amadou Oumar Hass Diallo   **m**   *Counsellor*
Ms Fatoumata Diallo   *   *Counsellor (Communication)*
Mr Oumar Konate   **m**   *Counsellor (Consular)*

MALTA
Malta High Commission
Malta House 36-38 Piccadilly W1J OLE
020 7292 4800
Fax 020 7734 1831
maltahighcommission.london@gov.mt
www.foreign.gov.mt
Monday-Friday 09.00-13.00 & 14.00-17.00

High Commissioner's Private Secretary
020 7292 4827

Political/Commonwealth
020 7292 4811

EU/Trade Section
020 7292 4823

Consular/Information/Citizenship Section
020 7292 4822

Visa Section
020 7292 4800

Passport Section
020 7292 4807
Passports.london@gov.mt

Medical Section
020 7292 4829
Medical.london@gov.mt

Pensions Section
020 7292 4821

HIS EXCELLENCY MR NORMAN HAMILTON   **m**   *High Commissioner (since 31 August 2013)*
        Mrs Josephine (Josette) Hamilton
Mr Jonathan Galea   *1st Secretary*
Mr Clint Mario Borg   *1st Secretary (Consular)*
Ms Chirelle Sciberras   *2nd Secretary*

MAURITANIA

Embassy of the Islamic Republic of Mauritania
Carlyle House, 235-237 Vauxhall Bridge Road, SW1V 1EJ
020 7233 6158

Vacant *Ambassador Extraordinary & Plenipotentiary*
Mr Mohamed Yahya Sidi Haiba **m** *Chargé d'Affaires*
Mr Yahya Ould Dahah * *Second Counsellor*

MAURITIUS

Mauritius High Commission
32/33 Elvaston Place SW7 5NW
020 7581 0294/5
Fax 020 7823 8437 / 020 7584 9859
londonmhc@btinternet.com
Monday-Friday 09.30-13.00 & 14.00-17.00

HIS EXCELLENCY MR ABHIMANU KUNDASAMY **m** *High Commissioner (since 05 December 2005)*
          Mrs Mahalutchmee Kundasamy
Mr Mohamed Iqbal Latona **m** *Deputy High Commissioner*
Mr Rakesh Bhuckory **m** *1st Secretary*
Mr Keswar Dooraree **m** *Attaché*

MEXICO

Embassy of Mexico
16 St. George Street W1S 1FD
020 7499 8586
embgbretana@sre.gob.mx
www.sre.gob.mx/reinounido
Monday-Friday 09.00-13.00 & 15.00-18.00

Consular Section
16a St. George Street W1S 1FD
consulmexuk@sre.gob.mx

Military & Air Section
8 Halkin Street SW1X 7DW
Tel & Fax 020 7235 7898

Naval Affairs Section
8 Halkin Street SW1X 7DW
020 7235 6211

Maritime Affairs Section
8 Halkin Street SW1X 7DW
020 7235 8475

Commercial Section
8 Halkin Street SW1X 7DW
020 7811 5041

HIS EXCELLENCY MR DIEGO GÓMEZ PICKERING *Ambassador Extraordinary & Plenipotentiary*
Mr Alejandro Estivill-Castro **m** *Minister & Deputy Head of Mission*
Mr Miguel Angel Vilchis-Salgado **m** *Minister (Consular Affairs)*
General Angel Antonio Cabrera **m** *Military & Air Attaché*
Mr Daniel Diaz Salas **m** *Rear Admiral/Naval Attaché*
Mr Alberto Lozano-Merino **m** *Counsellor*

Mr Milko Archibaldo Rivera-Hope   *   *Counsellor (Tourism and Information)*
Mr Jose Neif Jury-Fabre   **m**   *Counsellor (Commercial Affairs)*
Mr José Alberto Rodrigues Cuevas   *Commander/Deputy Naval Attaché*
Ms Michael Ivonne Mendoza-Tirado   *1st Secretary (Administration Commercial)*
Mr Mario González Álvarez   *1st Secretary (Commercial Attaché)*
Ms Guadalupe Ayala Ontiveros   **m**   *1st Secretary/Tourism*
Ms Susana Garduno-Arana   *2nd Secretary (Multilateral Affairs)*
Mr Juan Carlos Arturo Lombardo Munoz Ledo   *3rd Secretary (Economic Affairs)*
Ms Evelyn Vera Barreto *Diplomatic*   **m**   *Attache/Scientific*
Mr Jaime Juarez-Cosio   **m**   *Sergeant Attaché Military*
Mr Antonio Alfredo Perez De Tejada-Ortega   **m**   *Administrative Attaché*
Mr Ernesto Antonio Del Rio Casarrubias   **m**   *Telecomunications Attaché*
Ms Marcelino Herrera Sánchez   **m**   *Consular Attaché*
Mr Miguel García-Zamudio   **m**   Counsellor
Lt. Col. Rodolfo Chiñas Rosales   **m**   *Deputy Military & Air Attaché*
Mr Alberto Vega-Maury   **m**   *Commander/Deputy Naval Attaché*
Mr Miguel Garcia Zambudio   **m**   *Cammander/Deputy Political Affairs*
Ms Alejandra Franco Rodriguez   *1st Secretary (Communication & Transport)*
Mrs Laura Elisa García-Querol   **m**   *2nd Secretary (Scientific & Technical Affairs)*
Mr Jerónimo Mohar-Volkow   *Attaché (Political Affairs)*
Ms Celia Alcaide Blanco   *(Attache Assistant to the Ambassador)*

MOLDOVA

Embassy of the Republic of Moldova
5 Dolphin Square Edensor Road W4 2ST
020 8995 6818
Fax 020 8995 6927
embassy.london@mfa.md
www.britania.mfa.gov.md
Monday-Friday 09.00-13.00 & 14.00-18.00

Consular & Visa section
020 8996 0546
Fax 020 8995 6927
Consul.london@mfa.md
Monday-Friday 09.00-13.00 & 14.00-18.00

HIS EXCELLENCY MR IULIAN FRUNTAŞU   *Ambassador Extraordinary & Plenipotentiary (since 14 December 2011)*
Mrs Oxana Borta   *   *Counsellor*
Mr Petru Alexei   **m**   *1st Secretary*

MONACO

Embassy of the Principality of Monaco
7 Upper Grosvenor Street London W1K 2LX
0207 318 1081
Fax 0207 493 4563
www.monaco-embassy-uk.gouv.mc
blevrier@gouv.mc
embassy.uk@gouv.mc

HER EXCELLENCY MRS EVELYNE GENTA   *Ambassador Extraordinary & Plenipotentiary (since 12 January 2010)*

MONGOLIA

Embassy of Mongolia
7-8 Kensington Court W8 5DL
020 7937 0150
Fax 020 7937 1117
office@embassyofmongolia.co.uk
www.embassyofmongolia.co.uk

HIS EXCELLENCY MR TULGA NARKHUU　**m**　*Ambassador Extraordinary & Plenipotentiary (since 6 June 2013)*
　　　　Mrs Burmaa Batbold
Mr Gankhuyag Sodnom　**m**　*Counsellor*
Mr Angar Davaasuren　**m**　*Counsellor (Finance, Trade & Economic Affairs)*
Mr Bold-Erdene Yadamsuren　**m**　*2nd Secretary*
Mr Munkhjin Batsumber　*3rd Secretary (Education & Cultural Affairs)*
Ms Sukhbaatar Uyanga　*Attaché (Visa & Consular Affairs)*

MONTENEGRO

Embassy of Montenegro
18 Callcott Street W8 7SU
020 7727 6007
Fax 020 7243 9358
UnitedKingdom@mfa.gov.me

HIS EXCELLENCY PROF LJUBIŠA STANKOVIĆ　**m**　*Ambassador Extraordinary & Plenipotentiary (since 27 March 2011)*
　　　　Mrs Snežana Stanković
Mrs Marija Stjepcevic　**m**　*Counsellor*
Ms Snezana Žeković　*First Secretary*

MOROCCO

Embassy of the Kingdom of Morocco
49 Queen's Gate Gardens SW7 5NE
020 7581 5001/5004
Fax 020 7225 3862
ambalondres@maec.gov.ma
www.moroccanembassylondon.org.uk
Monday-Friday 09.00-17.00

Consular Section
Diamond House 97/99 Praed Street Paddington W2
020 7724 0719/ 0624
Fax 020 7706 7407
Consmorocco.uk@lycos.co.uk

HER EXCELLENCY HH PRINCESS LALLA JOUMALA ALAOUI　**m**　*Ambassador Extraordinary & Plenipotentiary (since 10 February 2009)*
　　　　Mr Mohamad Reza Nouri Esfandiari
Mr Othmane Bahnini　*Minister Plenipotentiary & Deputy Head of Mission*
Col. Mustapha Mounir　**m**　*Military, Naval & Air Attaché*
Commander Khalil Bachiri　**m**　*Deputy Defence Attaché & Representative to the IMO*
Mr Larbi R'Miki　**m**　*Minister-Counsellor/Head of Press & Cultural Section*
Mr Larbi Bouattaf　**m**　*Minister-Counsellor*
Mr Omar El Khayari　**m**　*Counsellor*

Mr Abdelghani Ambari   *Minister-Counsellor*
Mr Mohamed Amine El Alami   **m**   *Vice Consul (Consular Affairs)*
Mr Ismail Oudghiri Idrissi   **m**   *Counsellor*
Mrs Naima Senna   *   *Counsellor*
Mr Mohammed Farhane   **m**   *Counsellor*
Mrs Mouna Benomar   **m**   *Counsellor*
Mr Mohamed Reda Oudghiri Idrissi   **m**   *1st Secretary*
Miss Zeineb Bentahila   *1st Secretary*
Mr Abderrahman   **m**   *2nd Attaché (Consular Affairs)*
Mr Rabii Mohaiddine   *2nd Secretary*
Mr Mustapha Aalou   **m**   *Financial Attaché*
Mr Rachid Agassim   **m**   *Consul General*
Mrs Habiba Zemmouri   *Vice Consul (Consular Affairs)*
Mr Zein Rachid   **m**   *Vice Consul*
Mr Seddiq Bani   **m**   *Attaché*
Mr Said El Fenniri   **m**   *Attaché*

MOZAMBIQUE

High Commission for the Republic of Mozambique
21 Fitzroy Square W1T 6EL
020 7383 3800
Fax 020 7383 3801
www.mozambiquehighcommission.org.uk
Monday-Friday 09.30-13.00 & 14.00-17.00
HIS EXCELLENCY MR CARLOS DOS SANTOS   **m**   *High Commissioner (since 20 September 2011)*
        Mrs Isabel dos Santos
Mr Omar Remane   *   *Counsellor*
Mr Acácio Dinis Chacate   *   *3rd Secretary*
Ms Hanifa Ibraimo   *Consular Attaché*
Mr Filimao Langa   **m**   *Financial & Administrative Attaché*

MYANMAR see BURMA

NAMIBIA

High Commission for the Republic of Namibia
6 Chandos Street W1G 9LU
020 7636 6244
Fax 020 7637 5694
info@namibiahc.org.uk
Monday to Friday 09.00-13.00 & 14.00-17.00
HIS EXCELLENCY MR STEVE V. KATJIUANJO   **m**   *High Commissioner (since 21 October 2013)*
        Mrs Christophene Katjiuanjo
Mr Michael Ndivayele   **m**   *Minister Counsellor*
Ms Berenice Dentlinger   *1st Secretary (Commonwealth, Education & Culture & Politics)*
Ms Taati-Ester Matengu   *1st Secretary (Consular Affairs, IMO & Protocol)*
Ms Toini Ndapewa Fillemon   *   *2nd Secretary (Finance & Administration)*
Ms Angela Pavaza   *   *3rd Secretary*

NEPAL

Embassy of Nepal
12a Kensington Palace Gardens W8 4QU
020 7229 1594/6231/5352
Fax 020 7792 9861
eon@nepembassy.org.uk
www.nepembassy.org.uk
Monday-Friday 09.00-13.00 & 14.00-17.00

HIS EXCELLENCY DR SURESH CHANDRA CHALISE   m   *Ambassador Extraordinary & Plenipotentiary*
(since 26 January 2010)
               Mrs Dr Milan Adhikary (Chalise)
Mr Tej Bahadur Chhetri   m   *Counsellor / Deputy Chief of Mission*
Col. Bishawnath Ghimire   m   *Military Attaché*
Mr Babukaji Dongol   m   *Attaché (Consular)*
Mr Surya Bahadur Thapa   m   *Attaché (Accounts and Administration)*

NETHERLANDS

Royal Netherlands Embassy
38 Hyde Park Gate SW7 5DP
020 7590 3200
lon@minbuza.nl
www.dutchembassyuk.org
Monday-Friday 09.00-17.00
Passport & visa section: Please visit the Embassy's website for information on the opening hours of
the passport & visa section

Ambassador's Office
020 7590 3299
Fax 020 7590 3262

Political Department
020 7590 3294
Fax 020 7590 3262

Economic Department
020 7590 3259
Fax 020 7581 3450

Press & Cultural Department
020 7590 3269
Fax 020 7581 0053

Management Department
020 7590 3252
Fax 020 7225 0947

Consular Department
020 7590 3200
Fax 020 7581 3458

Defence Attaché's Office
020 7590 3244
Fax 020 7581 9614

Army Attaché's Office
020 7590 3244
Fax 020 7581 9614

Agricultural, Nature & Food Quality Department
020 7590 3279
Fax 020 7581 5276

Industrial Department
020 7590 3286
Fax 020 7584 3396

HER EXCELLENCY MS LAETITIA VAN DEN ASSUM   *Ambassador Extraordinary & Plenipotentiary (since 02 October 2012)*
Mrs Margriet Leemhuis   **m**   *Minister Plenipotentiary*
Mrs Carmen Gonsalves   **m**   *Counsellor (Political Affairs)*
Mrs Charlotte Talens   **m**   *1st Secretary (Political Affairs)*
Mr Sander van Schilt   **m**   *Counsellor (Home Affairs)*
Mr Fred Olthof   **m**   *Counsellor (Economic Affairs)*
Ms Ceta Noland   *1st Secretary (European & Economic Affairs)*
Ms jannet Dujjndam   *Counsellor (Press & Cultural Affairs)*
Mr Willem van Arnhem   **m**   *1st Secretary (Consular Affairs)*
Ms Janneke Pulleman   *Vice Consul (Consuar Affairs)*
Ms Meike de Jong   *Attaché (Consular Affairs)*
Mr Felix Kremer   **m**   *2nd Secretary (Management Affairs)*
Captain Harrie Welmer   **m**   *Defence and Naval Attaché*
Lt Colonel Ronald van de Put   *Military, Air and Deputy Defence Attaché*
Mr Paul Vlaanderen   **m**   *Counsellor (Finance)*
Mr Henk de Jong   **m**   *Counsellor (Agriculture, Nature and Food Quality)*

NEW ZEALAND

New Zealand High Commission
2nd Floor New Zealand House 80 Haymarket SW1Y 4TQ
Monday-Friday 09.00-17.00

Chancery
020 7930 8422
Fax 020 7839 4580
www.nzembassy.com/uk
Public Affairs: aboutnz@newzealandhc.org.uk
Consular: consular@newzealandhc.org.uk

Defence Staff & Defence Purchasing Office
020 7930 8400
Fax 020 7930 8401

Immigration New Zealand
09069 100 100 (Premium Rate)
020 3582 7499 (Visa Application Centre)
Fax 020 7973 0370

Passport Office
020 7968 2730
Fax 020 7968 2739

New Zealand Trade & Enterprise
020 7973 0380
Fax 020 7973 0104

HIS EXCELLENCY THE RT HON SIR ALEXANDER LOCKWOOD SMITH   *High Commissioner (since 22 March 2013)*
Lady Alexandra Jane Smith
Mr Robert Taylor   *Deputy High Commissioner*

Brigadier Anthony Hayward   **m**   *Defence Adviser & Head New Zealand Defence Staff*
Mr Sam Lewis   **m**   *Counsellor (Commercial)*
Mr Gary Smith   **m**   *Counsellor (Police)*
Mrs Jeannie Melville   **m**   *Counsellor (Immigration)*
Mrs Janice Galvin   *Counsellor*
Mr Jeremy Palmer   **m**   *1st Secretary (Management)*
Mr Richard Kay   **m**   *1st Secretary (Political)*
Mr Kenneth Ryan   *1st Secretary (Tade & Economic)*
Mr Carl Berendsen   **m**   *1st Secretary*
Mr Steven Ainsworth   *Counsellor (Veterinary Services) (Resident in Brussels)*
Mr Matthew Roseingrave   **m**   *Counsellor (Customs) (Resident in Brussels)*
Ms Shelley Robertson   *Counsellor (Education) (Resident in Brussels)*
Mr Bruce McCallum   **m**   *Counsellor (Science & Innovation) (Resident in Brussels)*
Commander Andrew McMillan   **m**   *Naval Adviser*
Wing commander Nicholas Olney   **m**   *Air Adviser*
Lieutenant Colonel Michael Beale   **m**   *Military Adviser*
Lieutenant Colonel Alastair Howieson RNZN   *Assistant Defence Adviser*
Squadron Leader Susie Barns   **m**   *Logistics Adviser*
Mr David Lilly   **m**   *2nd Secretary (Multilateral)*
Mr Ben Carter   **m**   *Attaché*

NICARAGUA

Embassy of Nicaragua
Suite 31 Vicarage House 58-60 Kensington Church Street W8 4DB
020 7938 2373
Fax 020 7937 0952
embaniclondon@btconnect.com
www.cancilleria.gob.ni

Consular Section
consulnic.uk@btconnect.com

His Excellency Mr Carlos Arguello- Gomez   **m**   *Ambassador Extraordinary & Plenipotentiary (since 17 May 2010)*
            Mrs Sherly Noguera de Arguello-Gomez
Ms Guisell Morales Echaverry   *Minister-Counsellor & Deputy Head of Mission*
Miss Gabriela Urrutia   *1st Secretary (Consular affairs)*

NIGER

Embassy of the Republic of Niger
154 Rue de Longchamp 75116 Paris FRANCE
(00) 331 45 04 80 60
Fax (00) 331 45 04 79 73

Vacant   *Ambassador Extraordinary & Plenipotentiary*
Mr Bakary Yaou Sangare   **m**   *1st Counsellor*
Mrs Aminatou Batouré Gaoh   **m**   *Counsellor*
Mr Eric Chamchoum   **m**   *Counsellor*
Mr Oudou Harouna   **m**   *Head of Protocol*
Colonel Oumarou Mallam Daouda   **m**   *Defence Attaché*
Mr Lestenau Ibrahim   **m**   *Attaché (Press)*
Mr Mamane Sidi   **m**   *Attaché (Financial)*
Mrs Zeinabou Abdoulaye Garba   *Attaché (Social Affairs)*
Mrs Fatoumata Oumarou   **m**   *Attaché (Education)*

NIGERIA
High Commission for the Federal Republic of Nigeria
Nigeria House 9 Northumberland Avenue WC2N 5BX
020 7839 1244
Fax 020 7839 8746
Monday-Friday 09.30-17.30
chancery@nigeriahc.org
information@nigeriahc.org.uk
www.nigeria.org.uk

Immigration Section
9 Northumberland Avenue WC2N 5BX
020 7839 1244
Fax 020 7925 0990
passport@nigeriahc.org.uk
visa@nigeriahc.org.uk
Monday-Friday 10.00-13.00

Defence Section
9 Northumberland Avenue WC2N 5BX
020 7839 1244
Fax 020 7925 1483

His Excellency Dr Dalhatu S. Tafida **m** *High Commissioner (since 12 April 2008)*
Mrs Salamatu Tafida
Ambassador Oluwatoyin K. Lawal **m** *Deputy High Commissioner*
Mr V.E. Udoyen **m** *Minister, Head of Immigration*
Mr S.A Adelemi **m** *Minister, Head of Trade and Investment*
Dr C.U. Gwam **m** *Minister, Head of Political Affairs*
Mr A.S. Ogah **m** *Minister, Information, Culture and Sports*
Mr T.G. Adeniyi **m** *Minister, Special Assistant to the High Commissioner*
Mr T.O Aje **m** *Minister, Chief of Protocol*
Mr M.M.B Aliyu **m** *Minister, Head of Consular, Education and Welfare*
Mr Ahmed Inusa **m** *Minister, Head of Chancery*
Mr S.F. Alege **m** *Minister, Deputy Head of Political Affairs*
Mrs A.A. Musa **m** *Minister, Administration*
Miss L.I. Onoh *Minister, Trade & Economy*
Mrs M AbdulRaheem **m** *Minister, Immigration*
Mrs H.I. Nze **m** *Senior Counsellor, Information*
Mr U. I. Bashir **m** *Minister, Education and Welfare*
Mr F.N. Enya **m** *Counsellor, Consular, Education and Welfare*
Mr M.D. Galadima **m** *Counsellor, Protocol*
Mr L.B. Riskuwa **m** *2nd Secretary*
Mr O. Olonijolu **m** *2nd Secretary*
Mrs E.G. Philips-Umezurike **m** *2nd Secretary*
Mrs O.B. Ejiwale **m** *2nd Secretary*
Mr Emmanuel Nweke **m** *2nd Secretary*
Mr E.M. Edache **m** *Finance Attaché*
Mrs A.N. Nwagu **m** *Administrative Attaché*
Mr M.A. Muhammad **m** *Immigration Attaché*
Mrs C.I. Ngere **m** *Deputy Immigration Attaché*
Mr Mustapha Ahmed **m** *Immigration Attaché I*
Mr E.J. Tariah **m** *Immigration Attaché II*
Mr E. Chibueze **m** *Immigration Attaché III*
Maj. Gen. J.M. Ogidi **m** *Defence Adviser*
Capt. (NN) I.M. Albara **m** *Deputy Defence Adviser (Navy)*

Col. K.K. Abobarin   **m**   *Deputy Defence Adviser (Finance)*
Wg. Cdr S.A. Bukar   **m**   *Deputy Defence Adviser (Air)*
Lt. Col. O.M. Azuikpe   **m**   *Deputy Defence Adviser (Library)*
Capt. Ibrahim Olugbade, mni   **m**   *Alternate Permanent Representative to the IMO*
Engr. Anas Kawu Suleiman   **m**   *Deputy Alternate Permanent Representative to the IMO*

NORWAY

Royal Norwegian Embassy
25 Belgrave Square SW1X 8QD
020 7591 5500
Fax 020 7245 6993
emb.london@mfa.no
www.norway.org.uk

HIS EXCELLENCY MR KIM TRAAVIK   **m**   *Ambassador Extraordinary & Plenipotentiary (since 31 August 2010)*
       Mrs Astrid Bente Brodtkorb
Mr Olav Myklebust   *Minister-Counsellor (Deputy Head of Mission)*
Ms Eva Vincent   *Minister-Counsellor (Press, Information & Cultural Affairs)*
Mrs Tove Sylstad Iversen   **m**   *Counsellor (Administrative)*
Mr Tom Holter   **m**   *Counsellor (Security & Defence Policy)*
Ms Terese Holm   *1st Secretary (Political & Economic Affairs)*
Mrs Marit Bækkelund Randsborg   **m**   *1st Secretary*
Mr Baard Vandvik   **m**   *1st Secretary*
Ms Grethe Knudsen   *Consul*
Mr Ronny Samsonstuen   **m**   Police *Attaché*
Captain Øystein Wemberg   **m**   *Defence Attaché*

OMAN

Embassy of the Sultanate of Oman
167 Queens Gate SW7 5HE
020 7225 0001
Fax 020 7589 2505
Monday-Friday 09.00-15.30

Information Attaché
020 7225 5233
Fax 020 7589 7751

Military Attaché
64 Ennismore Gardens SW7 1NH
020 7589 0202
Fax 020 7584 3653

Culture Attaché
64 Ennismore Gardens SW7 1NH
020 7589 0220
Fax 020 7584 6435/7589 3810

Health Attaché
64 Ennismore Gardens SW7 1NH
020 7589 0002
Fax 020 75812489

His Excellency Mr Abdulaziz Abdullah Zahir Al Hinai   **m**   *Ambassador Extraordinary &*
Plenipotentiary (*since 12 November 2009*)
   Mrs Maryam Al Hinai
Shaikh Ghassan Shaker   **m**   *Minister Plenipotentiary*
Dr Omar Zawawi   **m**   *Counsellor*
Mr Ahmed Said Omer Al-Kathairi   **m**   *Deputy Head of Mission*
Mr Humaid Ali Obiad Al-Mujaini   **m**   *Minister Plenipotentiary*
Mr Ahmed Ali Al-Rashdi   **m**   *Minister Plenipotentiary Head of Adminitrative & Finance*
Sayyis Mohamed Badar Saud Al-Busaid   **m**   *(Counsellor)*
Mr Jamil Haji Isma'il Al-Balushi   **m**   *Counsellor*
Mr Issa Saleh Adbullah Al-Sheibani   **m**   *1st Secretary*
Mr Mohamed Saif Hamed Al-Humaidi   **m**   *1st Secretary*
Mr Hatem HIlal Ali Al-Ya'qoubi   **m**   *1st Secretary*
Mr Mohamed Mubarak Al-Kalbani   **m**   *1st Secretary*
Mr Asad Issa Abdullah Al-Harthy   **m**   *1st Secretary*
Sayyid Ammar Abdullah Sultan Al-Busaidi   **m**   *1st Secretary*
Sheikh Saud Mustahail Al-Mashani   *2nd Secretary*
Air Commodore Ibrahim Ali Al-Farsi   **m**   *Military Attaché*
Wing Commander Ali Ahmed Al-Jawhari   **m**   *Assistant Military Attaché*
Lt Commander Mohamed Rasheed Al-Juma   **m**   *Administration & Finance Officer*
Dr Mohamed Sulaiman Abdullah Al-Bandari   **m**   *Cultural Attaché*
Mr Musallam Taman Al-Amri   **m**   *Assistant Cultural Attaché*
Mr Abdullah Sulaiman Saif Al-Abri   **m**   *Information Attaché*
Mr Saif Mohamed Khalifa Al-Busaidi   **m**   *Health Attaché*

PAKISTAN

High Commission for the Islamic Republic of Pakistan
35-36 Lowndes Square SW1X 9JN
020 7664 9284
Fax 020 7664 9224
poldiv@phclondon.org
www.phclondon.org
Monday-Friday 09.30-17.30

Consular Division
34 Lowndes Square SW1X 9JN
Monday-Thursday 10.00-12.30 & Friday 10.00-12.00

His Excellency Mr Wajid Shamsul Hasan   **m**   *High Commissioner* (*since 22 June 2008*)
   Mrs Zarina Hasan
Mr Mohammad Imran   **m**   *Deputy High Commissioner*
Mr Israr Hussain   **m**   *Counsellor (Political)*
Mr Khalid Majid   **m**   *Counsellor (Political)*
Mr Syed Mustafa Rabbani   **m**   *Head of Chancery, 1st Secretary*
Mr Shozab Abbas   **m**   *1st Secretary*
Mr Raheel Tariq   **m**   *3rd Secretary (Education)*
Mr Taj Muhammad Khan   **m**   *3rd Secretary*
Commodore Mushtaq Ahmed   **m**   *Defence & Naval Adviser*
Colonel Zulfiqar Ali Bhatty   **m**   *Army & Air Adviser*
Colonel Osamah Majeed   **m**   *PATLO*
Major Faisal Arif   **m**   *PATLO-I*
Syed Najeeb Hussain Nabeel Pasha   **m**   *Adviser Defence Procurement*
Mr Shafiq Ahmad   **m**   *Technical Attaché*
Mr Muhammad Ashraf Alam   **m**   *ACMA*

Mr Mian Shabbir Anwer **m** *Minister Press*
Mr Muneer Ahmad **m** *Press Attaché*
Mr Amjad Javaid Bajwa **m** *Minister (Coord)*
Mr Liaquat Ali Waseem **m** *Counsellor (Coord)*
Mr Hafeez Ullah Khan **m** *2nd Secretary (Coord)*
Mr Anjum Sohail **m** *1st Secretary (Coord)*
Mr Ijlal Ahmed Khattak **m** *Commercial Counsellor*
Mr Salas Raza Kiani **m** *Minister (Community Welfare Wing)*
Mr Sardar Balakh Sher Khosa **m** *Community Welfare Counsellor*
Mr Shahid Ali Baig **m** *Director (Audit & Accounts)*
Mr Waqas Ahmed Khan **m** *Third Secretary*
Mr Tariq Ahmad Lodhi **m** *GM (NADRA) UK & Europe*
Mr Muhammad Iqbal * *Manager (NADRA)*
Mr Fiaz Hussain **m** *Dy Director (Immigration & Passports)*
Ms Nadia Qadir Patel **m** *Education Attaché*

PALAU
London Honorary Consulate (see page 136)

PANAMA
Embassy of Panama
40 Hertford Street W1J 7SH
020 7493 4646
Fax 020 7493 4333
panama1@btconnect.com

Consulate General
40 Hertford Street W1J 7SH
020 7409 2255
Fax 020 7493 4499
legalizations@panamaconsul.co.uk

HER EXCELLENCY MS ANA IRENE DELGADO *Ambassador Extraordinary & Plenipotentiary, Consul General & Permanent Representative to the IMO (since 11 November 2011)*
Ms Margarita del C Zurita T *3rd Secretary, Deputy Head of Mission*
Miss Monique Vega Padilla *Commercial Attaché*
Miss Laura Montenegro *Attaché*
Mr Jaime Gilinski Bacal **m** *Political Affairs Attaché*

PAPUA NEW GUINEA
Papua New Guinea High Commission
14 Waterloo Place SW1Y 4AR
020 7930 0922
Fax 020 7930 0828
kunduldn3@btconnect.com
www.pnghighcomm.org.uk
Monday-Friday 09.00-17.00

HER EXCELLENCY MS WINNIE ANNA KIAP *High Commissioner (since 24 August 2011)*

PARAGUAY

Embassy of the Republic of Paraguay
3rd Floor 344 Kensington High Street W14 8NS
020 7610 4180
Fax 020 7371 4297
embapar@btconnect.com
www.paraguayembassy.co.uk
Monday-Friday 09.30-17.00

Consular Section
020 7610 4180
Fax 020 7371 4297
Monday-Friday 10.00-16.00

HIS EXCELLENCY MR MIGUEL ANGEL SOLANO LOPEZ CASCO **m** *Ambassador Extraordinary & Plenipotentiary (since 14 December 2009)*
        Mrs Maria Mercedes Troxler-Correa
Mr Bernardo José Balbuena Prieto **m** *Minister (Consular Affairs)*
Mr Hugo Diosnel Chaparro-Gonzalez *2nd Secretary*

PERU

Embassy of Peru
52 Sloane Street SW1X 9SP
020 7235 1917/8340/3802
Fax 020 7235 4463
postmaster@peruembassy-uk.com
www.peruembassy-uk.com
Monday-Friday 09.00-17.00

Defence Attaché's Office
5 Fallstaff House 24 Bardolph Road Richmond TW9 2LH
020 8940 7773
Fax 020 8940 7735
peruattache@yahoo.co.uk

Consulate General
52 Sloane Street SW1X 9SP
020 7838 9223/9224
Fax 020 7823 2789
peruconsulate-uk@btconnect.com
Monday-Friday 09.30-13.00

HIS EXCELLENCY MR JULIO MUÑOZ-DEACON **m** *Ambassador Extraordinary & Plenipotentiary* (since 30 March 2012)
        Mrs Laura Marcela Chavez Garcia
Mr Daniel Roca *Minister, Deputy Head of Mission*
Rear Admiral Pablo Monzón **m** *Defence Attaché & Alternate Permanent Representative to the IMO*
Mrs Ruth Saif de Preperier * *Minister (Consul General)*
Captain Jorge Vargas **m** *Deputy Defence Attaché & Alternate Permanent Representative to the IMO*
Miss Julissa Macciaello *Counsellor (Political & Multilateral Affairs) & Alternate Permanent Representative to the IMO*
Captain Roberto Carlos Teixeira **m** *Alternate Permanent Representative to the IMO*
Miss Claudia Lapeyre *2nd Secretary (Vice Consul)*
Mr Alejandro Manrique *2nd Secretary (Trade, Investment & Co-operation Affairs)*
Mr Vidal Eduardo Choroco *3rd Secretary and Alternate Permanent Representative to the IMO*

PHILIPPINES

Embassy of the Republic of the Philippines
6-8 Suffolk Street SW1Y 4HG
Tel: 020 7451 1780
Fax: 020 7930 9787
embassy@philemb.co.uk
philembassy-uk.org
Monday-Friday 09.00-13.00 & 14.00-17.00

Consular Section: 020 7451 1803/1805/1814/1815/1819
Political (Bilateral) Section: 020 7451 1806
Political (Multilateral) Section: 020 7451 1808
Economic /Administration Section : 020 7451 1807

Trade Section
1a Cumberland House Kensington Court W8 5NX
020 7937 1898/7998
Fax 020 7937 2747
info@ivestphilippines.org.uk
www.investphilippines.org.uk

Office of the Defence & Armed Forces Attaché
8 Suffolk Street SW1Y 4HG
020 7451 1831
Fax 020 7839 5401
defence@philemb.co.uk

Labour Section
3rd Floor 6 Suffolk Street SW1Y 4HG
020 7839 8078/020 7451 1832
Fax 020 7839 7345

HIS EXCELLENCY MR ENRIQUE MANALO   **m**   *Ambassador Extraordinary & Plenipotentiary and Permanent Representative to the IMO (since 04 October 2011)*
          Mrs Pamela Louise Manalo
Ms Maria Fe Pangilinan   *Deputy Chief of Mission & Deputy Permanent Representative to the IMO*
Mr Senen Tiemsin Mangalile   **m**   *Minister and Consul General*
Mr Francisco Noel Fernandez   **m**   *Minister & Alternate Permanent Representative to the IMO*
Miss Myla Grace Ragenia Macahilig   *1st Secretary & Consul*
Ms Emma Sarne   *1st Secretary & Consul*
Mr Voltaire Maurico   *1st Secretary & Consul*
Mr Emmanuel Donato Guzman   **m**   *3rd Secretary & Vice Consul*
Mr Rommel Romato   *3rd Secretary & Vice Consul*
Mrs Perlita Tabisaura   **m**   *2nd Secretary*
Mrs Joan Lourdes Lavilla   **m**   *Attaché (Labour)*
Ms Anne Marie Kristine Umali   *Attaché (Commercial)*
Captain Robert Patrimonio   *   *Maritime Attaché*
Cdr Eustacio Nimrod Enriquez   **m**   *Maritime Techincal Adviser*
Mrs Edith Mallillin   **m**   *Attaché*
Mr Tomas Raiz   **m**   *Attaché*
Mr Rico Garcia   *   *Attaché*
Mrs Vivian Pascua   *   *Attaché*
Mr Federico Silao Jr   **m**   *Attaché*
Mr Rosendo Rodriguez   **m**   *Attaché*
Mrs Cecilia Santos   **m**   *Attaché*
Mrs Teresa Modesto   **m**   *Attaché*
Mrs Emillet Palomique   *Attaché*

Mrs Marilyn Galanza   **m**   *Attaché*
Ms Millecent Verceles   *Attaché*
Mr Panteleon Lucas   **m**   *Attaché*
Mrs Flora Magdalena Gorordo   **m**   *Attaché*
Mrs Esperanza C. Cobarrubias   *   *Welfare Officer*

POLAND

Embassy of the Republic of Poland
47 Portland Place W1B 1JH
020 7291 3520
Fax 020 7291 3576
london@msz.gov.pl
www.london.mfa.gov.pl

Economic & Commercial Department
73 New Cavendish Street W1W 6LS
020 7291 3917
Fax 020 7291 3968
london.we@msz.gov.pl

Trade & Investment Promotion Department
90 Gloucester Place W1U 6HS
020 7317 2700/2
Fax 020 7486 9840
london@trade.gov.pl
www.london.trade.gov.pl

Polish Cultural Institute
52-53 Poland Street W1F 7LX
020 3206 2004
Fax 020 7434 0139
pci@polishculture.org.uk
www.polishculture.org.uk

Consular Section
73 New Cavendish Street W1W 6LS
020 7291 3914
Fax 020 7323 2320
londyn.amb.wk@msz.gov.pl
www.londynkg.polemb.net

His Excellency Mr Witold Sobków   *Ambassador Extraordinary & Plenipotentiary (since 03 September 2012)*
      Mrs Iwona Sobków
Mr Dariusz Laska   **m**   *Deputy Head of Mission, Minister-Counsellor*
Mr Ireneusz Truszkowski   **m**   *Minister-Counsellor, Consul General*
Col Ryszard Tomczak   *   *Defence, Military, Naval & Air Attaché*
Mrs Anna Wypych-Namiotko   **m**   *Minister Counsellor (IMO)*
Ms Anna Godlewska   *Counsellor, Director of the Polish Cultural Institute*
Mr Michal Mazurek   *1st Counsellor (Consular Affairs)*
Mrs Iwona Woicka-Żulawska   **m**   *Counsellor, Head of Economic & Commercial Department*
Mr Katarzyna Krause   *Counsellor, Head of Political Section*
Lt Col Piotr Pacek   **m**   *Deputy Defence Military, Naval & Air Attaché*
Mr Piotr Pacek   **m**   *Deputy Defence Attaché*
Ms Ewa Wiśniewska   *Counsellor (Financial)*
Mr Paweł Olczak   **m**   *Counsellor*
Mr Robert Szaniawski   **m**   *Counsellor (Promotion, Media & Information)*

Mr Mariusz Stus **m** *Counsellor (Political)*
Ms Justyna Stańczewska *Counsellor (Consular Affairs)*
Mr Rafal Siemianowski **m** *Counsellor (Science & Education)*
Mr Tomasz Stachurski * *Counsellor (Consular Affairs)*
Mr Cezary Jurek **m** *Counsellor (Political)*
Mr Leszek Banaszak **m** *Counsellor (Trade & Investment Promotions)*
Mr Rafal Czarnecki *1st Secretary (Administration)*
Ms Jolanta Srebrakowska *1st Secretary (Consular Affairs)*
Mrs Renata Wasilewska – Mazur **m** *1st Secretary (Consular Affairs)*
Mrs Helena Jurek **m** *1st Secretary (Political)*
Ms Monika Sobotka *1st Secretary (Consular)*
Miss Agnieszka Skolimowska **m** *1st Secretary (Political)*
Mr Marcin Tatarzyński * *2nd Secretary (Commercial)*
Mr Grzegorz Sala *2nd Secretary (Consular Affairs)*
Ms Agnieszka Hirsch *2nd Secretary (Trade & Investment Promotion)*
Mrs Monika Sadkowska **m** *2nd Secretary*
Mr Bartosz Tymkowski *2nd Secretary (Economic Affairs)*
Magdalena Karolak **m** *2nd Secretary (Administration)*
Mr Bartlomiej Druzinski * *2nd Secretary*
Mr Sergiusz Wolski **m** *3rd Secretary (Consular Affairs)*
Mrs Ines Czajczynska-Da Costa **m** *3rd Secretary (Consular)*
Zbigniew Chrzanowski *3rd Secretary*
Mr Tomasz Pazura **m** *Attaché*

PORTUGAL

Embassy of Portugal
11 Belgrave Square SW1X 8PP
020 7235 5331
Fax 020 7245 1287
londres@mne.pt

Trade & Tourism
020 7201 6666
Fax 020 7201 6633
trade.london@portugalglobal.pt
tourism.london@portugalglobal.pt

Consular Section
3 Portland Place W1B 1HR
020 7291 3770
Fax 020 7291 3799
mail@cglon.dgaccp.pt

HIS EXCELLENCY MR JOÃO DE VALLERA **m** *Ambassador Extraordinary & Plenipotentiary (since 19 January 2011)*
       Mrs Maria Margarida Azevedo
Ms Maria Cristina Xavier Castanheta *Minister-Counsellor, Deputy Head of Mission*
Mr Fernando d'Orey de Brito e Cunha Figueirinhas **m** *Consul General*
Mr Tiago Adão Alves Araújo **m** *1st Secretary*
Mr Luís Miguel Fontoura **m** *Economic & Commercial Counsellor*
Mr José António Galaz **m** *Social Affairs and Transport Attaché*
Mrs Maria Leite Pinto Monteiro **m** *Press & Political Affairs Attaché*
Mr Filipe Christensen-Roed Gonçalves da Silva **m** *Tourism Attaché*
Mrs Regina Duarte **m** *Educational Affairs Attaché*

QATAR

Embassy of the State of Qatar
1 South Audley Street W1K 1NB
020 7493 2200
Fax 020 7493 2661
ambassador@qatarembassy.org.uk
Monday-Friday 09.30-16.00

Cultural Section
21 Hertford Street W1Y 7RY
020 7495 8677
020 7495 8770
Fax 020 7495 8660
qatarcultural@hotmail.com
m.alkaabi@sec.gov.qa

Medical Section
30 Collingham Gardens SW5 0HN
020 7370 6871
Fax 020 7835 1469
qatmeduk@qatarhealth.co.uk

Military Section
21 Hertford Street W1J 7RY
020 7409 2229
Fax 020 7629 0740
Mil505@qa-daoffice.co.uk
Mil.da.london@mofa.gov.qa
mfahmi@qa-daoffice.co.uk

HIS EXCELLENCY MR KHALID RASHID AL-HAMOUDI AL-MANSOURI KCVO   **m**   *Ambassador Extraordinary & Plenipotentiary (since 26 August 2005)*
          Mrs Mooza Saif Al-Mansoori
Sheikh Hamad Bin Khalifa Al-Thani   **m**   *Counsellor*
Sheikh Hamad Bin Jassim Bin Jabr Al Thani   **m**   *Counsellor*
Mr Hamad Mohamed Hussein Ali Al-Muftah   *Counsellor*
Mr Rashid Abdulla Al-Dehaimi   **m**   *1st Secretary*
Sheikh Khalid Ahmed Kh. A Al-Thani   **m**   *2nd Secretary (Political & Legal Affairs)*
Mr Mubarak Ajlan Al-Kuwari   *3rd Secretary*
Mrs Leila Fanous MVO   *Attaché (Press)*
Mr Mohamed Hamad M.S. Al-Nuaimi   **m**   *Defence Attaché*
Mr Mohammed Rashid Al-Kuwari   **m**   *Assistant Defence Attaché*
Mr Mohamed Abdulla Al-Kaabi   **m**   *Cultural Attaché*
Mr Abdulla Ali Al-Ansari   **m**   *Medical Attaché*

ROMANIA

Embassy of Romania
Arundel House 4 Palace Green W8 4QD
020 7937 9666
Fax 020 7937 8069
londra@mae.ro
www.londra.mae.ro
Monday-Friday 09.00-17.00

Commercial Section
Arundel House 4 Palace Green W8 4QD
020 7937 9668
Fax 020 7937 8069
londra.economic@mae.ro

Defence Attaché's Office
Arundel House 4 Palace Green W8 4QD
020 7937 4379
Fax 020 7937 4379
londrabaap@yahoo.co.uk

Consular Section - London
M.E.I.C. House 344 Kensington High Street W14 8NS
020 7602 9833
Fax 020 7602 4229
londra.cons@mae.ro

Consular Section - Edinburgh
7-9 North Street EH2 1AW
0131 524 9498
Fax 0131 524 9499
edingburh@mae.ro

Romanian Cultural Institute
1 Belgrave Square SW1X 8PH
020 7752 0134
Fax 020 7235 0383
office@icr-london.co.uk
www.icr-london.co.uk

HIS EXCELLENCY DR ION JINGA   **m**   *Ambassador Extraordinary & Plenipotentiary (since 07 March 2008)*
            Mrs Daniela Doina Jinga
Mr Theodor Cosmin Onisii   **m**   *Counsellor (Deputy Head of Mission)*
Mr Marius-Ioan Dragolea   **m**   *Minister-Counsellor*
Mrs Mary-Eliana Teodorescu   *Counsellor (Political Affairs)*
Mrs Petronela Corina Iordănescu   **m**   *Counsellor*
Ms Simona Spinaru   *Counsellor (Political Affairs)*
Miss Dorina Orzac   *1st Secretary (Cultural Affairs)*
Miss Alexandra Damian   *2nd Secretary (Political Affairs)*
Mr Radu Oniga   **m**   *2nd Secretary (Political Affairs)*
Miss Vasilica-Vali Staicu   *3rd Secretary*
Mrs Oana Gheorghiu   *   *1st Secretary (Head of Consular Section London)*
Mr Mihai Delcea   **m**   *Minister-Counsellor (Head of Consular Section London)*
Mr Paul Hussar   **m**   *1st Secretary (Consular Affairs)*
Mrs Andreea Ioana Berechet   **m**   1st Secretary *(Consular)*
Ms Iulia Mocanu   *(Consular Attaché)*
Mr Dorian Branea   **m**   *Minister-Counsellor (Cultural Institute Director)*
Colonel Constantin Iacobiţă   **m**   *Defence, Military, Air & Naval Attaché*
Cdr(N) Gabriel Corneliu Oncioiu   **m**   *Deputy Defence, Military, Air & Naval Attaché*
Mrs Cecilia Deaconescu   *   *(Economic Counsellor)*
Ms Ileana Stanica   *(Social & Labour Affairs Attaché)*
Mr Ioan Dascalu   **m**   *(Home Affairs Attaché)*
Mr Robert Marin   **m**   *(Home Affairs Attaché)*

RUSSIA

Embassy of the Russian Federation (Residence of the Ambassador)
13 Kensington Palace Gardens W8 4QX
020 7229 3620
020 7792 1408
Fax 020 7229 5804

Embassy of the Russian Federation (Main Building)
6/7 Kensington Palace Gardens W8 4QP
020 7229 3628
020 7229 6412
Fax 020 7727 8625
www.great-britain.mid.ru
office@rusemblon.org

Consular Department
5 Kensington Palace Gardens W8 4QS
020 7792 8473
020 3051 1199
0845 868 1199
0905 889 0149 (visa information)
www.rusemblon.org
info@rusemblon.org

Defence Attaché's Office
44 Millfield Lane N6 6JB
020 8341 7979
Fax 020 8341 7744

Office of the Trade Representative
33 Highgate West Hill N6 6NL
020 8340 1907
Fax 020 8348 0112

HIS EXCELLENCY MR ALEXANDER V. YAKOVENKO   *Ambassador Extraordinary & Plenipotentiary (since 31 January 2011)*

      Mrs Nana Yakovenko
Mr Alexander M. Kramarenko   **m**   *Minister-Counsellor*
Mr Victor V. Spasskiy   **m**   *Trade Representative*
Mr Dmitry I. Lebedev   **m**   *Deputy Trade Representative*
Colonel Mikhail P. Klimuk   **m**   *Naval Attaché*
Mr Oieg Kornienko   **m**   *Senior Counsellor*
Mr Igor Elkin   **m**   *Naval Attaché Assistant*
Mr Karen K. Malayan   **m**   *Senior Counsellor*
Mr Ernest Chernukhin   *   *Counsellor*
Mr Vladimir A. Ananyev   **m**   *Senior Counsellor*
Mr Valery V. Rodichkin   **m**   *Senior Counsellor*
Mr Sergey Rodichkin   **m**   *Counsellor*
Mr Artem Kozhin   **m**   *Counsellor*
Mr Sergey F. Byvshev   **m**   *Senior Counsellor*
Mr Maxim Elovik   **m**   *Military Attaché*
Mr Andrey K. Batmanov   **m**   *Counsellor & Head of Consular Section*
Mr Vladimir Derbenskiy   **m**   *Counsellor*
Mr Vladimir Lutsenko   **m**   *Assistant Attaché*
Mr Sergey K. Andriashin   **m**   *1st Secretary*
Mr Dmitry Sharapov   **m**   *Military Attaché Assistant*
Mr Gennady G. Antonov   **m**   *1st Secretary*
Mr Sergey N. Kustov   **m**   *1st Secretary*

Mr Konstantin V. Shlykov   **m**   *1st Secretary*
Mr Sergey N. Nalobin   **m**   *1st Secretary*
Mr Pavel Vnukov   **m**   *2nd Secretary*
Mr Denis M. Temnikov   **m**   *1st Secretary*
Mr Alexander B. Shoshnikov   *1st Secretary*
Mr Vadim Y. Petrov   **m**   *1st Secretary*
Mr Ivan A. Volodin   **m**   *1st Secretary*
Mr Anton Chesnokov   **m**   *1st Secretary*
Lieutenant-Colonel Alexey P. Vertakov   **m**   *Assistant Military Attaché*
Lieutenant-Colonel Igor Lyashenko   **m**   *Assistant Defence & Military Attaché Assistant*
Mr Igor Mirtalibov   **m**   *Assistant Military Attaché*
Mr Dmitry V. Kalmykov   **m**   *2nd Secretary*
Mr Alexey O. Sheklakov   **m**   *2nd Secretary*
Mr Roman A. Zizin   **m**   *2nd Secretary*
Mr Viacheslav P. Petelin   **m**   *2nd Secretary*
Mr Andrey A. Ledenev   **m**   *2nd Secretary*
Mr Vitaly Zubkov   **m**   *3rd Secretary*
Mr Yaroslav V. Kon'kov   **m**   *3rd Secretary*
Mr Dmitry K. Lavrov   **m**   *2nd Secretary*
Ms Marina Ryazanova   *3rd Secretary (Consular Section)*
Mr Dmitry Grunenko   **m**   *2nd Secretary*
Mr Alexey I. Dobrinskiy   **m**   *2nd Secretary*
Mr Timofey N. Filonchik   **m**   *3rd Secretary*
Mr Andrey M. Pavlov   **m**   *3rd Secretary*
Mr Andrey A. Makarenko   **m**   *3rd Secretary*
Mr Alexander S. Karavaytsev   *3rd Secretary*
Mr Sergey Peshiy   **m**   *Attaché*
Mr Sergey Lukiyanov   **m**   *Attaché*
Mr Igor Sergeev   **m**   *Attaché*
Mr Sergey Korostelev   **m**   *Attaché*
Mr Alexy Zharov   **m**   *Attaché*
Mrs Larisa K. Linnik   **m**   *Attaché*
Mr Denis N. Ukhanov   **m**   *Attaché*
Mr Igor G. Prolygin   **m**   *Attaché*
Mr Alexei G. Tikolkin   **m**   *Attaché*
Mr Sergey O. Anufriev   **m**   *Attaché*
Mr Vasiliy I. Guliev   **m**   *Attaché*
Mr Eduard V. Orzhelskiy   **m**   *Attaché*
Mr Igor V. Chamov   *Attaché*
Mr Dmitry Y. Gorbunov   **m**   *Attaché*
Mr Andrey S. Chuprakov   **m**   *Attaché*
Mr Alexander Tomilov   **m**   *Attaché*
Mr Dmitry A. Kiselev   **m**   *Attaché*
Ms Anna Koshman   *Attaché*
Mr Denis S. Klevtsov   **m**   *Attaché*
Mr Oleg V. Shor   **m**   *Attaché*
Mr Vladimir Kudriashov   **m**   *Attaché*
Mr Andrey A. Kuznetsov   **m**   *Attaché*
Mrs Elizaveta V. Vokorina   **m**   *Attaché*
Mr Alexander I. Kochergin   *Attaché*
Ms Anna S. Koshman   *Attaché*

RWANDA
High Commission for the Republic of Rwanda
120-122 Seymour Place W1H 1NR
020 7224 9832
Fax 020 7724 8642
uk@ambarwanda.org.uk
www.ambarwanda.org.uk

His Excellency Mr Williams Nkurunizza   **m**   *High Commissioner (since 04 April 2013)*
      Mrs Leonia Nkuruh
Mrs Linda Kalimba   **m**   *1st Counsellor*
Brig. General Kanyambo Frank Rusagara   **m**   *Defence Attaché*
Mr James Wizeye   **m**   *1st Secretary*
Mr Patrick Gihana-Mulenga   **m**   *Commercial Attaché*

SAINT CHRISTOPHER & NEVIS
High Commission for Saint Christopher & Nevis
10 Kensington Court W8 5DL
020 7937 9718
Fax 020 937 7484
info@sknhc.co.uk
www.stkittsnevisuk.com

His Excellency Dr Kevin Monroe Isaac   **m**   *High Commissioner (since 12 January 2011)*
      Mrs Prangtip Isaac
Ms Wanda Connor   *1st Secretary*

SAINT LUCIA
High Commission for Saint Lucia
1 Collingham Gardens SW5 0HW
020 7370 7123
Fax 020 7370 1905
enquiries@stluciahcuk.org

His Excellency Dr Ernest Hilaire   **m**   *High Commissioner*
Mr Albert Fregis   *Minister-Counsellor*
Miss Kim Emmanuel   *1st Secretary*
Ms Clerona Compton   *Consul*
Mr Verne Augustin   *Vice Consul*
Mrs Esther Robinson-Bello   **m**   *Attaché/Administrative Secretary*

SAINT VINCENT & THE GRENADINES
High Commission for Saint Vincent & the Grenadines
10 Kensington Court W8 5DL
020 7460 1256
020 7565 2874
Fax 020 7937 6040
info@svghighcom.co.uk
www.svghighcom.co.uk
www.facebook.com/pages/SVG-High-Commission/113786951801
www.twitter.com/svghighcom
www.gov.vc

High Commissioner's Office
020 7565 2545
office@svghighcom.co.uk

Political & Commercial Section
020 7565 2885
mc@svghighcom.co.uk

Consular Section
020 7460 2588
info@svghighcom.co.uk

HIS EXCELLENCY MR CENIO E. LEWIS   **m**   *High Commissioner (since 24 April 2001)*
            Mrs Ita Lewis
Mrs Doris Charles   *   *Minister-Counsellor*
Ms Carolin de Freitas-Sawh   **m**   *Counsellor*

SAMOA

Embassy of Samoa
Avenue de l'Oree 20 Bte 4 Brussels 1000
0032 2 660 8454
Fax 0032 2 675 0336
samoanembassy@skynet.be

HIS EXCELLENCY FATUMANAVA DR PA'OLELEI H LUTERU   **m**   *High Commissioner (since 14 August 2012)*
Ms Amorette Posini   *Deputy Head of Mission/Counsellor*
Ms Anastasia Amoa   *Counsellor*
Mr Oliver Joseph Chan Ting   **m**   *1st Secretary*

SAN MARINO

Embassy of the Republic of San Marino
All correspondence should be addressed to the Department of Foreign Affairs
Palazzo Begni – Contrada Omerelli 47890 San Marino – Republic of San Marino
+378 (0549) 882422
Fax +378 (0549) 992018
dipartimentoaffariesteri@pa.sm

HER EXCELLENCY MS FEDERICA BIGI   *Ambassador Extraordinary & Plenipotentiary (since 31 October 2012)*

SÃO TOMÉ & PRINCIPE

Embassy of São Tomé & Principe
175 Avenue de Tervuren 1150 Brussels
00322 734 8966
Fax 00322 734 8815
Ambassade@saotomeeprincipe.be

Vacant   *Ambassador Extraordinary & Plenipotentiary*
Mr Armindo de Brito   **m**   *Chargé d'Affaires a.i.*
Mr Horatio Fernando da Forseca   **m**   *2nd Secretary*

SAUDI ARABIA

Royal Embassy of Saudi Arabia
30 Charles Street Mayfair W1J 5DZ
020 7917 3000

Defence Attaché's Office
26 Queens Gate SW7 5JE
020 7581 7070

Diplomatic Office of the Cultural Bureau
630 Chiswick High Road W4 5RY
020 3249 7000

Medical Section
60 Queen Anne Street W1G 8HP
020 7935 9931

Consular Office
32 Charles Street Mayfair W1J 5DZ
020 7917 3000

Economic Section
30 Charles Street Mayfair W1J 5DZ
020 7917 3000

Commercial Section
15/16 Queens Street Mayfair W1J 5PQ
020 7917 3000

Islamic Affairs Section
2nd Floor Park Lorne 111 Park Road NW8 7JL
020 7723 7817

Information Section
18 Seymour Street W1H 7HU
020 7486 8324

HIS EXCELLENCY HRH PRINCE MOHAMED BIN NAWAF BIN ABDULAZIZ   **m**   *Ambassador Extraordinary & Plenipotentiary (since 01 December 2005)*
        HH Princess Fadwa bint Khalid bin Abdullah bin Abdulrahman
Mr Abdulrahman A.A. Al-Suhaibani   **m**   *Minister Plenipotentiary*
Dr Saud Al Ammari   **m**   *Minister Plenipotentiary*
Mr Abdulrahman Al-Anezi   **m**   *Counsellor*
Mr Abdulaziz Al-Faleh   **m**   *Counsellor*
Mr Abdullah Zayed Assiri   **m**   *Counsellor*
Mr Abdulmomen Mohammad Sharaf   *   *Counsellor*
Mr Zainalabdeen Ali Ahmed Melebari   **m**   *Counsellor*
Mr Saud bin Fahd M. Al-Suwailem   **m**   *Counsellor*
Mr Ahmed Ali A. Kattouah   **m**   *Counsellor*
Mr Waleed Al-Hamoudi   **m**   *Counsellor*
Mr Khalid Abdullah A. Al-Rajhi   **m**   *Counsellor*
HH Prince Sultan Fahd Al-Saud   **m**   *1st Secretary*
Mr Musaid Sulaiman M. Al-Marwany   **m**   *1st Secretary*
Mr Mazen Abdulaziz Al Shaikh   **m**   *1st Secretary*
Mr Osamah D. R. Al-Ahmadi   **m**   *1st Secretary*
Mr Anas Abdulrahman Al-Wasedy   **m**   *1st Secretary*
Mr Mohamed S Al-Romih   *   *1st Secretary*
Mr Rajeh Tami H Al-Bugamy   *1st Secretary*
Mr Sultan Fahad A. Bin Khuzaim   **m**   *1st Secretary*
Mr Waleed Omar A. Baasem   **m**   *1st Secretary*
Mr Hessam Mohammed Al-Oqil   **m**   *2nd Secretary*

Mr Abdullah Abdulrahman A. Al-Fozan   **m**   *2nd Secretary*
Miss Norah Abdulaziz H El Gibreen   *2nd Secretary*
Ms Nouf Fahd Al-Khaldi   *   *2nd Secretary*
Mr Bander Sulaiman Al-Moqbel   **m**   *2nd Secretary*
Mr Fahad Khalid E Al-Khamali   **m**   *2nd Secretary*
Mr Yousef Shazle   **m**   *3rd Secretary*
Mr Fouad Sebaih   **m**   *3rd Secretary*
Mr Faisl Mohammed Al-Housaini   **m**   *3rd Secretary*
Mr Emad H. Zahim   **m**   *3rd Secretary*
HRH Princess Madawil bint Mohamed Al-Saud   *3rd Secretary*
Dr Abdulrahman bin Asad Hussain   **m**   *3rd Secretary*
Mr Ibrahim Omar Al-Dayel   **m**   *3rd Secretary*
Mr Majed Awah Al-Sulami   **m**   *3rd Secretary*
Mr Abdulmonem Mohammed Al-Ghamadi   **m**   *3rd Secretary*
Dr Dinah M Khayat   *3rd Secretary*
Mr Abdullah S. Al-Sallal   **m**   *Attaché*
Mr Mohammed Salem Al-Zubaidi   **m**   *Attaché*
HRH Princess Mashael bint Mohamed Al-Saud   *Attaché*
Mr Saad Mohammed Al-Othman   **m**   *Attaché*
Mr Ali Khalid Al-Humaidan   **m**   *Attaché*
Mr Nasser Thnayan Al-Thnayan   *Attaché*
Mr Khalid Yousef J. Bin Mohsen   *Attaché*
Brig. Gen. Abdullah S. Al-Zughaibi   **m**   *Defence Attaché*
Col. Abdullah Hamed M. Al-Ghoreibi   **m**   *Assistant Attaché (Naval Affairs)*
Col. Sajer Rafeed M. Al-Enazi   **m**   *Attaché (Defence)*
Col. Mohammed Salem R Al-Anazi   **m**   *Attaché (Defence)*
Col. Abdulaziz bin Abdullah bin I Al-Hamlan   **m**   *Assistant Attaché (Defence)*
Col. Omar I. Al-Seif   **m**   *Assistant Attaché (Defence)*
Col. Ahmed Mohammed A Al-Mulhim   **m**   *Assistant Military Attaché*
Mr Mohammed Abdulwahab Al-Nemer   **m**   *Attaché (Defence)*
Lt Col. Abdulrahman bin Abdullah Al-Zamel   **m**   *Attaché (Defence)*
Major Fahad Abdullah Al-Ruwayti   **m**   *Attaché (Defence)*
Major Ahmed Abu Hadi   **m**   *Attaché (Defence)*
Eng Lt Col Saeed Al-Rasheed   **m**   *Attaché (Defence)*
Capt. Saad Mohammed Al-Toaimy   **m**   *Attaché (Defence)*
Major Fahd Saud Al-Obeikan   **m**   *Attaché (Defence)*
Capt. Mohammed Abdullah A. Al-Arfaj   **m**   *Attaché (Defence)*
Mr Mohamed Abdullah Al-Burih   **m**   *Attaché (Defence)*
Mr Mohammed Yahya A Fagihi   *Attaché (Defence)*
Mr Abdullah Al-Daowas   **m**   *Attaché (Defence)*
Mr Hassan Abdullah Al-Azhari   **m**   *Attaché (Defence)*
Mr Mohammad Hamad bin Salem Al-Qahtany   **m**   *Assistant Attaché (Defence)*
Mr Ali bin Ibrahim F Al-Onazy   **m**   *Attache (Defence)*
Mr Saad Alduhaimi   **m**   *Attaché (Defence)*
Mr Soliman M S Al-Malki   **m**   *Attaché (Defence)*
Mr Badr bin Abdullah Al-Anazi   **m**   *Attaché (Defence)*
Mr Musleh Al-Garni   **m**   *Attaché (Defence)*
Mr Faisal Al Otaibi   **m**   *Attaché (Defence)*
Mr Ahmed Hamed H. Al-Mutairi   **m**   *Attaché (Defence)*
Mr Abdullah Turki Al-Osaimi   **m**   *Attaché (Defence)*
Mr Fahd bin Abdulrahman Al-Arfaj   **m**   *Attaché (Defence)*
Mr Bander Owaid Al-Otaibi   **m**   *Attaché (Defence)*
Dr Faisal Mohammed Abaalkail   **m**   *Attaché (Defence)*
Dr Othman Ali Al-Zamil   *   Vice Cultural *Attaché*

Mr Saleh Abdullah S Al-Monif   **m**   *Attaché Cultural)*
Dr Ahmed S A Turkistani   **m**   *Attaché (Cultural)*
Dr Mohammad Omar Abdulaziz Al-Subael   **m**   *Attaché (Cultural)*
Dr Khalid bin Saleh M Al-Subaiei   **m**   *Attaché (Cultural)*
Dr Mohammed Saeed Qasi Al-Ahmadi   **m**   *Attaché (Cultural)*
Dr Adbulghani Abdulhassan G Al-Harbi   **m**   *Attaché (Cultural)*
Dr Abdulrahman Abdullah Al-Obaid   **m**   *Attaché (Cultural)*
Dr Mustafa Abdulrahman Al-bar   **m**   *Attaché (Cultural)*
Dr Amal Saleh Al-Hamli   **m**   *Attaché (Cultural)*
Dr Neamah Habbas S Al-Mutairi   **m**   *Attaché (Cultural)*
Mr Abdulrahman A A Al-Angari   **m**   *Assistant Attaché (Cultural)*
Mr Nassir Fahadi Al-Bishr   **m**   *Attaché (Cultural)*
Mr Maree Al-Shahrani   **m**   *Attaché (Cultural)*
Mr Abdullah Adbulrahman Al-Jallal   **m**   *Attaché (Cultural)*
Mr Khalid Al-Sarami   **m**   *Attaché (Cultural)*
Mr Mohamed Ibrahim Aba Al-Khail   **m**   *Assistant Attaché (Cultural)*
Mr Mohammed Khalifah M Al-Khalifah   **m**   *Attaché (Cultural)*
Mr Eyad Ibrahim A Al-Fadel   *Attaché (Cultural)*
Mr Abdulaziz Al-Hindi   **m**   *Assistant Attaché (Information)*
Mr Munther Mohammad Al-Amrani   **m**   *Administrative Officer (Information)*
Mr Fawaz Saad Al-Ghamdi   **m**   *Attaché (Commercial)*
Mr Nasser Abdulaziz Al-Mugbil   *Attaché (Commercial)*
Dr Ali Hamed S. Al-Ghamdi   *   *Health Attaché*
Dr Ahmed Al-Dubayan   **m**   *Attaché (Islamic Affairs)*
Mr Abdulaziz Al-Harbi   **m**   *Attaché (Islamic Affairs)*
Mr Mazen Al-Malik   **m**   *Attaché*
Mr Turki bin Abdulaziz Al-Nasser   **m**   *Attaché*
Mr Eddies Abdullah Al-Oteibi   *Attaché*
Mr Fahd Abdu Ibrahim Shetaifi   *Attaché*
Mr Ibrahim Mohamed Jabali   **m**   *Attaché*
Mr Abdulaziz Mohamed bin Qann   **m**   *Attaché*
Mr Mohamed Al-Tuayan   **m**   *Attaché*
Mr Sultan bin Mohammed H. Al-Hulwah   **m**   *Attaché*
Mr Saad bin Mohammed M. Al-Qahtani   **m**   *Attaché*
Mr Sattam bin Menwer J. Al-Harbi   **m**   *Attaché*
Mr Nasser bin Salem Ayed Al-Baqami   **m**   *Attaché*
Mr Jarallah bin Hassan Al-Malki   **m**   *Attaché*
Mr Hossain Alqahtani   **m**   *Attaché*
Mr Muqrin Abdullah M. Al-Malki   **m**   *Attaché*
Mr Mohsen Yousef Al-Baqami   **m**   *Attaché*
Mr Daifallah Al-Harbi   **m**   *Attaché*
Mr Abdullah bin Shallah Al-Matrafi   **m**   *Attaché*
Mr Saeed bin Awad Al-Harbi   **m**   *Attaché*
Mr Bader bin Saad Al-Tilasi   **m**   *Attaché*
Brig Gen Hussein S Al-Kahtani   **m**   *Assistant Defence Attaché*

SENEGAL

Embassy of the Republic of Senegal

39 Marloes Road W8 6LA
020 7938 4048/020 7937 7237
Fax 020 7938 2546
senegalembassy@hotmail.co.uk
www.senegalembassy.com

His Excellency Mr Abdou Sourang **m** *Ambassador Extraordinary & Plenipotentiary (since 04 December 2007)*
Mrs Marieme Mbengue
Mr Youssouph Diallo **m** *1st Counsellor*
Mr Sara Ndiaye **m** *1st Counsellor*
Mr Aliou Ndiaye **m** *1st Secretary*
Mr Djibril Dia **m** *1st Secretary*

SERBIA

Embassy of the Republic of Serbia
28 Belgrave Square SW1X 8QB
020 7235 9049
Fax 020 7235 7092
london@serbianembassy.org.uk
www.serbianembassy.org.uk

His Excellency Dr Ognjen Pribićević **m** *Ambassador Extraordinary & Plenipotentiary (since 17 October 2013)*
Mrs Dragana Pribićević
Mr Nebojša Radojičić * *Minister-Counsellor*
Colonel Saša Perović **m** *Defence Attaché*
Ms Nataša Marić **m** *1st Counsellor (Political Affairs and Press)*
Mr Saša Uzelac * *1st Counsellor (Economic Affairs)*
Mrs Ljiljana Zarubica * *Counsellor (Consular Affairs)*
Major Bojan Velickovic **m** *Assistant Defence Attaché*
Mrs Branislava Perin Jarić * *1st Secretary*
Miss Emilija Marinkov *2nd Secretary*
Mrs Neda Mijajlović **m** *2nd Secretary*

SEYCHELLES

The High Commission of the Republic of Seychelles
4th Floor 130-132 Buckingham Palace Road SW1W 9SA
020 7245 0680
Fax 020 7730 0087
seyhc.london@btconnect.com
Monday-Friday 09.00-17.00

Consular Section
4th Floor 111 Baker Street W1U 6RR
020 7935 7770
Fax 020 7486 3272
consulate@seychelles-gov.net
www.seychelles-gov.net
Monday-Thursday 09.30-17.30, Friday 09.30-15.00

Commercial Section
4th Floor 130-132 Buckingham Palace Road SW1W 9SA
020 7297 2128
seychelles@uksto.co.uk
www.seychelles.travel
Monday-Friday 09.00-17.00

Her Excellency Mrs Marie-Pierre Lloyd *High Commissioner (since 21 November 2012)*
Mrs Lalatina Accouche **m** *Principal Counsellor*
Mr Bernard Silver **m** *Consul (Head of Consular Section)*

Ms Tinaz Wadia   *Commercial Attaché*
Mrs Lena Hoareau   **m**   *Commercial Attaché (Public Relations & News Bureau)*

SIERRA LEONE
Sierra Leone High Commission
41 Eagle Street WC1R 4TL
020 7404 0140
Fax 020 7430 9862
info@slhc-uk.org.uk
www.slhc-uk.org.uk
Monday-Friday 09.30-13.00 & 14.00-17.00

HIS EXCELLENCY MR EDWARD MOHAMED TURAY   *High Commissioner (since 09 January 2010)*
      Mrs Isatu Turay
Mr Tamba Mansa Ngegba   **m**   *Deputy High Commissioner*
Mr Sahr Prince Demba   **m**   Minister *Counsellor/Head of Chancery*
Mr Obai Taylor-Kamara   **m**   *Counsellor*
Mrs Clara Koroma   *   *1st Secretary*
Mrs Sia Tejan   **m**   *1st Secretary*
Mr Musa Bai Sesay   **m**   *2nd Secretary (Consular)*
Mr John Ellie   **m**   *Financial Attaché*
Mr Sorie Sudan Sesay   **m**   *Information* Attaché

SINGAPORE
High Commission for the Republic of Singapore
9 Wilton Crescent SW1X 8SP
020 7235 8315
Fax 020 7245 6583
singhc_lon@sgmfa.gov.sg
http://mfa.gov.sg/london
Monday-Friday 09.00-17.00

Consular Section
Basement 9 Wilton Crescent SW1X 8SP
020 7235 8315
Fax 020 7235 9850
Singhc_con_lon@sgmfa.gov.sg
Monday-Friday 09:30-12:30

Liaison Office
10 Greycoat Place SW1P 1SB
020 7960 6655/6656
Fax 020 7283 4024

Commercial Section
Singapore Centre Grand Buildings1-3 The Strand WC2N 5HR
020 7484 2730
Fax 020 7839 6162
http://www.iesingapore.gov.sg

Maritime Affairs
Singapore Centre Grand Buildings 1-3 The Strand WC2N 5HR
020 7484 2738
Fax 020 7484 2739

His Excellency Mr Thambynathan Jasudasen   *High Commissioner (since 22 August 2011)*
    Mrs Patricia Jasudasen
Mr Stephen Quick   **m**   *Deputy High Commissioner*
Ms Han Yin Lee   **m**   *Counsellor*
Mr Swee Meng Ho   **m**   *1st Secretary (Admin & Consular)*
Mrs Karolyn Poon   **m**   *1st Secretary (Overseas Singaporeans)*
Mr Ranjeet Singh   *1st Secretary (Maritime)*
Ms Lee Fee Chong   *1st Secretary (Maritime)*
Ms Mei Ling Yeoh   *2nd Secretary (Commercial)*
Ms Sheena Chan Zi Roon   *2nd Secretary (Political)*
Mr Yong Yang Mak   *2nd Secretary (Political)*
Mr Bartholomew Goh   **m**   *Attaché (Admin & Consular)*

SLOVAK REPUBLIC

Embassy of the Slovak Republic
25 Kensington Palace Gardens W8 4QY
020 7313 6470
020 7313 6481
emb.london@mzv.sk
www.mzv.sk/londyn
Monday-Thursday 08.30-16.45, Friday 08.30-15.30

Consular & Visa Section
Cons.london@mzv.sk
Monday-Thursday 09.00-12.00 & 13.00-16.00, Friday 09.00-12.00

Commercial Department
020 7313 6493
020 7727 3009
Fax: 020 7727 3667
Slovaktrade@btconnect.com
www.slovakembassy-cd-london.co.uk

Defence Attaché's Office
Tel/Fax 020 7792 0215

His Excellency Mr Miroslav Wlachovský   *Ambassador Extraordinary & Plenipotentiary (since 28 March 2011)*
    Mrs Jaroslava Wlachovská
Ms Slavomíra Mašurová   *Deputy Head of Mission*
Mrs Alena Longauerová   **m**   *2nd Secretary (Political Affairs)*
Mr Igor Pokojný   **m**   *Counsellor-Minister*
Mr Miroslav Karvai   **m**   *Attaché (Consular Affairs)*
Mrs Natália Hrnćiarová   *Attaché (Consular Affairs)*
Colonel Vladimír Samek   **m**   *Defence Attaché*
Lieut Col Adriana Kolarikova   **m**   *Attaché (Police)*

SLOVENIA

Embassy of the Republic of Slovenia
10 Little College Street SW1P 3SH
020 7222 5700
Fax 020 7222 5277
vlo@gov.si
www.london.embassy.si

Consular Section (entrance from Cowley Street)
020 7227 9711
Fax 020 7222 5277
Monday 09.30-13.00, Wednesday 09.30-13.00, 14.00-16.00 Thursday 10.00 -13.00.

HIS EXCELLENCY MR IZTOK JARC   **m**   *Ambassador Extraordinary & Plenipotentiary*
(since 02 February 2009)
            Mrs Helena Jarc
Mr Milko Dolinšek   **m**   *Minister Plenipontentiary*
Mrs Renata Cvelbar Bek   **m**   *Minister Plenipotentiary (Economics)*
Mrs Mateja Kračun   *   *Minister Counsellor*
Mr Miha Erman   *1st Counsellor*

SOLOMON ISLANDS
High Commission for the Solomon Islands
Avenue Edouard Lacombe 17B 1040 Brussels Belgium
00 32 2 732 7085
Fax 00 32 2 732 6885

HIS EXCELLENCY MR JOSEPH MA'AHANUA   *High Commissioner (since 30 June 2006)*
            Mrs Noelyn Ma'ahanua

SOMALIA
No official Embassy address at present time
HIS EXCELLENCY MR ABDULLAHI MOHAMED ALI   *   *(since 3 September 2013)*

SOUTH AFRICA
South African High Commission
South Africa House
Trafalgar Square WC2N 5DP
020 7451 7299
Fax 020 7839 5670

Immigration Section
15 Whitehall
SW1A 2DD
020 7925 89800/01
Fax 020 7839 5198

Vacant   *High Commissioner*
Ms Bongiwe Qwabe   *Deputy High Commissioner*
Mr Simphiwe Mhlekwa   **m**   *Minister (Corporate Services)*
Mr Dumisani Theohelus Ntuli   **m**   *Minister*
Mr Yusuf Ismail Timol   **m**   *Minister (Economic)*
Mrs Mandy Eileen Solomon   **m**   *Counsellor*
Mr Daniel Oliphant   **m**   *Counsellor*
Ms Phindile Wilhelmina Xaba   **m**   *Counsellor*
Mr Johannes Petrus Cornet   **m**   *Counsellor (ICT)*
Col Itumeleng Esther Kgole   *Counsellor*
Mr Henry Sipho Nkosi   **m**   *1st Secretary*
Mrs Wambambane Cathrine Moruke   **m**   *1st Secretary*
Ms Carol Mabuza   *1st Secretary*
Mr Phumudzo Ratshitanga   **m**   *1st Secretary*

91

Mr Oarabile Motlhaga   *3rd Secretary*
Mr Oupa Hendrik Mashaba   **m**   *1st Secretary (Corporate Services)*
Ms Selebaleng Maria Coerty Mongoegelwa   *1st Secretary (Corporate Services)*
Ms Thandi Audrey Vilane   *1st Secretary (ICT)*
Mr Thandi Ngcwabe   **m**   *1st Secretary (ICT)*
Ms Sithandiwe Zondo   *3rd Secretary (Corporate Services)*
Mrs Naomi Carmen Cornet   **m**   *3rd Secretary (Corporate Services)*
Brig-Gen GeraldSandile Sizani   *Defence & Naval Advisor*
Col Nompumelelo Daisy Tshiloane   *Deputy Defence Attaché*
WO1 Rodney Thomas Marks   **m**   *WO1*
Mr Rapelang Moses Malekanyo   **m**   *2nd Secretary (Immigration & Civic Affairs)*
Mr Kgomotso Ngoma   **m**   *2nd Secretary (Immigration & Civic Affairs)*

SPAIN

Embassy of Spain
39 Chesham Place SW1X 8SB
020 7235 5555
Fax 020 7259 5392
emb.londres@maec.es
www.exteriores.gob.es/embajadas/londres/en

Consulate General
20 Draycott Place SW3 2RZ
020 7589 8989
0871 376 0023 (Visa Information)
Fax 020 7581 7888
cog.londres@maec.es
www.consulateinlondon.maec.es

Cultural Office
39 Chesham Place SW1X 8SB
020 7201 5522/5517/5524
Fax 020 7259 6487
emb.londres.ofc@maec.es

Defence Office
3 Hans Crescent SW1X 0LN
020 7589 5731
Fax 020 7823 7926
agredlon@oc.mde.es

Financial Office
39 Chesham Place SW1X 8SB
020 7201 5551

Transport Office – Permanent Representation to International Maritime Organization
39 Chesham Place SW1X 8SB
020 7201 5539
Fax 020 7235 9303
imo.spain@fomento.es

Education Office
20 Peel Street W8 7PD
020 7727 2462
Fax 020 7229 4965
info.uk@meed.es
www.educacion.gob.es/reinounido

Employment and Social Affairs Office
20 Peel Street W8 7PD
020 7221 0098 / 020 7243 9897
Fax 020 7229 7270
constrab.londres@meyss.es
www.empleo.gob.es/reinounido

Agriculture, Food and the Environment Office
39 Chesham Place SW1X 8SB
020 7235 5005
Fax 020 7259 6897
londres@magrama.es

Information and Press Office
39 Chesham Place SW1X 8SB
020 7235 7537
Fax 020 7235 2263
consejeria.londres@mpr.es

Economic and Commercial Section
66 Chiltern Street W1U 4LS
020 7467 2330
Fax 020 7487 5586
Fax 020 7224 6409
londres@comercio.mineco.es

HIS EXCELLENCY MR FREDERICO TRILLO-FIGUEROA   m   Ambassador *Extraordinary & Plenipotentiary (since 16 May 2012)*
        Mrs Maria José Molinuevo
Mr Ramón Gandarias   m   *Minister-Counsellor*
Captain Pablo A. Lewick-Carazo   m   *Defence & Naval Attaché*
Mrs Mercedes Rico Carabias   *Minister (Consular Affairs)*
Mr Fidel López Álvarez   m   *Minister (Cultural & Scientific Affairs)*
Mr Enrique Ojeda Vila   m   *Counsellor*
Mr Jose Manuel Gutiérrez Delgado   m   *Counsellor (Finance)*
Mr Félix Álvarez Saavedra   m   *Counsellor*
Dr Ismael Cobos   *Counsellor for Transport (Maritime Affairs)*
Mr Liborio López García   m   *Counsellor (Education)*
Ms Blanca Sánchez-Robles Rute   *Counsellor (Employment & Social Affairs)*
Mr Enrique Ruiz   *Counsellor (Commerce & Tourism)*
Mr Luis González-Quevedo   m   *Counsellor (Agriculture, Food and the Environment)*
Ms Esther Corral Cortés   *Counsellor (Information and Press)*
Mr José Antonio Zamora   m   *Counsellor (Economic & Commercial)*
Mr Marcos Gómez   m   *Counsellor (Consul)*
Mr José Antonio González-Bueno   *Counsellor (Political Affairs)*
Mr Alberto Miranda   *First Secretary (Politcal Affairs)*
Ms Natividad Isabel Peña   m   *First Secretary (Political Affairs)*
Mr Damián Dávila Baena   m   *Counsellor*
Mr Ödön Pálla   *Counsellor (Economic & Commercial)*
Mr José González   m   *Attaché (Administrative Affairs)*
Mrs María Sanjurjo   m   *Attaché*
Ms Raquel Jorge   *Attaché*
Mr Oscar Asensi   m   *Attaché*
Mr Carlos Neito   *Attaché*
Mr Miguel Núñez Sanchez   m   *Maritime Attaché*
Ms Beatriz Monge   *Deputy Counsellor (Information & Press)*
Mrs Nuria Guzmán   m   *Deputy Counsellor (Commerce & Tourism)*

Mrs Carmen Sanz   *   *Commercial Attaché*
Mr Julio Crespo MacLennan   **m**   *Director Instituto Cervantes*

SRI LANKA

High Commission of the Democratic Socialist Republic of Sri Lanka
13 Hyde Park Gardens W2 2LU
020 7262 1841
Fax 020 7262 7970
mail@slhc-london.co.uk
www.srilankahighcommission.co.uk
Monday-Friday 09.00-17.00

HIS EXCELLENCY DR CHRISANTHA NICHOLAS ANTHONY NONIS   *High Commissioner (since 30 August 2011)*
Mr Neville Gladwin De Silva   **m**   *Deputy High Commissioner*
Mrs Sonali Nelum Ilangakkone Wijeratne   **m**   *Minister (Commerce)*
Dr Hashini Kokila Waidyaratne   **m**   *Minister (Education)*
Mrs S.A.P.P. Saram   **m**   *Minister-Counsellor (Administration)*
Mrs Undugodage C. P. Prasangani Rodrigo   **m**   *Minister-Counsellor (Media and Commonwealth)*
Mr G. Kodikara Appuhamilage Chaminda Kumara Kularatne   **m**   *Minister-Counsellor (Consular)*
Mr K. K. Yoganaadan   **m**   *Counsellor (Public Affairs)*
Mr H.M.K. Herath   **m**   *1st Secretary (Culture)*
Miss Muthu Padmakumara   *2nd Secretary (Media)*
Mrs Seevali Wijewantha   **m**   *3nd Secretary (Commerce)*

SOUTH SUDAN

Embassy of the Republic of South Sudan
28-32 Wellington Road NW8 9SF
020 7483 9260
info@goss-london.com
www.goss-london.com

HIS EXCELLENCY MR SABIT ABBE ALLEY   *   *Ambassador Extraordinary & Plenipotentiary (since 18 October 2012)*
Mr Chol Mawud Unguec Ajongo   **m**   *Deputy Head of Mission*
Mr Maker Ayuel Deng   *   *Minister Plenipotentiary*
Mr Akok Madut Manyuat   *   *Counsellor*
Mr William Ajang De Chan Chan   *   *Counsellor*
Mr Michael Saki Longwa   *   *First Secretary*
Mr David Laku Darious   *   *Second Secretary*
Mr Jacob Nhial Reath   *   *Third Secretary*
Ms Adhieu Elizabeth Yaak Dut   *Third Secretary*
Mr Kuol Nyok Kuol   *   *Defence Attaché*
Mr Kuir Dau Atem   *   *Administrative Attaché*

SUDAN

Embassy of the Republic of the Sudan
3 Cleveland Row St James's SW1A 1DD
020 7839 8080
Fax 020 7839 7560
admin@sudanembassy.co.uk
www.sudanembassy.co.uk

HIS EXCELLENCY MR ABDULLAHI HAMAD ALI ALAZREG   *Ambassador Extraordinary &*
Plenipotentiary (since 10 August 2010)
   Mrs Sumaya Omer Husain Abdelrahman
Mr Bukhari Ghanim Mohamed Afandi   **m**   *Deputy Head of Mission*
Mr Gaffar Somi Tutu Kuku   **m**   *Counsellor*
Mr Mohamed Osman Akasha El Hussain Mohamed   **m**   *Counsellor*
Mr Omer Hamid Abdalla Hamid   **m**   *2nd Secretary*
Mr Mekki Awad Mohamed Mohamedean   **m**   *Counsellor*
Dr Khalid Al Mubarak   **m**   *Press Counsellor*
Mr Mahmoud Suliman Mohamed Easa   **m**   *1st Secretary*
Mr Ibrahim Elbadawi Mohamed Ali   **m**   *Attaché*
Mr Adil Abdelfadeel Alhaj Khamis   **m**   *Attaché*
Mr Mamdouh Elfaki Khalf Alla Nour Elgalel   **m**   *Administrative Attaché*
Mrs Naila Dafa Alla Ali Babiker   **m**   *Financial Attaché*
Mr Mohamed Abdelhamid Ibrahim Abdelkarim   **m**   *Attaché*
Mr Abazr Sidahmed Mohamed Ahmed   *   *Administrative Attaché*

SURINAME

Embassy of the Republic of Suriname
Alexander Gogelweg 2 2517 JH The Hague The Netherlands
(00) 31 703650844
Fax (00) 31 703617445
ambassade.suriname@wxs.nl

HIS EXCELLENCY MR HARVEY HAROLD NAARENDORP   *Ambassador Extraordinary & Plenipotentiary*
(since 18 February 2012)
Mr Howard Rudy Patrick Nooitmeer   **m**   *Attaché*

SWAZILAND

Kingdom of Swaziland High Commission
20 Buckingham Gate SW1E 6LB
Tel: 020 7630 6611
Fax 020 7630 6564
Email: enquiries@swaziland.org.uk
Monday-Thursday 09.00-16.30 & Friday 09.00-16.00

HER EXCELLENCY MRS DUMSILE T. SUKATI   *   *High Commissioner (since 28 July 2010)*
Mr Henry Zeeman   **m**   *Counsellor*
Mr Themba Simelane   **m**   *1st Secretary (Information)*
Mr Muzi Joseph Nhlabatsi   *3rd Secretary*
Mrs Ruth Ntombikayise Kunene   **m**   *Administrative Attaché*

SWEDEN

Embassy of Sweden
11 Montagu Place W1H 2AL
Main Switchboard 020 7917 6400
Passports 020 7917 6410
Visas 020 7917 6413
Defence 020 7917 6426
Fax 020 7724 4174
Passports & Visas Fax 020 7917 6475
ambassaden.london@foreign.ministry.se
www.swedenabroad.com/london
Monday-Friday 09.00-12.00 & 14.00-16.00

Swedish Trade Council
259-269 Old Marylebone Road NW1 5RA
020 7616 4070
Fax 020 7616 4099

HER EXCELLENCY MS NICOLA CLASE **m** *Ambassador Extraordinary & Plenipotentiary (since 03 June 2010)*
       Dr Andrew Schenkel
Mrs Ulrika Funered **m** *Minister-Counsellor, Deputy Chief of Mission*
Mrs Christel Makarowski **m** *Counsellor (Administrative & Consular Affairs)*
Ms Leena Jaanson *Counsellor (Consular Affairs)*
Ms Helena Reitberger *Counsellor (Foreign & Security Policy)*
Mr Ulf Samuelsson *Counsellor (Political & Foreign European Affairs)*
Ms Sara Dahlsten *1st Secretary (Economic Affairs & Trade Policy)*
Ms Margareta Wrang *3rd Secretary*
Ms Santa Nokrach *3rd Secretary*
Ms Ellen Wettmark *Counsellor (Cultural Affairs)*
Mr Magnus Krumlinde **m** *Counsellor*
Colonel Mats Danielsson **m** *Defence Attaché*
Mr Fredrik Häggström **m** *Commercial Counsellor & Trade Commissioner*

SWITZERLAND

Embassy of Switzerland
16/18 Montagu Place W1H 2BQ
020 7616 6000
Fax 020 7724 7001
lon.swissembassy@eda.admin.ch
www.eda.admin.ch/london
Monday-Friday 09.00-12.00

Regional Consular Centre London
c/o Embassy of Switzerland in the United Kingdom
16-18 Montagu Place W1H 2BQ
020 7616 6000
Fax 020 7723 9581
rcclondon@eda.admin.ch
www.eda.admin.chrcclondon

HIS EXCELLENCY MR DOMINIK ROBERT FURGLER **m** *Ambassador Extraordinary & Plenipotentiary (since 26 June 2013)*
       Mrs Hayam Furgler
Mr Frank Othmar Grütter **m** *Minister*
Mr Hans Eberhart **m** *Defence, Military, Naval & Air Attaché*

Mr Nicholas C Niggi **m** *Counsellor (Economics, Finance & Scientific Affairs)*
Mrs Margrit Ledermann Prestofelippo **m** *Counsellor & Consul General*
Mr Denis Roland Charriére *Counsellor (Cultural Affairs)*
Mr Stephan Lauper **m** *1st Secretary (Legal & Political Affairs)*
Mr Conradin Mathis Rasi **m** *2nd Secretary (Economics, Financial & Scientific Affairs)*
Mrs Rebekka Barbara Benesch **m** *2nd Secretary (Financial Affairs)*
Ms Susanne Hemund *2nd Secretary, Consul (Consular & visa Affairs)*
Mr Hans-Rudolf Bolli **m** *3rd Secretary (Visa Affairs)*
Ms Martina Garamendi-Laim **m** *3rd Secretary (Consular Affairs)*
Mrs Liliana Varani Perrenoud **m** *Attaché (Administative Affairs)*
Mr Matthias Kuehni *Attaché (IT Affairs)*

SYRIA

(Temporarily closed by the Syrian Government)
Embassy of the Syrian Arab Republic
8 Belgrave Square SW1X 8PH
020 7245 9012
Fax 020 7235 4621
www.syrianembassy.co.uk

TAJIKISTAN

Embassy of the Republic of Tajikistan
26-28 Hammersmith Grove W6 7BA
020 8834 1003
Fax 020 8834 1100
info@tajembassy.org.uk
www.tajembassy.org.uk

HIS EXCELLENCY MR ERKIN KASYMOV **m** *Ambassador Extraordinary & Plenipotentiary (since 16 May 2008)*
      Mrs Eleonora Kasymova
Mr Jonibek Hikmatov **m** *1st Secretary*
Mrs Rukshona Rahmonova * *1st Secretary*

TANZANIA

High Commission of the United Republic of Tanzania
3 Stratford Place W1C 1AS
020 7569 1470
Fax 020 7491 3710
balozi@tanzania-online.gov.uk
www.tanzania-online.gov.uk

HIS EXCELLENCY MR PETER ALLAN KALLAGHE **m** *High Commissioner (since 19 August 2010)*
      Mrs Joyce D. Kallaghe
Mr Chabaka Kilumanga *Deputy High Commissioner*
Mr Yusuf Kashangwa **m** *Minister Plenipotentiary (Commerce)*
Col. Pellegreen Jacob Mrope **m** *Defence Adviser*
Mr Idrissa Zahran **m** *Minister-Counsellor (Information)*
Mr Sylvester Ambokile **m** *Counsellor*
Mrs Caroline Kitana Chipeta **m** *Minister-Counsellor (Head of Chancery)*
Mr Amos Daudi Msanjila **m** *Minister-Counsellor (Political)*
Mr Allen Fanuel Kuzilwa **m** *2nd Secretary*

Mr Wema Kibona   **m**   *Financial Attaché*

THAILAND
Royal Thai Embassy
29-30 Queen's Gate SW7 5JB
020 7589 2944
Fax 020 7823 9695
thaiduto@btinternet.com
www.thaiembassyuk.org.uk
Monday-Friday 09.30-12.30 & 14.00-17.00

Consular Section
29-30 Queen's Gate SW7 5JB
020 7589 2944 ext 5505
Fax 020 7823 7492
Monday-Friday 09.30-12.30

Office of the Defence & Naval Attaché
29-30 Queen's Gate SW7 5JB
020 7589 0492
Fax 020 7225 3782

Office of the Air Attaché
2 Victoria Road W8 5RD
020 7589 0369
Fax 020 7584 2618

Office of the Military Attaché
29-30 Queen's Gate SW7 5JB
020 7589 0492
Fax 020 7225 3782

Office of Financial Attaché
29-30 Queen's Gate SW7 5JB
020 7589 7266
Fax 020 7589 2624

Office of Commercial Attaché
11 Hertford Street W1Y 7DX
020 7493 5749
Fax 020 7493 7416

Office of Educational Attaché
28 Prince's Gate SW7 1QF
020 7584 4538
Fax 020 7823 9896

HIS EXCELLENCY MR PASAN TEPARAK   **m**   *Ambassador Extraordinary & Plenipotentiary (since 1 November 2012)*
          Mrs Paradee Teparak
Captain Worawut Pruksarungruang   **m**   *Defence & Naval Attaché*
Colonel Apichat Chaiyadar   **m**   *Military Attaché & Assistant Defence Attaché*
Group Captain Punpakdee Pattanakul   **m**   *Air Attaché & Assistance Defence Attaché*
Dr Piyawat Sivaraks   **m**   *Education Attaché/Minister (Education)*
Mr Chulit Stavorn   **m**   *Commercial Attaché/Minister-Counsellor (Commercial)*
Dr Ketsuda Supradit   *Financial Attaché/Minister (Financial)*
Mrs Piyapin Niyomreks   **m**   *Minister-Counsellor*
Mr Thanut Suvarnananda   **m**   *Minster-Counsellor*
Captain Chittapan Sudaprasert   *Assistant Defence & Naval Attaché*

Mr Jirakarn Bejrajati   m   *Assistant Commercial Attaché/Minister-Counsellor (Commercial)*
Mr Phuchphop Mongkolnavin   m   *Counsellor*
Miss Tarichaya Kamperayanon   *Assistant Commercial Attaché/Counsellor (Commercial)*
Mr Kittipod Hongsombud   *1st Secretary*
Mr Natthapol Na Songkhla   m   *1st Secretary*
Miss Jidapa Lumyong   *1st Secretary*
Miss Duansib Pathamasoonthorn   *1st Secretary*
Mr Nathawut Malisuwan   *1st Secretary*
Ms Kemawadee Osthaphan   *1st Secretary*
Mrs Kwanjit Pongamphai   m   *Attaché (Administrative)*

TIMOR-LESTE

Embassy of the Democratic Republic of Timor-Leste
4 Cavendish Square, Paddington W1G 0PG

HIS EXCELLENCY MR JOAQUIM ANTÓNIO MARIA LOPES DA FONSECA   m   *Ambassador Extraordinary & Plenipotentiary (since 07 October 2013)*
        Mrs Barbara Nazareth Andrade de Oliveira
Ms Milena Maria da Costa Rangel   m   *Counsellor*
Ms Amy Maree McMullen   *Counsellor (Legal Affairs)*

TOGO

Embassy of the Republic of Togo
8 Rue Alfred Roll 75017 Paris
(00) 331 43 80 12 13
Fax (00) 331 43 80 06 05
Monday-Friday 09.00-13.00 & 14.00-17.00

HIS EXCELLENCY MR CALIXTE MADJOULBA   m   *Ambassador Extraordinary & Plenipotentiary (since 06 June 2011)*
        Madame Kossiwa Madjoulba
Mr Assiongbor K. Folivi   m   *Minister-Counsellor*
Mrs Biam Didinabe Hodjo   *Minister-Counsellor*
Mr Koffi Adjeoda Maxime Assah   m   *Minister-Counsellor*
Mr Batossie Madjoulba   m   *Minister-Counsellor (Consular Affairs)*
Mr Mustapha Allani   *Counsellor (Economic Affairs)*
Mr Akela-Esso Tonaga   m   *1st Counsellor (Protocol)*
Mr Kokou Agboli   m   *Cultural Attaché*
Mr Koutolbema Batawila Tassou   m   *Financial Attaché*
Mrs Edoh Gadegbekou épouse Amabley   *Financial Attaché*
Mrs Kambarenne Viviane épouse Kpabre-Sylli Kombath   m   *Consular Attaché*
Mrs Afua Toviakou épouse Fiagbe   m   *Administrative Attaché*
Mr Bédouénou Atcho   m   *Attaché (Consular Affairs)*
Mr Issifa Zakariyao Kolobe   m   *Attaché (Consular Affairs)*
Mr Komi Sapey   m   *Attaché (Consular Affairs)*
Mr Koudjo Edjamtoli   m   *Attaché (Consular Affairs)*
Mr M. Yao Malou   m   *Attaché*
Mr Labatibè Douti   *Attaché (Consular Affairs)*

TONGA

Tonga High Commission
36 Molyneux Street W1H 5BQ
020 7724 5828
Fax 020 7723 9074
Monday-Friday 09.00-13.00 & 14.00-17.00

Vacant   *High Commissioner*
Mr Sione Sonata Tupou   *Acting High Commissioner (since 13th December 2012}*
Mr Siale Vuki Bain Vete   *1st Secretary*

TRINIDAD & TOBAGO

High Commission of the Republic of Trinidad & Tobago
42 Belgrave Square SW1X 8NT
020 7245 9351
Fax 020 7823 1065
tthc@btconnect.com
www.tthighcommission.co.uk
Monday-Friday 09.00-17.00

HIS EXCELLENCY MR GARVIN EDWARD TIMOTHY NICHOLAS   **m**   *High Commissioner (since 05 December 2010)*
   Dr Nicola Alcalá
Mrs Reshma Bissoon-Deokie   *   *1st Secretary*
Ms Keisha Rochford-Hawkins   *2nd Secretary*
Ms Nickesha Smith   *2nd Secretary*
Mr David Hinkson   **m**   *Immigration Attaché*
Mr Marlon Choo Ying   *Immigration Attaché*
Ms Wendy Ann Austin   *Financial Attaché*
Ms Beverly Allen   *Administrative Attaché*

TUNISIA

Embassy of Tunisia
29 Prince's Gate SW7 1QG
020 7584 8117
Fax 020 7584 3205
London@tunisianembassy.co.uk

HIS EXCELLENCY MR NABIL AMMAR   **m**   *Ambassador Extraordinary & Plenipotentiary (since 11 December 2012)*
   Mrs Hager Ammar
Mr Riadh Dridi   **m**   *Counsellor*
Mr Naoufel Hdia   **m**   *Counsellor*
Mr Karim Boussaha   *Counsellor*
Ms Aida Toumi   *   *1st Secretary*
Mr Imed Dinar   **m**   *1st Secretary*
Mr Amor Majbri   **m**   *1st Secretary*
Miss Zahra Rebii   *Administrator*
Mr Nasereddine Neji   **m**   *Attaché*
Mr Ezzine Chehidi   *Attaché*
Colonel Major Mohamed Meddeb Military   *Attaché (Resident in Paris)*

TURKEY

Embassy of the Republic of Turkey
43 Belgrave Square SW1X 8PA
020 7393 0202
Fax 020 7393 0066
embassy.london@mfa.gov.tr
www.turkishembassylondon.org

Office of the Ambassador
020 7393 0222
Fax 0207393 9213

Military Attaché's Office
020 7235 1959

Office of the Counsellor for Security
020 7235 7085

Press Counsellor's Office
020 7235 6968

Commercial Counsellor's Office
020 7235 4991

Economic Counsellor's Office
020 7235 2743

Financial & Customs Counsellor's Office
020 7245 6318

Cultural & Information Counsellor's Office
020 7839 7778

Educational Counsellor's Office
020 7724 1511

Religious Affairs Counsellor's Office
020 7823 1632

Consulate General of the Republic of Turkey
Rutland Lodge Rutland Gardens Knightsbridge SW7 1BW
020 7591 6900
Fax 020 7591 6922
consulate.london@mfa.gov.tr
www.turkishconsulate.org.uk

HIS EXCELLENCY MR ÜNAL ÇEVIKÖZ **m** *Ambassador Extraordinary & Plenipotentiary (since 16 July 2010)*
      Mrs Emel Çeviköz
Mr Fatih Ulusoy *Minister-Counsellor, Deputy Head of Mission*
Capt. (N) Erdal Ergün **m** *Defence & Naval Attaché*
Col. Ömer Özkan **m** *Air Attaché*
Col. Mehmet Çalkayiş **m** *Army Attaché*
Mr Mustafa İlhan * *Counsellor for Security Affairs*
Mr Yavuz Mollasalihoğlu **m** *Chief Commercial Counsellor*
Dr M. Coşkun Cangöz **m** *Chief Economic Counsellor*
Mr Ömer Faruk Altintaş * *Legal Counsellor*
Mr Emin Tuğrul **m** *Press Counsellor*
Mr Mehmet Akkul **m** *Economic Counsellor*
Mr Ahmet Gülhan Gücel **m** *Expert Counsellor for Maritime Affairs*
Mrs Fikriye Asli Güven *Counsellor (Political Officer)*
Mr Ferit Orçun Başaran **m** *Counsellor (Political Officer)*
Mr Alper Aktaş **m** *Counsellor (Political Officer)*

Mrs Nazmiye Başaran **m** *Counsellor (Political Officer)*
Miss Cemile Elvan Haciefendioğlu *Counsellor (Political Officer)*
Mr Recep Kalpak *1st Secretary (Political Officer)*
Mr Ahmet Çelik **m** *Deputy Counsellor (Security Affairs)*
Mrs Zeynep Arslan **m** *Deputy Commercial Counsellor*
Mr Fatih Topçu *Consul*
Mr Murat Nalçaci **m** *Consul*
Mr Yusuf Kenan Küçük **m** *2nd Secretary (Political Officer)*
Mr Serkan Kiramanlioğlu *2nd Secretary (Political Officer)*
Mr Murat Sümer *2nd Secretary (Political Officer)*
Mr Mehmet Burak Koşaner *2nd Secretary (Political Officer)*
Mr Beşir Murat **m** *2nd Secretary (Consular & Technical Officer)*
Mrs Banu Nalçaci **m** *2nd Secretary (Consular & Technical Officer)*
Mrs Ayşen Atan **m** *2nd Secretary (Consular & Technical Officer)*
Mr Ahmet Eyyüp Kalafat **m** *3rd Secretary (Political Officer)*
Mr Numan Kodal **m** *Labour and Social Security Attaché*
Mr Ahmet Duran **m** *Press Attaché*
NCO Halil Yildiz **m** *Military Administrative Attaché*
Mr Fatih Alper **m** *Attaché*
Mr Orhan Ağtaş **m** *Attaché*
Mrs İlknur Özcan **m** *Attaché*
Mr Süleyman Taşkin *Attaché*
Mr Ayhan Yilmaz **m** *Attaché*
Mr Ahmet Güler **m** *Attaché*

TURKMENISTAN
Embassy of Turkmenistan
131 Holland Park Avenue W11 4UT
020 7610 5239
Fax 020 7751 1903
Monday-Friday 09.30-18.00
Consular Section Monday-Friday 10.00-12.00 & 14.00-16.00 (Closed Wednesday)
tkm-embassy-uk@btconnect.org.uk
www.turkmenembassy.org.uk

HIS EXCELLENCY MR YAZMURAD N. SERYAEV **m** *Ambassador Extraordinary & Plenipotentiary (since 02 July 2003)*
      Mrs Djennetgozel Seryaeva
Mr Dovlet Atabayev **m** *Counsellor*
Mrs Oguljahan Atabayeva **m** *1st Secretary*
Mr Bayram Aganyyazov **m** *1st Secretary/Consul*

TUVALU
London Honorary Consulate (see page 137)

UGANDA

Uganda High Commission
Uganda House 58-59 Trafalgar Square WC2N 5DX
020 7839 5783
Fax 020 7839 8925
info@ugandahighcomission.co.uk
www.ugandahighcommission.co.uk

HER EXCELLENCY MRS JOYCE KAKURAMATSI KIKAFUNDA **m** *High Commissioner (since*
12 July 2013)
        Dr Joseph Kikafuna-Twine
Mr Isaac Biruma Sebulime *Chargé d'Affaires a.i.*
Mr Fred Moses Mukhooli **m** *Counsellor*
Mr Alfred Balinda **m** *1st Secretary*
Mr Innocent Opio * *2nd Secretary*
Ms Judith Asiimwe **m** *2nd Secretary*
Mr Sam Muhwezi *2nd Secretary*
Miss Irene Luyiga *Attaché*

UKRAINE

Embassy of Ukraine
60 Holland Park W11 3SJ
020 7727 6312
Fax 020 7792 1708
emb_gb@mfa.gov.ua
www.ukremb.org.uk
Monday-Friday 09.00-13.00 & 14.00-18.00

Ambassador's Office
60 Holland Park W11 3SJ
020 7727 6312
Fax 020 7792 1708
mve@ukremb.org.uk

Economic Section
60 Holland Park W11 3SJ
020 7727 6312
Fax 020 7792 1708
economy@ukremb.org.uk

Consular and Visa Section
78 Kensington Park Road W11 2PL
020 7243 8923
Fax 020 7727 3567
gc_gb@mfa.gov.ua
Monday-Friday 09.00-13.00 & 14.00-18.00
Reception Hours Monday-Friday 09.00-13.00 (Last admission 12.30)

Military Section
60 Holland Park W11 3SJ
020 7727 6312
Fax 020 7792 1708
dao@ukremb.org.uk

Cultural Section
60 Holland Park W11 3SJ
020 7727 6312
Fax 020 7792 1708
y.rubashov@ukremb.org.uk

Press Section
60 Holland Park W11 3SJ
020 7727 6312
Fax 020 7792 1708
o.kyzyma@ukremb.org.uk

HIS EXCELLENCY MR VOLODYMYR KHANDOGIY   **m**   *Ambassador Extraordinary & Plenipotentiary, Permanent Representative to the International Maritime Organisation (since 31 August 2010)*
Mrs Nataliia Shevchenko
Mr Andrii Kuzmenko   **m**   *Minister-Counsellor*
Mr Volodymyr Khomanets   **m**   *Minister-Counsellor (Head of Economic Section)*
Colonel Pavlo Tertytskyi   **m**   *Defence & Air Attaché*
Colonel Maksym Soroka   **m**   *Military Attaché*
Lieutenant Colonel Vitalii Kraskovskyi   **m**   *Naval Attaché*
Mr Volodymyr Soshnikov   **m**   *Counsellor (Security Affairs)*
Mr Kostiantyn Billiar   **m**   *Counsellor (Maritime Affairs)*
Mr Anatolii Solovei   **m**   *Counsellor (Political Affairs)*
Mr Volodymyr Kovalenko   **m**   *Counsellor (Consular Affairs)*
Mr Rostyslav Ogryzko   **m**   *Counsellor (Political Affairs)*
Mr Oleksandr Rak   **m**   *1st Secretary (Science & Technology)*
Mr Yuriy Rubashov   *1st Secretary (Cultural Affairs & Information)*
Mr Oleksandr Pukhliak   **m**   *1st Secretary (Political Affairs)*
Mr Maksym Yemelianov   *2nd Secretary (Protocol & Administrative Affairs, PA to Ambassador)*
Mr Yurii Makukha   *2nd Secretary (Trade & Economic Affairs)*
Mr Denys Buhera   **m**   *2nd Secretary (Security Affairs)*
Ms Yulia Pomazan   *   *3rd Secretary*
Mr Serhii Krasnoschok   **m**   *3rd Secretary (Information)*
Mrs Oksana Kyzyma   **m**   *3rd Secretary (Press Attaché)*
Mr Volodymyr Pavlichenko   *Attaché (Legal Affairs)*

UNITED ARAB EMIRATES

Embassy of the United Arab Emirates
30 Prince's Gate SW7 1PT
020 7581 1281
Fax 020 7581 9616
www.uae-embassy.ae
Monday-Friday 09.00-16.00

Consular Section
48 Prince's Gate SW7 2QA
020 7581 1281
Fax 020 7584 0989

Military Attaché's Office
6 Queen's Gate Terrace SW7 5PF
020 7581 4113

Cultural Attaché's Office
48 Prince's Gate SW7 2QA
020 7581 1281
Fax 020 7581 1870

Medical Attaché's Office
71 Harley Street W1G 8DE
020 7486 6281
Fax 020 7224 3575

Police Liasion Office
48 Prince's Gate SW7 2QA
020 7486 6281
Fax 020 7823 7716

HIS EXCELLENCY MR ABDULRAHMAN GHANEM A. ALMUTAIWEE   *   *Ambassador Extraordinary & Plenipotentiary (since 20 April 2009)*
Shaikh Mohammed bin Maktoum bin R. Almaktoum   *1st Secretary*
Mr Mohamed Ahmed Salem Farea Alharbi   *1st Secretary*
Mr Sultan Rashed Saeed M. Al Darmaki   *   *2nd Secretary*
Miss Sara Ghazi Abdulla Salem Bin Ashoor Al Mahri   *3rd Secretary*
Mr Ali Abdulla Juma Abdulla Alhaj   *Consul 3rd Secretary*
Khalid Mohamed Amer Salmeen Alhajeri   m   *3rd Secretary*
Major Dr Mohamed Ahmed Mohammed N Albreiki   m   *Police Attaché*
Mr Abdulla Hamad Suail Awaida Alkhyeli   *Vice Police Attaché*
Mr Ahmed Awad Sultan Balghamisa Alshamsi   m   *Administrative Attaché (Police)*
Mr Jamal Abdulaziz Nasser Alowais   m   *Medical Attaché*
Mr Mohamed Aslam Rahma Albulooshi   m   *Administrative Attaché (Medical)*
Mr Jamal Yousuf Adbdulrahman Almulla   m   *Administrative Attaché (Medical)*
Mr Ismail Amin Abdelrahim Alawadi   m   *Military Attaché*
Mr Jamal Mohamed Karama Mohamed Alameri   m   *Vice Military Attaché*
Mr Wissa Ramadhan Shareef Eissa   *   *Assistant Military Attaché*
Mr Ahmed Yaqoub Abdulla Aljesmi   m   *Assistant Military Attaché*
Mr Abdullah Ali Salh Almehrezi   m   *Assistant Military Attaché*
Mr Rashed Mohamed Rashed Saif A. Alshehhi   *   *Assistant Military Attaché*
Engineer fayad rasheed Abdu Aldhaheri   *   *Assistant Military Attaché*
Mr Ali Ali Rashed Mohammed Alkuwaiti   m   *Assistant Military Attaché*
Salem Abdullah Salem Alkaabi   m   *Assistant Military Attaché*
Mr Majid Omair Husain Abdulla Alharthi   m   *Assistant Military Attaché*
Mr Mobarak Rashed Humaid Khameis Alyammahi   *Assistant Military Attaché*
Mr Hussain Jasim Abdalla Mohamed Al Ali   m   *Assistant Military Attaché*
Mr Jasem Hassam Mohamed Alyammahi   m   *Assistant Military Attaché*
Mr Abdulla Salem Mohammed Sultan Aljaberi   m   *Assistant Military Attaché*
Mr Khalfan Saeed Khalfan Buajail Almheri   m   *Assistant Military Attaché*
Mr Khalid Abdulla Hassan Mohamed Al-Ali   m   *Assistant Military attaché*
Mr Mohammed Obaid Shahdad A Alneyadi   m   *Administrative Attaché (Military)*
Mr Mohammed Ibrahim A Alshaibani   m   *Administative Attaché*
Mr Abdulla Saeed bin Nassar Almansoori   m   *Administative Attaché*
Mr Yousuf Bakhit Mohammad Abdulla   *Administrative Attaché*
Mr Yaser Abdulrahman Ahmed Zayed   m   *Administative Attaché*

UNITED STATES OF AMERICA

American Embassy
24 Grosvenor Square W1A 1AE
020 7499 9000
Monday-Friday 08.30-17.30

Diplomatic Visas
5 Upper Grosvenor Street W1
020 7499 9000 Ext 3050

United States Department of Agriculture, Foreign Agricultural Service
020 7894 0464

United States Commercial Service
020 7408 8019

United States Public Affairs
020 7499 9000

United States Information Service
55-56 Upper Brook Street W1A 2LH
020 7499 9000

His Excellency The Honourable Matthew Barzun   **m**   *Ambassador Extraordinary &*
Plenipotentiary (Since 27 August 2013)
      Mrs Brooke Barzun
Mrs Elizabeth Dibble   **m**   *Deputy Chief of Mission*
Mr Thomas Tiernan   **m**   *Minister-Counsellor for Management Affairs*
Mr David Stewart   **m**   *Minister-Counsellor for Consular Affairs*
Mr Thomas Leary   **m**   *Minister-Counsellor for Public Affairs*
Mr Mark Tokola   **m**   *Minister Counsellor for Political Affairs*
Mr Lawrence Richter   **m**   *Minister Counsellor for Management Affairs*
Ms Julie Nutter   *Minister-Counsellor for Economic Affairs*
Mr Philip Reilly   **m**   *Minister-Counsellor for Coordination Affairs*
Mr John Breidenstine   **m**   *Minister Counsellor for Commercial Affairs*
Dr Larry Padget   **m**   *Counsellor for Medical Affairs*
Mr Douglas Quiram   **m**   *Minister for Regional Security*
Mr Eugene Philhower   **m**   *Minister Counsellor for Argricultural Affairs*
Ms Kelly Adams-Smith   **m**   *Counsellor*
Brig Gen John Quintas   **m**   *Defence Attaché*
Mr David Stracener   **m**   *Naval Attaché*
Col Joseph Halisky   **m**   *Army Attaché*
Col Travis Willis Jr   **m**   *Air Attaché*
Lt Col Tiley Nunnink   **m**   *Marine Attaché*
Mr Scott Cruse   **m**   *Legal Attaché*
Mr Robert Paschall   **m**   *Attaché*
Mr George Barnes   **m**   *Attaché*
Mr Glen Alberro   **m**   *Attaché*
Mr Daniel O'Brien   **m**   *Attaché*
Dr Wayne Julian   **m**   *1st Secretary*
Mr Rodney Evans   **m**   *1st Secretary*
Mr Ronald Larsen   **m**   *Attaché*
Mr William Centre Jr   *1st Secretary*
Ms Lynne Platt   **m**   *1st Secretary*
Mr Michael Pate   **m**   *1st Secretary*
Ms Karyn Eliot   **m**   *1st Secretary*
Mr William Babash   *Attaché*
Ms Cynthia Rapp   **m**   *1st Secretary*
Mr Charles Wilson   **m**   *1st Secretary*
Mr Edwin Daly   **m**   *Attaché*
Ms Kathleen Lively   **m**   *1st Secretary*
Ms Donna Chapin   *Attaché*
Mr Matthew   **m**   *Attaché*
Mr Gregory Olsavsky   **m**   *Attaché*
Mr Craig Lynes   **m**   *Attaché*
Mr Dean Burke   **m**   *Attaché*
Mr Thomas Sobocinski   **m**   *Attaché*

Mr William Fallin   **m**   *Attaché*
Ms Stephanie Okimoto   **m**   *Attaché*
Ms Clasissa Balmaseda   **m**   *Attaché*
Mr Joel Seltzer   *Attaché*
Mr Charles Hamblett   **m**   *Attaché*
Ms Monique Quesada   *1st Secretary*
Ms Gwendolyn Sawyer   **m**   *Attaché*
Mr Raymond Bassi   **m**   *Attaché*
Mr Scott Cecil   **m**   *1st Secretary*
Mr steven Lemelin   **m**   *Attaché*
Mr Jeffrey Lodinsky   **m**   *1st Secretary*
Mr Ranbier S Smagh   **m**   *1st Secretary*
Mr Steven Adams-Smith   **m**   *1st Secretary*
Mr Ranbier Smagh   **m**   *1st Secretary*
Ms Lisa Letendre   *1st Secretary*
Ms Margaret Kane   *1st Secretary*
Mr Herbert S. Traub III   **m**   *1st Secretary*
Ms Susan Haley   **m**   *1st Secretary*
Mr Michael Cicere   **m**   *1st Secretary*
Mr Alan Eyre   **m**   *1st Secretary*
Mr Edward Heartney   **m**   *1st Secretary*
Ms Christine Bell   **m**   *1st Secretary*
Ms Victoria King   **m**   *1st Secretary*
Mr Ryan Gliha   **m**   *1st Secretary*
Ms Larilyn Reffett   *1st Secretary*
Ms Marisa Plowden   **m**   *1st Secretary*
Mr William Tuttle   **m**   *1st Secretary*
Mr Eric Geelan   **m**   *1st Secretary*
Mr Craig Miller   *1st Secretary*
Mrs Victoria King   **m**   *1st Secretary*
Ms Jozlyn Schroeder   **m**   *1st Secretary*
Ms Heida Starbuck   **m**   *1st Secretary*
Ms Sandra Labarge   **m**   *1st Secretary*
Mr Raymond White   **m**   *1st Secretary*
Ms Mary Beth Reincke   *1st Secretary*
Mr Jonathan Peccia   *1st Secretary*
Mr James Minicozzi   **m**   *1st Secretary*
Mrs Cara Martin-Cumpler   **m**   *1st Secretary*
Ms Elaine French   *1st Secretary*
Mr Fleur Cowan   *1st Secretary*
Ms Deborah Maclean   **m**   *1st Secretary*
Mr Brian Roundy   **m**   *Attaché*
Mr Kevan Higgins   **m**   *1st Secretary*
Mr Patrick Haley   **m**   *1st Secretary*
Ms Anne Seator   *2nd Secretary*
Mr Donald Parnell   **m**   *2nd Secretary*
Mr Daniel Fults   **m**   *Attaché*
Mr Steven L. Donnell   **m**   *Attaché*
Mr Peter Carlson   **m**   *Attaché*
Mr Timothy Lunardi   **m**   *Attaché*
Ms Jamie Martin   **m**   *2nd Secretary*
Ms Lisbeth Sandoy   *2nd Secretary*
Mr Charles Perdue   **m**   *2nd Secretary*
Mr James Neel   **m**   *2nd Secretary*

Mr Kevin Friloux   **m**   *2nd Secretary*
Mr John Ward Jr   **m**   *2nd Secretary*
Mr Perry Chen   **m**   *2nd Secretary*
Ms Jennifer   **m**   *2nd Secretary*
Mr Michael Rogers Prosser   **m**   *2nd Secretary & Vice Consul*
Ms Shannon Eskow   *2nd Secretary*
Ms Rachel Birthisel   **m**   *2nd Secretary*
Mr Eirik Sanness   **m**   *2nd Secretary*
Ms Laura Barker   *2nd Secretary*
Mr Thomas Legones   **m**   *2nd Secretary*
Ms Sara Martz   **m**   *2nd Secretary*
Mr Oliver Thomas   **m**   *2nd Secretary*
Ms Anne Salas   **m**   *2nd Secretary*
Ms Audra Keagle   **m**   *2nd Secretary*
Mr Kevin Gallagher   **m**   *2nd Secretary*
Mr Kevin Krimm   **m**   *2nd Secretary*
Ms Pamela Bentley   **m**   *2nd Secretary*
Mr Heath Ward   **m**   *Attaché*
Mr Eric Ros   **m**   *Attaché*
Ms Natalie Koza   *Attaché*
Mr Michael Wautlet   *2nd Secretary*
Mr Juan Martinez   **m**   *2nd Secretary*
Mr Michael Prosser   **m**   *2nd Secretary*
Ms Diana Braunschweig   *2nd Secretary*
Ms Sandra Dupuy   **m**   *2nd Secretary*
Mr Daniel Madar   **m**   *2nd Secretary*
Mr Richard McDaniel   *2nd Secretary*
Mr Stephen Mraz   **m**   *2nd Secretary*
Ms Christine Prince   *2nd Secretary*
Mr Kurt Updegraff   **m**   *2nd Secretary*
Mr Robert Adelson   *2nd Secretary*
Ms Lorraine Kramer   **m**   *2nd Secretary*
Ms Jodi Breisler   *2nd Secretary*
Mr Adam G.Heller   **m**   *2nd Secretary*
Mr Kitt Christopherson   **m**   *Attaché*
Ms Irene Onyeagbako   *2nd Secretary*
Mr Garrett Wilkerson   *2nd Secretary*
Mr James Kuykendall   *2nd Secretary*
Ms Anna Kerner   **m**   *2nd Secretary*
Mr Rufus Johnson   **m**   *2nd Secretary*
Mr John Kent   **m**   *2nd Secretary*
Ms Lauren Yost   *2nd Secretary*
Mr John Young-Anglim   **m**   *2nd Secretary*
Ms Lilla White   *2nd Secretary*
Mr Rafael Gonzalez   **m**   *2nd Secretary*
Mr Benjamin Partington   **m**   *2nd Secretary*
Mr Jay Thompson   **m**   *2nd Secretary*
Mr Michael Dubray   **m**   *2nd Secretary*
Mr Theodore Massey   **m**   *2nd Secretary*
Ms Anna Mirabile   **m**   *2nd Secretary*
Ms Sarah Lundquist Nuutinen   *2nd Secretary*
Ms Jaisha wray   *Attaché*
Mr Alan Kohler Jr   **m**   *Assistant Attaché*
Mr Michael Driscoll   **m**   *Assistant Legal Attaché*

Mr John Machin   **m**   *Assistant Attaché*
Ms Lynn Marsland   **m**   *Assistant Attaché*
Mr Mark Kodur   *Attaché*
Mr Jason Kidd   **m**   *Assistant Attaché*
LCDR Alan Brechbill   **m**   *Assistant Attaché*
LTC Travis Phillips   **m**   *Assistant Army Attaché*
Ms Joan Buckley   *Assistant Legal Attaché*
Mr John Kuchta   **m**   *Assistant Legal Attaché*
Lt Col Kyle Hurwitz   **m**   *Assistant Air Attaché*
Mr Davis Zimmermann   **m**   *Assistant Legal Attaché*
Mr Kevin O'Malley   **m**   *Assistant Attaché*
Mr Conor Dufrain   **m**   *Assistant Attaché*
Mr Jeffrey   **m**   *Assistant Attaché*
Mr John Patina   **m**   *Assistant Attaché*
Mr Michael McGonigle   **m**   *Assistant Attaché*
Mr Gregory Manoli   **m**   *Assistant Attaché*
Mr James Gee   **m**   *Assistant Attaché*
James Brenneman   **m**   *Assistant Attaché*
Ms Caitlin Finley   *3rd Secretary*
Mr Bradley Coley   *2nd Secretary*

URUGUAY

Embassy of Uruguay
150 Brompton Road SW3 1XH
020 7584 4200
Fax 020 7584 2947
emburuguay@emburuguay.org.uk

HIS EXCELLENCY MR JULIO MOREIRA MORÁN   **m**   *Ambassador Extraordinary & Plenipotentiary (since 16 September 2009)*
            Mrs Ana Medina-Novoa de Moreira-Morán
Mr Marcelo Bachechi Pavone   *Second Secretary and Head of Consular Affairs*
Captain Carlos Butteri   **m**   *Defence Attaché*
Mr Enrique Facelli   *Attaché for Cultural Affaires, Press & Tourism*

UZBEKISTAN

Embassy of the Republic of Uzbekistan
41 Holland Park W11 3RP
020 7229 7679
Fax 020 7229 7029
info@uzbekembassy.org
www.uzbekembassy.org
Monday-Friday 09.00-13.00 & 14.30-18.30

Ambassador's Office
020 7229 7679 (ext.7)

Political Affairs
020 7229 7679 (ext.2)

Trade & Investment
020 7229 7679 (ext.3)

Culture & Education
020 7229 7679 (ext.7)

Consular Section
020 7229 7679 (ext.1)
Monday, Wednesday & Friday 10.00-13.00

Administrative Section
020 7229 7679 (ext.4)

Financial Section
020 7229 7679 (ext.5)

HIS EXCELLENCY MR OTABEK AKBAROV   **m**   *Ambassador Extraordinary & Plenipotentiary (since 17 October 2007)*
              Mrs Khayrinisa Akbarova
Dr Jamshed Safarov   **m**   *Counsellor (Political Affairs)*
Mr Rustam Kayumov   **m**   *1st Secretary*
Mr Rustam Ismailov   **m**   *2nd Secretary (Consular Section)*
Mr Bakhtiyor Turayev   **m**   *Attaché (Press & Education)*

VANUATU

Embassy of Vanuatu
Avenue de Tervueren 380 Chemin de Ronde 1150 Brussels BELGIUM
Tel/Fax: 0032 2 771 74 94
info@vanuatuembassy.be

HIS EXCELLENCY MR ROY MICKEY JOY   **m**   *High Commissioner (since 11 April 2011)*

VENEZUELA

Embassy of the Bolivarian Republic of Venezuela
1 Cromwell Road SW7 2HW
020 7584 4206 or 020 7581 2776
Fax 020 7589 8887
info@venezlon.co.uk
www.embavenez-uk.org

Consular Section
56 Grafton Way W1T 5DL
020 7387 6727
Fax 020 7387 2979

Defence Attaché's Office
54 Grafton Way W1T 5DL
020 7387 0695
Fax 020 7916 1155

Cultural Section
52 & 58 Grafton Way W1T 5DJ
020 7388 5788
Fax 020 7383 4857

Vacant   *Ambassador Extraordinary & Plenipotentiary*
Mr Alvaro Sánchez   **m**   *Chargé d'Affaires*
Mr William Suárez   *1st Secretary*
Mr Henry Suárez   **m**   *1st Secretary*
Mr Yaruma Rodríguez   **m**   *2nd Secretary*
Mr Roberto Bayley   **m**   *2nd Secretary*
Mr Jhon Rafael Guerra Sansonetti   *2nd Secretary*
Ms Angela Emilia Chourio   *2nd Secretary*

VIETNAM

Embassy of the Socialist Republic of Vietnam
12-14 Victoria Road W8 5RD
020 7937 1912
Fax 020 7565 3853
vanphong@vietnamembassy.org.uk
www.vietnamembassy.org.uk

Commercial Section
108 Campden Hill Road W8 7AR
020 3524 1732
thuyngh@moit.gov.vn / nguyenhongthuy2012@gmail.com

His Excellency Mr Vu Quang Minh   **m**   *Ambassador (since 13 April 2011)*
          Mrs Nguyen Minh Hanh
Ms Le Thi Thu Hang   *Minister Counsellor (Deputy Chief of Mission)*
Mr Tran Thi Huong Lien   *Counsellor (Consular)*
Mrs Doan Phuong Lan   *Counsellor (Economy)*
Mr Nguyen Van Phong   **m**   *1st Secretary (Press)*
Mr Nguyen Xuan Hai   **m**   *1st Secretary (Education)*
Mr Le Mai Son   **m**   *2nd Secretary*
Mr Do Hoang Linh   *3rd Secretary (Political)*
Mrs Nguyen Ngoc Diep   *2nd Secretary (Administration)*
Mr Luu Nghia Phuong   *Attaché (Economy)*
Mrs Nguyen Thuy Thi Hong   **m**   *Commercial Counsellor*

YEMEN

Embassy of the Republic of Yemen
57 Cromwell Road SW7 2ED
020 7584 6607
Fax 020 7589 3350
Yemen.embassy@btconnect.com
Monday-Friday 09.30-16.00

His Excellency Mr Abdulla Ali Al-Radhi   **m**   *Ambassador Extraordinary & Plenipotentiary (since 28 September 2010)*
          Mrs Bilqis Ali Ali Al-Hadheri
Mr Abdulkader Ahmed Saeed Alsunadair   **m**   *Minister Plenipotentiary/Deputy Head*
Mr Fadhel Yahya Ahmed Alsunaidar   **m**   *Counsellor*
Mr Mohamed Hamood Mohamed Al-Bawab   *   *1st Secretary*
Miss Manal Zaid Mutttee Dammaj   *2nd Secretary*
Mr Waleed Hussain Saleh Al-Rwaishan   **m**   *3rd Secretary*
Mr Haytham Abdulsalam A Al-Shawkani   **m**   *3rd Secretary*
Ms Beilqes Yayha Mohammed Al-Zawm   *3rd Secretary*
Miss Ahlam Hamoud Saleh Al-Bashiri   *3rd Secretary*

YUGOSLAVIA, see SERBIA

ZAIRE, see CONGO (DEMOCRATIC REPUBLIC)

ZAMBIA

High Commission for the Republic of Zambia
Zambia House
2 Palace Gate W8 5NG
020 7589 6655
Fax 020 7581 1353
zhcl@btconnect.com
www.zhcl.org.uk
Monday-Friday 09.30-13.00 & 14.00-17.00

Immigration Office
Fax 020 7581 0546
immzhcl@btconnect.com

HIS EXCELLENCY MR PAUL WILLIAM LUMBI **m** *High Commissioner (since 14 April 2013)*
            Mrs Hilda Lumbi
Mr Chola Chama **m** *Deputy High Commissioner*
Brigadier General Martin Mumbi **m** *Defence Adviser*
Mr Muyangana Akalalambili Kaluwe **m** *Counsellor*
Mrs Ikayi Gertrude Sambondu Mushinge **m** *Counsellor (Economic)*
Mr Nkonde Michael Lombanya * *1st Secretary (Protocol/Admin)*
Mrs Beatrice Chilomo *1st Secretary (Finance)*
Miss Ruth Nyeji Chilembo *1st Secretary (Economics)*
Mr Anthony Mumba **m** *1st Secretary (Trade)*
Mr Steward Nchimunya **m** *1st Secretary (Consular)*
Ms Alice Mubanga Mulenga Shanshima *1st Secretary (Immigration)*
Mr Dick Mambwe Chibuye **m** *1st Secretary*
Ms Ines K.C. Manjimela * *2nd Secretary (Personal Secretary)*
Ms Chitamalika Beatrice Mukuka *2nd Secretary*

ZIMBABWE

Embassy of the Republic of Zimbabwe
Zimbabwe House 429 Strand WC2R 0JR
020 7836 7755
Fax 020 7379 1167
Telexes 262014/262115
zimlondon@yahoo.co.uk
zimebassy@zimlondon.gov.zw
www.zimlondon.gov.zw

HIS EXCELLENCY MR GABRIEL MHARADZE MACHINGA **m** *Ambassador Extraordinary & Plenipotentiary (since 31 October 2005)*
            Mrs Esteri Machinga
Mr Cecil Chinenere **m** *Deputy Head of Mission*
Mrs Mietani Chauke-Khumalo **m** *Counsellor*
Goup Captain Alinos Nhamoinesu **m** *Defence Attaché*
Mr Donald T Charumbira **m** *Counsellor*
Mr Clever Bangwayo **m** *Counsellor*
Mr Edmore Mudada **m** *Counsellor*
Mr Ndudzo Tugwete **m** *Counsellor*
Mrs Esther Kaisi **m** *3rd Secretary*
Mrs Miriam Mukai Panganayi **m** *3rd Secretary*

LIST OF THE REPRESENTATIVES IN LONDON OF FOREIGN STATES & COMMONWEALTH COUNTRIES

in Order of their Precedence in each Class

m Married
* Married but not accompanied by wife or husband
+ Unmarried
(R) Realms

This list is updated monthly on the Foreign & Commonwealth Office web-site: www.fco.gov.uk

AMBASSADORS & HIGH COMMISSIONERS

Kuwait.....................	m	H.E. Mr Khaled Al Duwaisan GCVO *(Ambassador & Dean of the Diplomatic Corps)*
Guyana	m	H.E. Laleshwar K.N. Singh *(Senior High Commissioner)*
Botswana...................	m	H.E. Mr Roy Warren Blackbeard *(High Commissioner)*
Congo, Republic of...........	m	H.E. Mr Henri Marie Joseph Lopes *(Ambassador, Resident in Paris)*
St Vincent & The Grenadines (R)	m	H.E. Mr Cenio Lewis *(High Commissioner)*
Burkina Faso	m	H.E. Mr Kadré Désiré Ouedraogo *(Ambassador, Resident in Brussels)*
Turkmenistan	m	H.E. Mr Yazmurad N. Seryaev *(Ambassador)*
Mali.......................	m	H.E. Mr Ibrahim Bocar Ba *(Ambassador, Resident in Brussels)*
Niger	m	H.E. Mr Adamou Seydou *(Ambassador, Resident in Paris)*
Antigua & Barbuda (R)........	m	H.E. Dr Carl Roberts CMG *(High Commissioner)*
Cambodia	m	H.E. Mr Hor Nambora *(Ambassador)*
Djibouti....................	m	H.E. Mr Rachad Farah *(Ambassador, Resident in Paris)*
Qatar......................	m	H.E. Mr Khalid bin Rashid bin Salim Al-Hamoudi Al-Mansouri *(Ambassador)*
Zimbabwe..................	m	H.E. Mr Gabriel Mharadze Machinga *(Ambassador)*
Saudi Arabia................	m	H.E. HRH Prince Mohammed bin Nawaf bin Abdulaziz Al-Saud *(Ambassador)*
Mauritius	m	H.E. Mr Abhimanu Mahendra Kundasamy *(High Commissioner)*
Ethiopia....................	m	H.E. Mr Ato Berhanu Kebede *(Ambassador)*
Solomon Islands (R)...........	m	H.E. Mr Joseph Ma'ahanua *(High Commissioner, Resident in Brussels)*
Costa Rica..................	m	H.E. Mrs Pilar Saborío Rocafort *(Ambassador)*
Liberia.....................	m	H.E. Mr Wesley Momo Johnson *(Ambassador)*
The Gambia	+	H.E. Mrs Elizabeth Ya Eli Harding *(Ambassador)*
Azerbaijan	m	H.E. Mr Fakhraddin Gurbanov *(Ambassador)*
Uzbekistan	m	H.E. Mr Otabek Akbarov *(Ambassador)*
Eritrea.....................	m	H.E. Mr Tesfamicael Gerahtu Ogbaghiorghis *(Ambassador)*

Senegal	m	H.E. Mr Abdou Sourang *(Ambassador)*
Honduras	m	H.E. Mr Ivan Romero-Martinez *(Ambassador)*
Romania	m	H.E. Dr Ion Jinga *(Ambassador)*
Kazakhstan	m	H.E. Mr Kairat Abusseitov *(Ambassador)*
New Zealand (R)	+	H.E. Mr Derek William Leask *(High Commissioner)*
Nigeria	m	H.E. Dr Dalhaltu S. Tafida *(High Commissioner)*
Tajikistan	m	H.E. Mr Erkin Kasymov *(Ambassador)*
Lebanon	+	H.E. Mrs Inaam Osseiran *(Ambassador)*
Pakistan	m	H.E. Mr Wajid Shamsul Hasan *(High Commissioner)*
Barbados (R)	+	H.E. Mr Hugh Anthony Arthur *(High Commissioner)*
Cameroon	m	H.E. Mr Nkwelle Ekaney *(High Commissioner)*
Slovenia	m	H.E. Mr Iztok Jarc *(Ambassador)*
Morocco	m	H.E. HH Princess Lalla Joumala Alaoui *(Ambassador)*
UAE	*	H.E. Mr Abdul Rahman Ghanim Al Mutaiwee *(Ambassador)*
Benin	m	H.E. Mr Albert Agossou *(Ambassador, Resident in Brussels)*
Central African Republic	*	H.E. Mr Jean Willybiro Sako *(Ambassador, Resident in Paris)*
Congo, Dem Republic	m	H.E. Dr Barnabe Kikaya Bin Karubi *(Ambassador)*
Uruguay	m	H.E. Mr Julio Moreira Morán *(Ambassador)*
Ghana	m	H.E. Professor Kwaku Danso-Boafo *(High Commissioner)*
Czech Republic	m	H.E. Mr Michael Žantovsky *(Ambassador)*
Iceland	m	H.E. Mr Benedikt Jonsson *(Ambassador)*
Kenya	m	H.E. Mr Ephraim W Ngare *(High Commisioner)*
Oman	m	H.E. Mr Abdul Aziz Al Hinai *(Ambassador)*
Paraguay	m	H.E.Mr Miguel Angel Solano Lopez Casco *(Ambassador)*
El Salvador		H.E. Mr Werner Matias Romero *(Ambassador)*
Guatemala	m	H.E. Mr Acisclo Valladares Molina *(Ambassador)*
Sierra Leone	m	H.E. Mr Edward Mohamed Turay *(High Commission)*
Monaco	m	H.E. Mrs Evelyne Genta *(Ambassador)*
Belgium	m	H.E. Mr Johan Verbeke *(Ambassador)*
Nepal	m	H.E. Dr Suresh Chandra Chalise *(Ambassador)*
China	m	H.E. Mr Liu Xiaoming *(Ambassador)*
Austria	m	H.E. Dr Emil Brix *(Ambasaador)*
Italy	m	H.E. Mr Alain Giorgio Maria Economides *(Ambassador)*
Nicaragua	m	H.E. Dr Carlos Argüello-Gómez *(Ambassador,Resident in The Hague)*
Malaysia	m	H.E. Datuk Zakaria bin Sulong *(High Commissioner)*
Finland	m	H.E. Mr Pekka Huhtaniemi *(Ambassador)*
Sweden	m	H.E. Ms Nicola Clase *(Ambassador)*
Turkey	m	Mr Ahmet Ünal Çeviköz *(Ambassador)*
Swaziland	*	H.E. Mrs Dumsile Thandi Sukati *(High Commissioner)*

Sudan......................	m	H.E. Mr Abdullahi Hamad Ali AlAzreg *(Ambassador)*
Brazil	m	H.E. Mr Roberto Jaguaribe *(Ambassador)*
Tanzania	m	H.E. Mr Peter Kallaghe *(High Commissioner)*
Norway	m	H.E. Mr Kim Traavik *(Ambassador)*
Estonia	m	H.E. Mrs Aino Lepik von Wirén *(Ambassador)*
Ukraine	m	H.E. Mr Volodymyr Khandogiy *(Ambassador)*
Chile	+	H.E. Mr Tomas Eduardo Müller Sproat *(Ambassador)*
Yemen	m	H.E. Mr Abdulla Ali Mohamed Al-Radhi *(Ambassador)*
Cuba	m	H.E. Mrs Esther Gloria Armenteros Cárdenas *(Ambassador)*
Brunei	m	H.E. Mr Mohd Aziyan bin Abdullah *(High Commissioner)*
Trinidad & Tobago...........	m	H.E. Mr Garvin Edward Timothy Nicholas *(High Commissioner)*
Algeria.....................	m	H.E. Mr Amar Abba *(Ambassador)*
St Christopher & Nevis (R).....	m	H.E. Mr Kevin Isaac *(High Commissioner)*
Portugal	m	H.E. Mr Joao de Vallera *(Ambassador)*
Japan......................	m	H.E. Mr Keiichi Hayashi *(Ambassador)*
Russia	m	H.E. Mr Alexander Yakovenko *(Ambassador)*
Hungary	m	H.E. Mr János Zoltán Csák *(Ambassador)*
Holy See....................	+	H.E. Archbishop Antonio Mennini *(Apostolic Nuncio)*
Montenegro..................	m	H.E. Prof. Dr. Ljubiša Stanković *(Ambassador)*
Slovak Republic	m	H.E. Mr Miroslav Wlachovský *(Ambassador)*
France	m	H.E. Mr Bernard Emié *(Ambassador)*
Vanuatu....................	m	H.E. Mr Roy Mickey Joy *(High Commissioner, Resident in Brussels)*
Vietnam....................	m	H.E. Mr Vu Quang Minh *(Ambassador)*
Chad	+	H.E. Mr Ahmat Awad Sakine *(Ambassador, Resident in Brussels)*
Togo.......................	m	H.E. Mr Calixte Madjoulba *(Ambassador, Resident in Paris)*
Jordan.....................	m	H.E. Mr Mazen Kemal al-Homoud *(Ambassador)*
Dominican Republic...........	m	H.E. Dr Federico Alberto Cuello Camilo *(Ambassador)*
Côte d'Ivoire................	m	H.E. Mr Claude Stanislaus Bouah-Kamon *(Ambassador)*
Singapore	m	H.E. Mr Thambynathan Jasudasen *(High Commissioner)*
Papua New Guinea (R)	+	H.E. Ms Winnie Anna Kiap *(High Commissioner)*
Sri Lanka	+	H.E. Dr Chris Nonis *(High Commissioner)*
Israel	m	H.E. Mr Daniel Taub *(Ambassador)*
Canada (R)	m	H.E. Mr Gordon Campbell *(High Commissioner)*
Bahrain	+	H.E. Ms Alice Samaan *(Ambassador)*
Mozambique.................	m	H.E. Mr Carlos dos Santos *(High Commissioner)*
Fiji	m	H.E. Mr Solo Mara *(High Commissioner)*
Philippines	m	H.E. Mr Enrique A. Manalo *(Ambassador)*
Laos.......................	m	H.E. Mr Khoutanta Phalivong *(Ambassador, Resident in Paris)*
Panama		H.E. Ms Ana Irene Delgado *(Ambssador)*
Moldova	m	H.E. Mr Iulian Fruntaşu *(Ambassador)*

Korea, DPR	m	H.E. Mr Hyon Hak Bong *(Ambassador)*
Indonesia...................		H.E. Mr Teuku Mhoammad Hamzah Thayeb *(Ambassador)*
Angola	m	H.E. Mr Miguel Neto *(Ambassador)*
Suriname		H.E. Harvey Harold Naarendorp *(Ambassador)*
Argentina		H.E. Ms Alicia Amalia Castro *(Ambassador)*
Bulgaria...................	m	H.E. Mr Konstantin Stefanov Dimitrov *(Ambassador)*
Peru	m	H.E. Mr Julio-Muñoz-Deacon *(Ambassador)*
Bosnia Herzegovina	m	H.E. Mr. Mustafa Mujezinović Ambassador
Spain	m	H.E. Mr Fererico Trillo-Figueroa Martinez-Conde *(Ambassador)*
Jamaica (R)................		H.E Mrs Aloun Ndombet-Assamba *(High Commissioner)*
Equatorial Guinea		H.E Mrs Maricruz Evuna Andeme *(Ambassador)*
Belize (R)...................		H.E. Ms Perla Perdomo *(High Commissioner)*
Afghanistan		H.E Dr Mohammad Daud Yaar Ambassador
Samoa		H.E Fatumanava Dr Pa'olelei H Luteru *(High Commissioner, Resident in Brussels)*
Dominica, Commowealth of		H.E. Mrs Francine Baron-Royer *(High Commissioner)*
Poland	m	H.E. Mr Witold Sobków *(Ambassador)*
Malawi	m	H.E Mr Bernard Herbert Sande *(High Commissioner)*
Libya	m	H.E Mr Mahmoud Mohammed al-Nacua *(Ambassador)*
Netherlands.................		H.E Ms Laetitia van den Assum *(Ambassador)*
Greece	m	H.E. Mr Konstantinos Bikas *(Ambassador)*
Croatia	m	H.E. Dr Ivan Grdešić *(Ambassador)*
South Sudan	m	H.E. Mr Sabit Abbe Alley *(Ambassador)*
San Marino		H.E. Ms Federica Bigi *(Ambassador, resident in San Marino)*
Thailand	m	H.E. Mr Pasan Teparak *(Ambassador)*
St Lucia (R)...............	m	H.E. Dr Earnest Hilaire *(High Commissioner)*
Lithuania	m	H.E. Mrs Asta Skaisgiryté Liauškiené *(Ambassador)*
Seychelles		H.E. Ms Marie-Pierre Lloyd *(High Commissioner)*
Australia (R)...............	m	H.E. The Hon Mike Rann CNZM *(High Commissioner)*
Bangladesh	m	H.E. Dr Mohamed Mijarul *(High Commissioner)*
Egypt	m	H.E. Mr Ashraf Elkholy *(Ambassador)*
Kosovo	m	H.E. Mr Lirim Greiçevci *(Ambassador)*
Tunisia	m	H.E. Mr Nabil Ammar *(Ambassador)*
Bahamas (R)	m	H.E. Mr Eldred E Bethel *(High Commissioner)*
Burkina Faso	m	H.E. Mr Frédéric Assomption Korsaga *(Ambassador)*
Belarus	m	H.E. Mr Sergei F Aleinik *(Ambassador)*
Macedonia	m	H.E. Mr Jovan Donev *(Ambassador)*
Albania	m	H.E. Mr Mal Berisha *(Ambassador)*
New Zealand...............	m	H.E. Dr the Rt Hon Sir Lockwood Smith *(High Commissioner)*
Rwanda	m	H.E. Mr Williams Nkurunziza *(High Commissioner)*
Zambia	m	H.E. Mr Paul Lumbi *(High Commissioner)*

Italy	m	H.E. Mr Pascuale Terracciano (*Ambassador*)
Latvia	m	H.E. Mr Andris Teikmanis (*Ambassador*)
Iraq	m	H.E. Mr Faik Ferik Abdilesis Nerweyi (*Ambassador*)
Mongolia	m	H.E. Mr Narkhuu Tulgu (*Ambassador*)
Switzerland	m	H.E. Mr Dominik Furgler (*Ambassador*)
Korea (Republic of)	m	H.E. Mr Sungnam Lim (*Ambassador*)
Uganda	m	H.E. Prof Joyce Kakuramatsi Kikafunda (*High Commissioner*)
Grenada(R)	m	H.E. Mr Joslyn Raphael Whiteman (*High Commissioner*)
Luxembourg	m	H.E. Mr Patrick Engelberg (*Ambassador*)
USA	m	H.E. Mr Matthew Barzun (*Ambassador*)
Malta	m	H.E. Mr Norman Hamilton (*High Commissioner*)
Somalia		H.E. Mr Abdullahi Mahamed Ali (*Ambassador*)
Ecuador	m	H.E. Mr Juan Falconi Puig (*Ambassador*)
Ireland	m	H.E. Mr Daniel Mulhall (*Ambassador*)
Denmark	m	H.E. Mr Claus Grube (*Ambassador*)
Lesotho		H.E. Mrs Felleng Mamakeka Makeka (*High Commissioner*)
Timor-Leste	m	H.E. Mr Joaquim Antonio Maria Lopes da Fonseca (*Ambassador*)
Serbia	m	H.E. Dr Ognjen Pribićević (*Ambassador*)
Namibia	m	H.E. Mr Steve Vemunavi Katiuanjo (*High Commissioner*)
Armenia	m	H.E. Dr Armen Sarkissian (*Ambassador*)
Burma	m	H.E. Mr U Kyaw Zwar Minn (*Ambassador*)
Cyprus	m	H.E. Mr Euripides L. Evriviades (*High Commissioner*)
Guinea		H.E. Mr Paul Goa Zoumanigui (*Ambassador*)

CHARGÉ D'AFFAIRES & ACTING HIGH COMMISSIONERS

São Tomé & Principe	m	Mr Armindo de Brito Fernandes (*Embassy, Resident in Brussels*)
Kiribati	+	Mrs Makurita Baaro (*High Commission*)
Andorra		Mrs Eva Descarrega Garcia (*Embassy*)
Cabo Verde		Ms Maria de Jesus Macarenhas (*Embassy*)
Burundi		Mr Bernard Ntahiraja (*Embassy*)
Maldives	m	Mr Ahmed Shiaan (*High Commission*)
Kyrgyzstan		Mr Aleiblek Tilebaliev (*Embassy*)
Gabon		Mr Medard Nze Ekome
Bolivia		Mrs Melendres Argote (*Embassy*)
Tonga		Mr Sone Sonata Tupou (*High Commission*)
Mauritania		Mr Mohamed Yahya Ould Sidi Haiba (*Embassy*)
Mexico		Mr Alejandro Estivill Castro (*Embassy*)
Haiti		Madame Valerie Pompee (*Embassy*)
Georgia		Ms Tamar Kapanadze (*Embassy*)
Germany		Dr Rudolf Adam (*Embassy*)
Venezuela		Mr Alvaro Sanchez (*Embassy*)
Chad		Mr Bedadrone Tombalbaye (*Embassy*)
South Africa		Ms Bongiwe Qwabe (*High Commission*)
India		Dr Virander Kumar Paul (*High Commission*)

Colombia...................	Mr Juan Manuel Uribe-Robledo *(Embassy)*
Syria	*Vacant*
Iran	*Vacant*
Guinea-Bissau	*Vacant*
Nauru	*Vacant*
Tuvalu (R)..................	*Vacant*
Madagascar	*Vacant*

NATIONAL DAYS

Date	Country	Title
January 1	Cuba	Day of Liberations
1	Haiti	National Day
1	Sudan	Independence Day
4	Burma (Myanmar)	Independence Day
26	India	Republic Day
26	Australia	Australia Day
31	Nauru	Independence Day
February 4	Sri Lanka	Independence Day
6	New Zealand	Waitangi Day
7	Grenada	Independence Day
11	Iran	Islamic Revolution Day
16	Lithuania	Independence Day
17	Kosovo	Independence Day
17	Libya	National Day
18	The Gambia	Independence Day
23	Brunei	National Day
23	Guyana	Republic Day
24	Estonia	Independence Day
25	Kuwait	National Day
27	Dominican Republic	Independence Day
March 1	Bosnia & Herzegovina	Independence Day
3	Bulgaria	National Day
6	Ghana	National Day
12	Mauritius	Republic Day
15	Hungary	National Day
17	Ireland	St Patrick's Day
20	Tunisia	Independence Day
21	Namibia	National Day
23	Pakistan	National Day
25	Greece	Independence Day
26	Bangladesh	Independence Day
April 3	Guinea	National Day
4	Senegal	National Day
16	Denmark	Royal Birthday
17	Syria	National Day
18	Zimbabwe	National Day
19	Swaziland	Royal Birthday
19	Holy See	Inauguration Day
26	Israel	National Day
26	Tanzania	Union Day
27	Sierra Leone	National Day
27	South Africa	Freedom Day
27	Togo	National Day
30	Netherlands	Official Birthday
May 3	Poland	National Day
5	Netherlands	Liberation Day
15	Paraguay	Independence Day
17	Norway	Constitution Day
20	Cameroon	National Day
22	Yemen	National Day

24	Eritrea	National Day
25	Jordan	Independence Day
25	Argentina	National Day
26	Guyana	Independence Day
26	Georgia	Independence Day
28	Azerbaijan	National Day
28	Ethiopia	National Day
29	Nepal	Republic Day
June 1	Samoa	Independence Day
2	Italy	National Day
5	Denmark	Constitution Day
6	Sweden	National Day
10	Portugal	National Day
12	Russia	National Day
12	Philippines	National Day
17	Iceland	National Day
18	Seychelles	National Day
23	Luxembourg	National Day
25	Mozambique	National Day
25	Croatia	National Day
25	Mozambique	National Day
25	Slovenia	National Day
26	Madagascar	Independence Day
27	Djibouti	National Day
30	Democratic Republic of Congo	National Day
July 1	Burundi	National Day
1	Somalia	National Day
1	Canada	National Day
1	Rwanda	National Day
1	British Virgin Islands	Territory Day
3	Belarus	National Day
4	Tonga	National Day
4	United States	Independence Day
5	Cabo Verde	National Day
5	Venezuela	Independence Day
6	Malawi	National Day
7	Nepal	Royal Birthday
10	Bahamas	National Day
11	Mongolia	National Day
12	São Tome & Principe	National Day
12	Kiribati	Independence Day
14	France	National Day
15	Brunei	Royal Birthday
17	Lesotho	Royal Birthday
20	Colombia	Independence Day
21	Belgium	National Day
23	Egypt	National Day
26	Maldives	National Day
26	Liberia	Independence Day
28	Peru	National Day
30	Vanuatu	Independence Day
30	Morocco	Date of Accession
August 1	Benin	National Day
1	Switzerland	National Day

2	Macedonia	National Day
6	Bolivia	Independence Day
6	Jamaica	Independence Day
7	Côte d'Ivoire	National Day
9	Singapore	National Day
10	Ecuador	Independence Day
11	Chad	Independence Day
15	Republic of Congo	National Day
15	Korea	National Day
15	Liechtenstein	National Day
17	Gabon	National Day
17	Indonesia	National Day
19	Afghanistan	National Day
20	Hungary	National Day
24	Ukraine	Independence Day
25	Uruguay	Independence Day
27	Moldova	National Day
31	Trinidad & Tobago	Independence Day
31	Kyrgyzstan	Independence Day
31	Malaysia	National Day
September 1	Slovak Republic	Constitution Day
1	Uzbekistan	Independence Day
2	Vietnam	National Day
3	San Marino	National Day
6	Swaziland	National Day
7	Brazil	Independence Day
8	Andorra	National Day
8	Macedonia	Independence Day
9	Democratic People's Republic of Korea	National Day
9	Tajikistan	Independence Day
15	Guatemala	Independence Day
15	Costa Rica	Independence Day
15	El Salvador	Independence Day
15	Honduras	Independence Day
15	Nicaragua	Independence Day
16	Mexico	Independence Day
16	Papua New Guinea	National Day
16	St Christopher & Nevis	National Heroes Day
18	Chile	National Day
19	St Christopher & Nevis	Independence Day
21	Malta	National Day
21	Armenia	National Day
21	Belize	National Day
22	Mali	National Day
23	Saudi Arabia	National Day
24	Guinea-Bissau	National Day
30	Botswana	Botswana Day
October 1	Nigeria	National Day
1	China	National Day
1	Cyprus	Independence Day
1	Palau	Independence Day
2	Guinea	National Day
3	Germany	National Day
4	Lesotho	Independence Day

9	Uganda	Independence Day
10	Fiji	National Day
12	Spain.	National Day
12	Equatorial Guinea.	National Day
23	Hungary	National Day
24	Zambia	Independence Day
24	United Nations Day	
26	Austria	National Day
27	Saint Vincent & the Grenadines	Independence Day
27	Turkmenistan	Independence Day
28	Czech Republic	National Day
29	Turkey	National Day
November 1	Antigua & Barbuda	National Day
1	Algeria	National Day
3	Panama.	Independence Day
3	Commonwealth of Dominica	Independence Day
4	Tonga	Constitution Day
9	Cambodia	National Day
11	Angola	Independence Day
18	Latvia	National Day
18	Oman	National DAy
19	Monaco.	National Day
22	Lebanon	National Day
25	Suriname	National Day
28	Mauritania	Independence Day
28	Albania.	National Day
30	Barbados.	National Day
December 1	Romania	National Day
1	Central Africa Republic	National Day
2	United Arab Emirates.	National Day
2	Laos	National Day
5	Thailand	Royal Birthday
6	Finland	National Day
11	Burkina Faso	National Day
12	Kenya.	Independence Day
12	Turkmenistan	Day of Turkmenistan Neutrality
16	Bahrain.	National Day
16	Kazakhstan	Independence Day
18	Niger.	National Day
18	Qatar.	National Day
23	Japan.	Emperor's Birthday

DIRECTORY OF INTERNATIONAL ORGANISATIONS

International Organisations & their staff do not enjoy privileges & immunities under the Diplomatic Privileges Act 1964 but under separate legislation, to which reference is made in each entry in this Directory.

m Married
* Married but not accompanied by wife or husband

CAB INTERNATIONAL
(International Organisations Acts 1968 & 1981-S.I. 1982/1071)

Wallingford Oxon OX10 8DE
01491 832111
Fax 01491 833508
corporate@cabi.org
www.cabi.org

Dr Trevor Nicholls   *   *Chief Executive Officer*
Mr Ian Barry   **m**   *Chief Financial Officer*
Ms Caroline McNamara   **m**   *Executive Director, Commercial*
Mrs Andrea Powell   **m**   *Executive Director, Publishing*
Mr Neil MacIntosh   **m**   *Executive Director, Human Resources*
Mr Tim Walsha   **m**   *Executive Director, Information Technology*
Mr Neil MacIntosh   **m**   *Executive Director, Human Resources*
Mr Dennis Rangi   **m**   *Executive Director, International Development*

COMMONWEALTH FOUNDATION
(International Organisations Act, 1968-S.I. 1983/143)

East Wing Marlborough House Pall Mall SW1Y 5HY
020 7747 6579
Fax 020 7839 8157
www.commonwealthfoundation.com

Mr Vijay Krishnarayan   **m**   *Director*
Ms Myn Garcia   *Deputy Director*

COMMONWEALTH SECRETARIAT
(Commonwealth Secretariat Act, 1966)

Marlborough House Pall Mall SW1Y 5HX
020 7747 6500
Fax 020 7930 0827
Quadrant House 55-58 Pall Mall SW1Y 5JH
020 7839 3411
www.thecommonwealth.org

HIS EXCELLENCY MR KAMALESH SHARMA   **m**   *Commonwealth Secretary-General*
       Mrs Babli Sharma
Mrs Mmasekgoa Masire-Mwamba   **m**   *Deputy Secretary-General*

Mr Amitav Banerji   **m**   *Director, Political Affairs Division*
Mr Simon Gimson   **m**   *Director & Head, Secretary-General's Office*
Dr Cyrus Rustomjee   **m**   *Director, Economic Affairs Division*
Mr Nabeel Goheer   **m**   *Director, Strategic Planning £ Evaluation Division*
Ms Katherine Ellis   *Director, Youth Affairs Division*
Mr Richard Uku   **m**   *Director, Communications & Public Affairs Division*
Ms Zarinah Davies   **m**   *Director, Human Resources Division*
Ms Paula Harris   *Director, Corporate Services Division*
Mr Arindam Roy   **m**   *Adviser & Head, Debt Management Section, Special Advisory Services Division*
Mrs Nishana Jayawickrama   **m**   *Adviser & Head of Asia/Europe Section, Political Affairs Division*
Ms Priyanka Chauhan   **m**   *Deputy Head, Secretary-General's Office*
Mrs Shirani Goonatilleke de Fontgalland   *Adviser & Head of Criminal Law Section, Legal & Constitutional Affairs Division*
Mrs Esther Eghobamien   **m**   *Head of Gender Equality, Social Transformation Programmes Division*
Mr Yogesh Bhatt   **m**   *Adviser & Head of Evaluation Section, Strategic Planning & Evaluation Division*
Mr Timothy Newman   **m**   *Head of Technical Cooperation & Strategic Response Group, Governance & Institutional Development Division*
Ms Nita Yawanarajah   *Adviser & Head, Good Offices Section, Political Affairs Division*
Ms Janet Strachan   **m**   *Adviser & Head of Small States, Environment & Economic Management Section, Economic Affairs Division*
Mr Joshua Brien   **m**   *Adviser & Head of Economic & Legal Section, Special Advisory Services Divison*
Dr Pauline Greaves   **m**   *Head of Education Section, Social Transformation Programmes Division*
Mr Jarvis Matiya   **m**   *Adviser & Head of Justice Section, Legal & Constitutional Affairs Division*
Mr Ibibia Worika   **m**   *Legal Adviser, Economic & Legal Section, Special Advisory Services Division*
Ms Norma MacIssac   **m**   *Adviser & Head, Planning Section, Strategic Planning & Evaluation Division*
Mr Julian Roberts   **m**   *Adviser (Ocean Governance), Economic & Legal Section, Special Advisory Services Division*
Ms Samantha Attridge   *Adviser & Head, International Finance & Capital Markets Section, Economic Affairs Division*
Mrs Joan Nwasike   **m**   *Head of Thematic Programmes Group, Governance & Institutional Development Division*
Mr Henry Nyambu   **m**   *Head of Information Technology Section, Corporate Services Division*
Ms Magna Aidoo   *Head of Health Section, Social Transformation Programmes Division*
Ms Kimberly Cliff   *Head of Finance & Management Information Sectiob, Corporate Services Division*
Ms Victoria Holdsworth   *Deputy Director Communications & Public Affairs Division*
Dr Ekpen Omonbude   **m**   *Economic Adviser (Natural Resources), Economic & Legal Section, Special Advisory Services Division*
Dr Mohammed Razzaque   **m**   *Adviser & Head, International Trade & Regional Co-operation Section, Economic Affairs Division*
Ms Yvonne Apea   **m**   *Head of office, Deputy Secretary-General's Office (MM), Secretary-General's Office*
Mr Adonia Ayebare   **m**   *Adviser & Head, Democracy Section, Political Affairs Division*
Mr Martin Kasirye   **m**   *Adviser & Head, Democracy Section, Political Affairs Division*

COMMONWEALTH TELECOMMUNICATIONS ORGANISATION
(International Organisations Acts 1968 & 1981-S.I. 1983/144)

64-66 Glenthorne Road W6 OLR
020 8600 3600
Fax: 020 8600 3819
www.cto.int
info@cto.int

Professor Tim Unwin   **m**   *Secretary General*
Mr Rakesh Luchmun   **m**   *Director/Head of Finance & Administration*
Mr Lasantha De Alwis   **m**   *Director/Head of Operations & Corporate Secretary*
Mr Marcel Belingue   **m**   *Head of Membership & Communocations*

THE EUROPEAN BANK FOR RECONSTRUCTION & DEVELOPMENT
(International Organisations Act, 1968-S.I. 1991/757)

1 Exchange Square EC2A 2JN
020 7338 6000
Fax 020 7338 6100
www.ebrd.com

Sir Suma Chakrabarti   **m**   *President*
Mr Philip Bennett   **m**   *1st Vice-President, Banking*
Mr Manfred Schepers   **m**   *Vice-President, Finance*
Dr Luise Hőlscher   *Vice-President & Chief Administration Officer, Human Resources & Corporate Services*
Mr András Simor   **m**   *Vice-President, Policy*
Miss Betsy Nelson   *Vice-President, Risk*

EUROPEAN BANKING AUTHORITY
(European Communities Act, 1972, Protocol on the Privileges & Immunities of the European Communities, 1965)

Floor 18 Tower 42 25 Old Broad Street EC2N 1HQ
020 7382 1770
Fax 020 7382 1771
info@eba.europa.eu

Mr Andrea Enria   **m**   *Chairperson*
Mr Adam Farkas   *Executive Director*
Ms Isabelle Vaillant   *Director (Regulation)*
Mr Peter Mihalik   **m**   *Director (Operations)*
Mr Piers Haben   *Director (Oversight)*

EUROPEAN CENTRE FOR MEDIUM-RANGE WEATHER FORECASTS (ECMWF)
(International Organisations Act, 1968 & 1981-S.I. 1975/158)

Shinfield Park Reading Berkshire RG2 9AX
0118 949 9000
Fax 0118 986 9450
www.ecmwf.int

Professor Alan Thorpe   **m**   *Director-General*
Professor Erland Källén   **m**   *Director of Research Department & Deputy Director-General*
Mr Nyall Farrell   *Director of Administration Department*
Dr Florence Rabier   **m**   *Director of Forecast Department*
Mrs Isabella Weger   **m**   *Acting Director of Computing Department*
Mrs Hilda Carr   *Head of Communications*

EUROPEAN COMMISSION
(European Communities Act, 1972-Protocol on the Privileges & Immunities of the European Communities, 1965)
Representation in the UK: Europe House 32 Smith Square SW1P 3EU
020 7973 1992
Fax 020 7973 1900
www.ec.europa.eu/uk

Mrs Jacqueline Minor   *Head of Representation*
Ms Christine Dalby   **m**   *Deputy Head of Representation & Head of Political Section*
Mr Mark English   **m**   *Head of Media*
Ms Antonia Mochan   *Head of Communication/Partnership & Networks*
Mr Kyle Galler   **m**   *Principal Economic Policy Analyst*
Ms Marie-Madeleine Kanellopoulou   **m**   *Political Officer*
Mr John Evans   *Multilingualism Officer*
Ms Angelique Petrits   **m**   *Multilingualism Officer*
Ms Maria Kelly   *Head of Administration*
Mr Vassili Lelakis   **m**   *Director in Charge of Relations with EBRD/Member of the Board representing the European Community*
Mr Richard Mason   **m**   *Accredited Representative of the European Commission to the International Maritime Organisation*

Regional Offices:
Ms Colette Fitzgerald   *Head of Office, Belfast   Tel 028 9024 0708*
Mr David Hughes   *Head of Office, Cardiff   Tel 029 2089 5020*
Mr Graham Blythe   *Head of Office, Edinburgh   Tel 0131 225 2058*

EUROPEAN INVESTMENT BANK
(European Communities Act, 1972-Protocol on the Privileges & Immunities of the European Communities, 1965)

3rd Floor Royal Exchange Buildings EC3V 3LF
020 7375 9660
Fax 020 7375 9699
www.eib.org

Mr Betrand Rossert   *   *Head of Office (Interim)*

EUROPEAN MEDICINES AGENCY

(European Communities Act, 1972-Protocol on the Privileges & Immunities of the European Communities, 1965)

7 Westferry Circus Canary Wharf E14 4HB
020 7418 8400
Fax 020 7418 8660
mail@emea.europa.eu

Mr Guido Rasi   **m**   *Executive Director*
Mr Andreas Pott   **m**   *Deputy Executive Director*
Mr Noel Wathion   **m**   *Head of Division, Stakeholder & Community/Chief Policy Officer*
Mr David Mackay   **m**   *Head of Division, Veterinary Medicines & Product Data Management*
Mr Fergus Sweeney   **m**   *Head of Division, inspections & Human Medicines Pharmacovigilance*
Ms Agnes Saint-Raymond   *Head of Programme Design Board*
Mr Luc Verhelst   **m**   *Head of Unit, Information and Communications Technology*
Ms Zaïde Frias   *Head of Division, Human Medicines Research & development Support*
Ms Enrica Alteri   **m**   *Head of Division, Human Medicines Evaluation*
Mr Alexis Nolte   *Head of Division, Procedure Management & Business Support Veterinary Medicines & Product*

EUROPEAN MOLECULAR BIOLOGY LABORATORY (OUTSTATION)
EUROPEAN BIOINFORMATICS INSTITUTE

(International Organisations Act, 1968 & 1981-S.I. 1994-1890)

Wellcome Trust Genome Campus Hinxton Cambridge CB10 1SD
01223 494444
Fax 01223 494468

Professor Iain Mattaj   **m**   *Director-General of EMBL, Non-Resident*
Professor Dame Janet Thornton   **m**   *Director of Outstation*
Dr Ewan Birney   **m**   *Joint Associate Director of Outstation*
Dr Rolf Apweiler   **m**   *Associate Director of Outstation*
Mr Mark Green   **m**   *Head of Outstation Administration*

EUROPEAN PARLIAMENT

(European Communities Act, 1972-Protocol on the Privileges & Immunities of the European Communities, 1965)

32 Smith Square SW1P 3EU
020 7227 4300
Fax 020 7227 4302
www.europarl.org.uk
eplondon@europarl.europa.eu

Björn Kjellström   **m**   *Head of Office*
Ms Zuzana Pavlickova   *Press Officer*

EUROPEAN PARLIAMENT OFFICE IN SCOTLAND
(European Communities Act, 1972-Protocol on the Privileges & Immunities of the European Communities, 1965)

The Tun 4 Jackson's Entry Holyrood Road Edinburgh EH8 8PJ
0131 557 7866
Fax 0131 557 4977
www.europarl.org.uk
epedinburgh@europarl.eu.int

Mr Per Johansson   **m**   *Head of Office*

EUROPEAN POLICE COLLEGE (CEPOL SECRETARIAT)
(International Organisations Act, 1968-S.I.2004/3334)

Bramshill House Hook Hampshire RG27 0JW
01256 602668
Fax 01256 602996
secretariat@cepol.europa.eu
www.cepol.europa.eu

Mr Ferenc Bánfi   **m**   *Director*
Mr Detlef Schroder   *****   *Deputy Director*
Mr Roeland Woldhuis   **m**   *Head of Corporate Services Department*

EUROPEAN SCHOOL
(European Communities Act, 1972-S.I. 1990/237)

Culham Abingdon Oxon OX14 3DZ
01235 522621
Fax 01235 554609
esculham@eursc.org
www.esculham.eu

Mr Simon Sharron   **m**   *Head*
Ms Leene Soekov   **m**   *Deputy Head (Secondary)*
Ms Maeve McCarthy   *Deputy Head (Primary)*
Mr Robin J Holcombe   **m**   *Bursar*

EUROPEAN SPACE AGENCY
(International Organisations Act, 1968-S.I.1978/1105)

ESA Harwell Centre ATLAS Building
Harwell Oxford Didcot OX11 OQX
01235 567 9000
harwellcentre@esa.int
www.esa.int

Mrs Magali Françoise Vaissiere-Serre   **m**   *Head of ECSAT Centre and Director of Telecommunications and Integrated Applications*
Mr Sergio Vazzana   **m**   *Head of Facilities Management Service*
Mr Pascal Lecomte   **m**   *Head of ESA Climate Office*
Dr Bruno Leone   **m**   *Physicist/Engineer*

HONG KONG ECONOMIC & TRADE OFFICE
(International Organisations Act, 1968-S.I.1997/1334)

6 Grafton Street
London W1S 4EQ
020 7499 9821
Fax 020 7495 5033
general@hketolondon.gov.hk
www.hketolondon.gov.hk

Miss Lai Man Erica Ng   *Director-General*
Mr Wai Kuen Lee   **m**   *Marine Adviser*
Miss Ching Yi Noel Pun   *Deputy Director-General*
Mr Chung Cham Ching   **m**   *Deputy Director-General*
Mr Chung Sing Lau   **m**   *Assistant Director-General*

INTERNATIONAL BANK FOR RECONSTRUCTION & DEVELOPMENT
(see under WORLD BANK GROUP)

INTERNATIONAL COCOA ORGANIZATION
(International Organisations Act, 1968-S.I.1975/411)

5th Floor, Westgate House, Westgate Road, London W5 1YY
020 8991 6000
Fax 020 8997 4372
www.icco.org
info@icco.org

Dr Jean-Marc Anga   **m**   *Executive Director*
Mr Laurent Pipitone   **m**   *Director of the Economics & Statistics Division*

INTERNATIONAL COFFEE ORGANIZATION
(International Organisations Act, 1968-S.I. 1969/733)
22 Berners Street, London W1T 3DD
020 7612 0600
Fax: 020 7612 0630
info@ico.org
www.ico.org

Mr Robério Oliveira Silva   *Executive Director*
Mr Mauricio Galindo   *Head of Operations*
Mr David P Moorhouse   **m**   *Head of Finance and Administration*

129

INTERNATIONAL DEVELOPMENT ASSOCIATION
(see under WORLD BANK GROUP)

INTERNATIONAL FINANCE CORPORATION
(see under WORLD BANK GROUP)

INTERNATIONAL GRAINS COUNCIL
(International Organisations Act, 1968 & 1981-S.I. 1968/1863)
1 Canada Square Canary Wharf E14 5AE
020 7513 1122
Fax 020 7513 0630
igc@igc.org.uk
www.igc.org.uk

Mr E Kitahara **m** *Executive Director*
Ms H Henton *Chief Economist*
Mr Y Makarov **m** *Senior Economist*
Ms A Reynolds *Senior Economist*
Mr D Cooper *Senior Economist*
Mr N Kemp **m** *Economist*

INTERNATIONAL MARITIME ORGANIZATION
(International Organisations Act, 1968-S.I. 2002/1826)

4 Albert Embankment SE1 7SR
020 7735 7611
Fax 020 7587 3210
www.imo.org

Mr K Sekimizu **m** *Secretary General*
      Mrs Chiho Sekimizu
Mr A Winbow *Assistant Secretary-General/Director, Maritime Safety Division (M.S.D.).*
Mrs O O'Neil **m** *Director, Conference Division (C.D.)*
Mr J O Espinoza Ferrey *Director, Administration Division (A.D.)*
Mr S Micallef *Director, Marine Environment Division (M.E.D.)*
Mr N L Charalambous *Director, Technical Co-operation Division (T.C.D.)*
Mr L Barchue, Sr. **m** *Head, Department of Member State Audit and Implementation Support, M.S.D.*
Mr Y Ito **m** *Special Adviser to the Secretary-General/Head of the Task Forces for the implementation of the Djibouti Code of Conduct, Office of the Secretary-General.*
Mr V Job **m** *Senior Deputy Director/Head, Information Technology and Information Systems Section, A.D.*
Mrs P Tansey **m** *Senior Deputy Director, T.C.D.*
Mr G Librando **m** *Senior Deputy Director, Sub-Division for Legal Affairs, L.E.D.*
Mr Min Kyung-Rae **m** *Senior Deputy Director, Internal Oversight and Ethics Office, Office of the Secretary General.*
Mr S-J Kim **m** *Deputy Director/Head, Management Accounting Services, A.D.*
Mr C Trelawny **m** *Senior Deputy Director, Sub-Division for Maritime Security and Facilitation, M.S.D.*
Mr J Westwood-Booth **m** *Senior Deputy Director, Sub-Division for MarineTechnology and Cargoes, M.S.D.*

130

Mr J Shiundu   m   *Deputy Director/Head, Programme Management, T.C.D.*
Mr A Mahapatra   m   *Senior Deputy Director, Sub-Division for Operational Safety and Human Element, M.S.D.*
Mr A Botsford   m   *Deputy Director/Chief, Office of General Services, A.D.*
Ms A Gireud   m   *Deputy Director/Head, French Translation Section, Translation Services, C.D.*
Mrs J Thompson   m   *Deputy Director/Head of the Executive Office of the Secretary-General.*
Mr E Vågslid   *Technical Adviser, Office of the Secretary-General.*
Mr M El Housseini-Hilal   m   *Deputy Director/Head, Arab and Africa (Francophone) Section, Geographical Focal Points, T.C.D*
Miss P A Richards   *Deputy Director/Head, Financial Services, A.D.*
Mr D Pughiuc   m   *Deputy Director/Head, Marine Biosafety Section, Sub-Division for Pollution Prevention, M.E.D.*
Mr C Dahoui   m   *Deputy Director/Head, Human Resources Services, A.D.*
Mr P Holihead   m   *Programme Director, Copunter-Piracy Programme (Djibouti Code of Conduc), Office of the Secretary-General.*
Mrs H Deggim   *Senior Deputy Directior, Sub-Division for Protective Measures, M.E.D*
Li Youqiang   m   *Deputy Director/Head, Chinese Translation Section, Sub-Division for Meeting Services, Interpretation and Translation (Arabic,Chinese and Russia), C.D*

THE FOLLOWING MEMBERS OF THE INTERNATIONAL MARITIME ORGANIZATION HAVE DESIGNATED PRINCIPAL PERMANENT REPRESENTATIVES TO THE ORGANIZATION IN THE UNITED KINGDOM:-

Brazilian
170 Upper Richmond Road
Putney SW15 2SH
020 8246 4493/82
Fax 020 8246 4495
BrazilianRepresentation.IMO@mar.org.uk

Admiral Luiz Umberto de Mendonça   m   *Head of the Representation & Permanent Representative*
Captain Marcelo Pamplona   m   *Alternate Permanent Representative*
Commander Vagner Belarmino de Oliveira   m   *Assistant to the Alternate Permanent Representative*

Democratic People's Republic of Korea
73 Gunnersbury Avenue W5 4LP
020 8992 8221
Fax 020 8992 2053

HIS EXCELLENCY MR HYON HAK BONG   m   *Permanent Representative*
Mr Ryong Sop Kim   m   *Deputy Permanent Representative*
Mr In Ryong Kim   m   *Counsellor (Maritime Affairs)*

France
6 Cromwell Place London SW7 2JN
020 7073 1393
Fax : 020 7073 1390

Mrs Elisabeth Barsacq   m   *Head of the Representation & Permanent Representative*
Mr Francois-Xavier Rubin de Cervens   m   *Maritime Counsellor*
Mr Eric Berder   m   *Deputy Permanent Representative*
Mr Charles-Henri de Barsac   *Alternate Permanent Representative*

Republic of Liberia
3rd Floor, 107 Fenchurch Street, EC3M 5JF
020 7702 1243
Fax 020 7702 2639
info@liberianpm.org.uk

Mr George M. Arku **m** *Permanent Representative*

Russian Federation
37 Harrington Gardens SW7 4JU
020 7370 6768/64
Fax 020 7370 0225
imo@mintrans.ru

Mr Yury Melenas *Permanent Representative*
Mr Vladimir Ananiev **m** *Deputy Permanent Representative*

INTERNATIONAL MOBILE SATELLITE ORGANIZATION
(International Organisations Act, 1968 & 1981-S.I. 1999/1125)

99 City Road EC1Y 1AX
020 7728 1249
Fax 020 7728 1172
www.imso.org
info@imso.org

Captain Esteban Pacha Vicente **m** *Director-General*
          Mrs. Pilar Dominguez
Mr Andrew Clement Fuller **m** *Deputy Director-General*
Ms Jennifer Jayne Ray **m** *Head of Administration, Finance & Conferences*
Mr Cafer Ozkan Istanbullu **m** *Technical Officer*
Mr Ibrahim Halil Keskin *IT Technical Officer*

INTERNATIONAL OIL POLLUTION COMPENSATION FUNDS
(International Organisations Acts, 1968 & 1981 - S.I. 1979/912 & S.I. 1996/1295)

Portland House Bressenden Place SW1E 5PN
020 7592 7100
Fax 020 7592 7111
info@iopcfund.org
www.iopcfund.org

Mr Jóse M Maura **m** *Director*
Mr Ranjit S P Pillai **m** *Deputy Director/Head, Finance & Administration Department*
Mrs Akiko Yoshida **m** *Legal Counsel*
Vacant *Head, Claims Department/Technical Adviser*
Mr Thomas Liebert **m** *Head, External Relations and Conference Department*

INTERNATIONAL ORGANIZATION FOR MIGRATION

Mission in the United Kingdom of Great Britain & Northern Ireland
(International Organisations Act 1968 - S.I. 2008/3124)

11 Begrave Road London SW1V 1RB
020 7811 6060
Fax: 020 7811 6043
iomuk@iom.int

Mrs Clarissa Azkoul   **m**   *Chief of Mission*

INTERNATIONAL SUGAR ORGANIZATION

(International Organisations Act, 1968 & 1981-S.I. 1969/734)

1 Canada Square Canary Wharf Docklands E14 5AA
020 7513 1144
Fax: 020 7513 1146
finance-admin@isosugar.org

Dr Peter Baron   **m**   *Executive Director*
Mr James Lowe   **m**   *Head, Finance & Adminstration*
Mr Sergey C Gudoshnikov   **m**   *Senior Economist*
Mr Lindsay O Jolly   **m**   *Senior Economist*
Dr Leonardo Bichara Rocha   *Senior Economist*

INTERNATIONAL TELECOMMUNICATIONS SATELLITE ORGANISATION (ITSO)

(International Organisations Act, 1968 & 1981-S.I. 1979/911)

ITSO - 3400 International Drive NW Washington DC 20008-3096 USA
(00)1 202 243 5096
itsomail@itso.int

Mr José Toscano   *Director General & Chief Executive Officer*

INTERNATIONAL WHALING COMMISSION

(International Organisations Act, 1968-S.I. 1975/1210)

The Red House 135 Station Road Impington Cambridge CB24 9NP
01223 233971
Fax 01223 232876
www.iwc.int
secretariat@iwc.int

Dr Simon Brockington   **m**   *Secretary to the Commission*

NORTH ATLANTIC SALMON CONSERVATION ORGANIZATION

(European Communities Act, 1972-S.1. 1985/1973)

11 Rutland Square Edinburgh EH1 2AS
013 1228 2551
Fax 01310228 4384
hq@nasco.int
www.nasco.int

Dr Peter Hutchinson   **m**   *Secretary*

NORTH EAST ATLANTIC FISHERIES COMMISSION
(International Organisations Act, 1968-S.I. 1999/278)
22 Berners Street W1T 3DY
020 7631 0016
Fax 020 7149 9950
www.neafc.org
info@neafc.org

Mr Stefán Ásmundsson   **m**   *Secretary*

THE OSPAR COMMISSION
(International Organisations Act, 1968-S.I. 1979/914)
Victoria House
37-63 Southampton Row WC1B 4DA
020 7430 5200
Fax 020 7242 3737
secretariat@ospar.org

Dr Darius Campbell   **m**   *Executive Secretary*
Ms L Rodriguez   **m**   *Deputy Secretary*
Ms E Corcoran   *Deputy Secretary*
Mr Gert Verreet   **m**   *Deputy Secretary*
Mr John Mouat   *Deputy Secretary*

OFFICE OF THE UNITED NATIONS HIGH COMMISSIONER FOR REFUGEES
(International Organisations Act, 1968-S.I. 1974/1261)
Strand Bridge House 138-142 Strand WC2R 1HH
020 7759 8090
Fax 020 7759 8119
www.unhcr.org
gbrlo@unhcr.org

Mr Roland Schilling   **m**   *Representative*
Ms Elizabeth Mpyisi-Nthengwe   *Senior Legal Officer*
Mr Måans Nyberg   **m**   *Senior External Relations Officer*
Ms Alexandra McDowall   **m**   *Legal Officer*

REGIONAL UNITED NATIONS INFORMATION CENTRE
(International Organisations Act, 1968-S.I. 1974/1261)
Office: Residence Palace Bloc C2. Rue de la Loi 155/1040 Brussels
0032 (0) 2 788 8484
Fax 0032 (0) 2 788 8485
Info@unric.org

Mrs Afsane Bassir-Pour   **m**   *Director*

UNITED NATIONS ENVIRONMENT PROGRAMME
WORLD CONSERVATION MONITORING CENTRE
(International Organisations Act, 1968 - S.I. 1974/1261)

219 Huntingdon Road Cambridge CB3 0DL
01223 277314
Fax 01223 277136
www.unep-wcmc.org

Dr Jonathan M Hutton **m** *Director*
Ms Monika MacDevette *Deputy Director*

THE UNITED NATIONS WORLD FOOD PROGRAMME
(International Organisations Act, 1968 - S.I. 1974/1261)

First Floor Strand Bridge House 138-142 Strand WC2R 1HH
020 7240 9001
Fax 020 7240 6662
http://www.wfp.org

Mr Gregory Barrow **m** *Senior Public Affairs Officer*

WORLD BANK GROUP
12th Floor Millbank Tower 21-24 Millbank SW1P 4QP

INTERNATIONAL DEVELOPMENT ASSOCIATION
INTERNATIONAL BANK FOR RECONSTRUCTION & DEVELOPMENT
(Overseas Development & Co-operation Act 1980-S.I. 1946/36 S.I. 1976/221)
(Overseas Development & Co-operation Act 1980-S.I. 1960/1383 S.I. 1976/221)

020 7592 8400
Fax: 020 7592 8420
www.worldbank.org

Mr Andrew J Felton **m** *Senior International Affairs Officer*

INTERNATIONAL FINANCE CORPORATION
(Overseas Development & Co-operation Act 1980-S.I. 1955/1954 S.I. 1976/221)

020 7592 8400
Fax 020 7592 8430
www.ifc.org

Mr Tomasz Telma **m** *Acting Director for Western Europe*

HONORARY CONSULS

Alphabetical list of Honorary Consular representatives of Foreign States & Commonwealth Countries not represented by a Diplomatic Mission in London. The persons listed have certain Privileges & Immunities under the Consular Relations Act 1968.

BENIN
Millenium House Humber Road NW2 6DW
020 8830 8612
Fax 020 7435 0665
TELEX 8830 8925

Mr Lawrence L. Landau   **m**   *Honorary Consul for the Republic of Benin*

BHUTAN
2 Windacres Warren Road Guildford GU1 2HG
01483 538 189
mrutland@aol.com

Mr Michael R. Rutland   *Honorary Consul for Bhutan*

BURKINA FASO
Lilacs Stane Street Ockley Surrey RH5 5LU
01306 627 225/0777 1984 680

Mr Colin Seelig   **m**   *Honorary Consul for the Republic for Burkina Faso*

CABO VERDE (REPBULIC OF)
7A The Grove N6 6JU
07876 232 305
CapeVerde@JonathanLux.co.uk

Mr Jonathan S. Lux   **m**   *Honorary Consul for Cabo Verde*

CONGO (REPUBLIC OF)
3rd Floor Holborn Gate (HRG) 26 Southampton Buildings WC2A 1PN
020 7922 0695
Fax 020 7401 2566/2545

Mr Louis Muzzu   **m**   *Honorary Consul for the Republic of Congo*

KIRIBATI
The Great House Llanddewi Rydderch Monmouthshire NP7 9UY
01873 840 375/01873 840 152
Fax 01873 840 375
mravellwalsh@btopenworld.com

Mr Michael Ravell Walsh   **m**   *Honorary Consul for the Republic of Kiribati*

NAURU
Romshed Courtyard Underriver Nr Sevenoaks Kent TN15 0SD
01732 746 061
Fax 01732 746062
nauru@weald.co.uk

Mr Martin W.L. Weston   *Honorary Consul for the Republic of Nauru*

NIGER
MPC House 15 Maple Mews NW6 5UZ
020 7328 8180
Fax 020 7328 8120
www.nigerconsulateuk.org
visa@nigerconsulateuk.org
consulate@nigerconsulateuk.org
mdikko.ladan@nigerconulateuk.org

Mr Ladan   *Honarary Consul for the Republic of Niger*

PALAU
Bankfoot Square Bankfoot Street Batley WF17 5LH
01924 470 786
Fax 01924 474 747
www.palauconsulate.org.uk

Mr. Q. Mohammed   **m**   Honorary Consul for the Republic of Palau

SAN MARINO
Flat 51 162 Sloane Street SW1
020 7259 9754
Fax 01268 292 629
Consulate.london.sm@gmail.com

Mr Eduardo Teodorani-Fabbri   *Honorary Consul for San Marino*

SAMOA
Church Cottage Pedlinge Nr Hythe Kent CT12 5JL
01303 260 541
Fax 01303 238 058

Mrs Prunella Scarlett LVO   *Honorary Consul for Samoa*

SÃO TOMÉ & PRINCIPE
Flat 8 Marsham Court 58 Victoria Drive Southfields SW19 6BB
020 8788 6139

Miss Natalie Galland-Burkl   *Honorary Consul for the Democratic Republic of São & Tomé & Principe in London*

SURINAME
89 Pier House 31 Cheyne Walk SW3 5HN
020 3 0847 143
07768 196 326
Fax: 0207 3490663

Dr Amwedhkar Jethu   **m**   *Honorary Consul for the Republic of Suriname*

TUVALU
Tuvalu House 230 Worple Road SW20 8RH
020 8879 0985
Fax 020 8879 0985
Tuvaluconsulate@netscape.net

Dr Iftikhar A. Ayaz   *Honorary Consul for Tuvalu*

CAREER CONSULS-GENERAL & CONSULS

Alphabetical list of Career Consular representatives of Foreign States & Commonwealth Countries notified under the Vienna Convention on Consular Relations. The persons listed have certain Privileges or Immunities under the Consular Relations Act, 1968.

AUSTRALIA

Agent-General for South Australia
Australia Centre Strand WC2B 4LG
020 7887 5124

Mr Bill Muirhead AM   *   *Agent-General for South Australia*

Agent-General for Queensland
Queensland House 392 Strand WC2R 0LZ
020 7836 1333

Mr Kenneth Smith   m   *Agent-General for Queensland*

Agent-General for Victoria
Australia Centre Strand WC2B 4LG
020 7836 2656

Ms Sally Anne Capp   m   *Agent-General for Victoria*

Agent-General for Western Australia
Australia Centre Strand WC2B 4LG
020 7240 2881

Mr Kevin Skipworth   m   *Agent-General for Western Australia*

CANADA

Agent-General for the Province of Québec
Québec House 59 Pall Mall London SW1Y 5JH
020 7766 5900

Monsieur Stéphane Paquet   *   *Agent-General for Québec*

REPRESENTATIVES OF BRITISH OVERSEAS TERRITORIES

This list is provided for information only. Some of the persons listed below may have an entitlement to certain Privileges & Immunities.

ANGUILLA

Government of Anguilla London Office
c/o Aequitas Consulting
M4 West Wing Somerset House Strand WC2R 1LA
020 7759 1141
ukeurep@anguillagovlondon.org

Ms Dorothea Hodge   *UK Representative*

BERMUDA

Government of Bermuda London Office
6 Arlington Street London SW1A 1RE
020 7518 9900
Fax: 020 7518 9901
www.gov.bm

Ms Kimberley Durrant   *UK Representative*

BRITISH VIRGIN ISLANDS

Government of the British Virgin Islands London Office
BVI House 15 Upper Grosvenor Street W1K 7PJ
020 7355 9570
Fax 020 7355 9575
kmalone@bvi.org.uk
www.bvi.gov.vg

Mr Kendrick Malone   *UK Representative*

CAYMAN ISLANDS

Cayman Islands Government Office
6 Arlington Street SW1A 1RE
020 7491 7772
Fax 020 7491 7944
blencathra@cigo.co.uk
www.gov.ky

The Rt Hon the Lord Blencathra   *Director*

FALKLAND ISLANDS

Falkland Islands Government Office
Falkland House 14 Broadway SW1H 0BH
020 7222 2542
Fax 020 7222 2375
representative@falklands.gov.fk
www.falklands.gov.fk

Ms Sukey Cameron MBE   **m**   *UK Representative*

GIBRALTAR

Government of Gibraltar
178-179 Strand London WC2R 1 EL
020 7836 0777
Fax 020 7240 6612
info@gibraltar.gov.uk
www.gibraltar.gov.uk

Mr Albert A. Poggio OBE   *UK Representative*

MONTSERRAT

Government of Montserrat
180-186 Kings Cross Road WC1X 9DE
020 7520 2622
Fax 020 7520 2624
j.panton@montserrat-gov.org

Mrs Janice Panton MBE   **m**   *UK Representative*

ST HELENA

Government of St Helena
16 Old Queen St SW1H 9HP
020 7031 0314
Fax 020 7031 0315
shgukrep@sthelenagov.com

Mrs Kedell Worboys MBE   **m**   *UK Representative*

TURKS & CAICOS ISLANDS

No representation

OTHER REPRESENTATIVE OFFICES & ORGANISATIONS IN THE UNITED KINGDOM

This list is provided for information only. Some of the persons listed may have certain privileges & immunities.

THE LEAGUE OF ARAB STATES

106 Gloucester Place London W1U 6HU
Tel: 020 7317 0393
Fax: 020 7486 7586
press@arableague.org.uk

Vacant
Mrs Mayssa Sleiman   **m**   *Counsellor (Arab League Affairs)*
Mr Sohail Elhuni   **m**   *2nd Secretary*
Mrs Salma Al-Feky   **m**   *2nd Secretary*

INDEPENDENT INTERNATIONAL COMMISSION ON DECOMMISSIONING

I.I.C.D Block 1 Knockview Building Stormont Estate Belfast BT4 3SL
028 904 88600
Fax 028 904 88601

General John de Chastelain   *   *Chairman*
Mr Andrew D Sens   *   *Commissioner*
Brigadier-General Tauno Nieminen   *   *Commissioner*
Mr Aaro Suonio   **m**   *Chef de Cabinet*
Ms Ricki Schoen   *   *Office Manager*
Mrs Taina Suonio   **m**   *Administrative Assistant*

PALESTINIAN MISSION TO THE UNITED KINGDOM

5 Galena Road Hammersmith W6 0LT
020 8563 0008
Fax 020 8563 0058
www.palestinianmissionuk.com
info@palestinianmissionuk.com
info@palgd.org.uk

Prof. Manuel S. Hassassian   **m**   *Head of Mission*
            Mrs Selwa Kazwini
Mr Ahmed Mansur   **m**   *Consular & Administrative Affairs*
Miss Meisoon El-Shorafa   *Political Affairs Counsellor*
Mrs Rana Abu Ayyash   **m**   *Information & Press Counsellor*
Miss Haya Alfarra   *Second Secretary, Parliamentary Affairs & Civil Society*
Mr Mohamed Masharqa   **m**   *Cultural Counsellor*